PIANO SERVICING, TUNING, & REBUILDING

For The Professional
The Student
The Hobbyist

by Arthur A. Reblitz

The Vestal Press — Vestal, New York 13850   USA

Opposite: Baldwin SD-10 Concert Grand Piano at Music Hall,
Cincinnati, Ohio

Library of Congress Cataloging in Publication Data

Reblitz, Arthur A
  Piano servicing, tuning, rebuilding.

  Bibliography: p.
  Includes index.
  1. Piano—Construction.   I. Title.
ML652.R3   786.2'3   76-21796
ISBN 0-911572-12-0

First Printing — September 1976
Second Printing — December 1976
Third Printing — May 1977
Fourth Printing — June 1978

Frontispiece:

Cincinnati Music Hall is famous for its fine acoustics. Built in 1878, it was recently renovated to its original splendor. Music Hall is the home of the internationally famous Cincinnati Symphony Orchestra led by the world-renowned conductor and recording artist Thomas Schippers, as well as the Cincinnati May Festival and the Cincinnati Summer Opera.

The Baldwin SD-10 piano on the stage is an outstanding product of one of America's best-known makers of quality instruments.

ACKNOWLEDGEMENTS

The author wishes to express thanks to the following individuals and organizations for help and support in many different ways:

Byron, Sr. and Lois Akers, Durrell Armstrong (Player Piano Company), Nelson Barden, Baldwin Piano and Organ Company, Bob Barns, Q. David Bowers (American International Galleries), Sen. Charles Bovey, James Bratton, Elmer Brooks (Aeolian Corporation), James Burton (Editor, *The Piano Technician's Journal*), Gene H. Clark, Gordon Curtis, George A. Defebaugh (Kawai Piano Corporation), LaRoy Edwards (Yamaha Pianos), John Farnsworth, Howard and Helen Fitch (Editors, *The Musical Box Society Bulletin*), Dan and Jerry Flanigan (The Colorado Springs Music Company), Don Galt (Technical Editor, *The Piano Technician's Journal*), Roger Garvin (Rhodes Musical Instruments), Donald J. Gass (The WurliTzer Company), Warren Groff, Charles S. Hausmann (First United Methodist Church, Colorado Springs), Dennis Hayes (House of Baldwin, Colorado Springs), Henry Heller (Aeolian Corporation), Lew Herwig (The WurliTzer Company), Herbert Johnson (Schaff Piano Supply Company), George King, Bob Lehrer (Aeolian Corporation), Gordon Lipe, Richard Marschner, Thomas Marshall, Marvin Masel (Berkshire Instruments, Inc.), Norman Neblett (Yamaha Pianos), Warrell Nelson, Jr., Roy Newstadt (The WurliTzer Company), The Piano Technicians Guild, Major Harry F. Powell, Don Shoffner, Willard Sims (Baldwin Piano and Organ Company), William T. Singleton, Harry J. Sohmer, Jr. (Sohmer and Co., Inc.), Henry Z. Steinway, John H. Steinway (both of Steinway and Sons, Inc.), Albert Svoboda, Neil Torrey, Gerald Volk (Tuners Supply Company), Roger Weisensteiner (Kimball Piano and Organ Company), Dana Johnson.

The following people deserve special recognition, and have my deepest gratitude. Without their help, this book would not have been possible:

David L. Junchen, Michael Kitner, David Ramey and Thomas Sprague, who have shared their experience generously.

John Ellingsen, for the line drawings, and Willie Wilson, for photographs not otherwise attributed.

Harvey and Marion Roehl, for continual help with the mechanics of writing and publishing.

Grace Petzke (my mother-in-law) for typing the manuscript.

Eleanor and Fred Reblitz (my parents) for instilling in me the love of music and things mechanical at an early age, and for proofreading the manuscript.

My lovely wife, Jeannie, for constant encouragement, motivation and patience.

A.A.R.

Biography

The author has studied music ever since he was old enough to reach a piano keyboard and pick out melodies in the right key, before entering kindergarten. A native of Riverdale, Illinois, he graduated with high honors from the University of Illinois in 1968 with a Bachelor of Science in Music Education, majoring in flute.

Player pianos, nickelodeons and band organs have fascinated the author ever since he saw a Seeburg KT Special orchestrion (a self-playing keyboardless piano with xylophone and drums), in Daytona Beach, Florida, at age seven. His continuing interest in music machines led him to learn piano servicing as a basis for the restoration of automatic pianos, and he is a registered craftsman member of the Piano Technicians Guild. Mr. Reblitz conducts a full-time tuning, servicing and rebuild-

ing business with home base in Colorado Springs, but he has also serviced instruments in many prominent collections all over the United States, including Bellm's Cars & Music of Yesterday in Sarasota, Florida, Svoboda's Nickelodeon Tavern & Museum in Chicago Heights, Illinois, and the Vestal Press collection in Vestal, New York. He is a musical consultant to The House On The Rock in Spring Green, Wisconsin, and part-time curator of the musical instrument collections of the Bovey restoration in Virginia City and Nevada City, Montana. He also arranges new music rolls, and has done so for Ringling Bros., Barnum & Bailey Circus, Steamboat Julia Belle Swain, Gay Nineties Village in Sikeston, Missouri, Knott's Berry Farm in Buena Park, California, and others.

Mr. Reblitz has written many articles for a number of collectors' publications, including a regular record review column for the "Bulletin" of the Musical Box Society International, and several technical and musical articles for Q. David Bowers' *Encyclopedia of Automatic Musical Instruments.*

CONTENTS

INTRODUCTION

The modern piano is a complex musical instrument containing mechanisms which are not found in any other device. Therefore, the piano technician must use specialized knowledge, tools and techniques which are unique to the piano servicing field.

Many piano servicing problems which look difficult to the uninitiated are simple, given the correct tools, knowledge of procedure and a certain amount of mechanical ability. Other problems are more difficult and should not be tackled in a fine piano until experience is gained on lesser-quality instruments. It is hoped that this book will give the mechanically minded student the necessary knowledge of procedures and tools, along with the insight to distinguish between those relatively easy skills which may be put to use immediately (like regulating the soft pedal in an old upright) and those which should be practiced first (like putting new hammers in a concert grand). In addition, it is hoped that the experienced tuner-technician will be inspired to try new areas of repair and rebuilding which had been avoided due to lack of knowledge.

Tuning is a skill which is not necessarily related to musical ability. A professional musician usually analyzes tone *subjectively,* using a sense of relative pitch to compare one note to another: "That note sounds like G and is a little flat." The professional tuner, on the other hand, usually analyzes tone *objectively,* using mathematical rules to compare tones: "Note #1 is two pulsations per second flat of note #2." This is not to say that a fine ear for music does not help the tuner, because the best tuners use both types of listening to check their work. The fact that musical ability is not absolutely essential is only mentioned as a bit of encouragement to those who think they will never be able to tune a piano because they were not born with perfect pitch.

The quality of one's piano servicing, like anything else, is a reflection of his overall philosophy, and leads him around in ever-widening circles on whatever plateau he chooses. If one is content to get by with poor quality, he will attract customers who want no more than this. On the other hand, if he is dedicated to excellence in every facet of his work, he will slowly build a reputation which will attract the most desirable kind of customers.

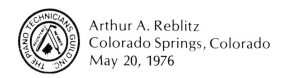

Arthur A. Reblitz
Colorado Springs, Colorado
May 20, 1976

Preface

Why this book?

It's pretty easy to show with some estimates and statistics that there is plenty of room for improvement of piano service in the United States and elsewhere, and they make interesting reading.

As this book is published, the American Music Conference has judged that there are perhaps ten million pianos in American homes, businesses, and institutions—and new ones are being added at a rate of about 175,000 per year. In The Piano Technician's Journal about the same time, Editor James H. Burton estimates that there are about 5,000 technicians working in the U. S. who match the "Craftsman Member" qualifications of The Piano Technician's Guild, although only about half of these are members of that organization. It is further estimated, based on surveys within the Guild, that suggest that the average tuner who works full-time at the trade tunes about 750 instruments per year.

A little simple arithmetic with these figures, and it's quickly apparent that if every piano in the United States were to be tuned only once each year that it would take an army of 15 to 20 thousand technicians to do the work!

This obviously means that a lot of pianos simply don't get serviced and tuned, and it also could mean that there's a lot of work available if there were a sufficient number of qualified people to do the work. And what the statistics don't show is what every good piano man knows—that a lot of work is being done by persons who are in no way properly qualified to take money from an unsuspecting public for working on their instruments.

Against this obvious need for qualified technicians to service these many instruments, there's a surprising dearth of good published information on the subject. This book illustrates and describes many normal jobs that a technician has to do which, to the best of our knowledge, have never before been published in book form.

Fortunately, most piano technicians want to learn more about pianos and how to service them, because they know that it's a complex machine and a person can work on them for an entire lifetime and really not know everything there is to know. The active participation in workshops conducted by the Technician's Guild is ample evidence of this desire to learn more; this publisher hopes that the book will serve to assist all of those—from beginner to full-time professional—to learn whatever is in these covers that may have escaped him previously.

For every technician who is capable of "concert tuning and regulating" a fine grand piano to satisfy the critical demands for the public performance of a Van Cliburn or a Liberace, there are scores who would aspire to that level of technical competence. All that knowledge is not necessarily between the covers of this volume, but it's fair to say that most of it is and the person who has mastered its contents is surely well on his way to becoming a master of his profession.

The modern piano is a surprisingly complex piece of apparatus considering that it is common in American homes, as well as elsewhere around the world. Not as complex as an automobile, perhaps, but in a way more mysterious—and certainly every bit as much of a challenge to understand and service properly. Broken down to its elements, it's a machine which behaves according to the rules of physics which pertain to it, as do all machines, and there's no reason why anyone willing to take some time to study its mechanisms can't learn to repair and tune it well. It's somewhat more complex than most machinery in the sense that it combines an unusual number of components which are subject to the vagaries of changing moisture content of the air and its temperature, as well as time itself, but there's no reason at all why a person with persistence, common sense, and a bit of mechanical aptitude cannot do this type of work.

If the insides of a piano seem a bit mysterious, perhaps it is because in past years some elements in the trade have tried to keep it that way in the mistaken notion that in so doing, those active in the field would somehow best secure their own employment. This publisher has taken quite the contrary view that the more people know about a subject, the more it will interest them; the more general interest there is about a given subject, the more everyone associated with the trade will benefit in the long run. This has proven quite true in the field of automatically-played pianos. In recent years the rebuilding and servicing of these has been left almost entirely to hobbyists, and some of the finest examples of rebuilding craftsmanship imaginable have been done by people who have no intention of becoming workers in the piano trade—but who are completely content to take all the time necessary to put a one-time gorgeous instrument back to its original condition for their own personal satisfaction and enjoyment.

This book is intended to serve that market as well as those who make their living at the servicing and rebuilding of pianos, and without question the fact that thousands of hobbyists have been seeking facts about proper techniques to do this means that interest of the public in general will be strengthened where these instruments are concerned; the piano trade in general cannot but benefit as a result. This publisher is pleased to play a part in this, and hopes that this book will assist in some small way to elevate the standards of service of all pianos to their owners as well as to the music-loving public.

Harvey N. Roehl
Craftsman Member,
Piano Technicians Guild
Owner, The Vestal Press

TELEPHONE (212) 721-2600

STEINWAY & SONS
PIANO MAKERS
STEINWAY PLACE
LONG ISLAND CITY, N.Y. 11105

May 21, 1976

Mr. Harvey Roehl
Vestal Press
P. O. Box 97
3533 Stratford Drive
Vestal, N. Y. 13850

Dear Harvey:-

This book by Arthur A. Reblitz fills a void that has existed for too long a time. I realize that it is not possible to cover in one volume every detail that might cause a problem in servicing, but Mr. Reblitz' research and personal experience has peculiarly endowed him to create a manual that can be very useful to piano owners and piano service people everywhere.

Of course, there is no way to supplant practice and experience in acquiring any skill. This is particularly true in piano technology. The best technicians have always learned by <u>doing</u>.

I feel, however, that this book can help the apprentice - either a professional or an advanced amateur - to gain the kind of knowledge that will make his practice or experience in this field more meaningful. As such I recommend it highly.

John H. Steinway

s/m

viii

Chapter One
Piano History and Classification

The piano is a unique keyboard instrument. Only the piano has hammers which strike tuned strings and rebound away from them, allowing the strings to vibrate and produce sustained musical tones. In order for the hammers to rebound, there is an *escapement* mechanism between each key and its hammer, which releases the hammer from the key just before the string is struck, allowing the hammer to bounce away from the strings. The pianist may play loudly or softly by varying the force with which he presses the keys, thus varying the blows of the hammers on the strings.

The first practical piano with an escapement mechanism for the hammers and capable of being played softly or loudly was built in 1726 by an Italian, Bartolomeo Cristofori (1655–1731). The name *piano* is an abbreviation of Cristofori's original name for the instrument: *piano et forte* or *soft and loud*. It stems from the fact that Cristofori's new instrument has a much wider range of expressive capabilities than did either of its predecessor keyboard instruments, the clavichord or the harpsichord.

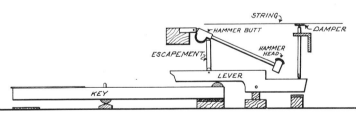

Illus. 1-1 Approximation of early escapement action by Cristofori. When the key is depressed, the escapement lever raises the hammer to a certain point and then releases it. The hammer "escapes" from control of the key, and rebounds from the strings. This escapement action sets the piano apart from all other keyboard instruments.

The history of the piano may be divided into three periods, each overlapping somewhat with the next: 1720–1850, 1850–1900, and 1900 to the present. For purposes of this book, the pianos made during these periods are called *antique*, *Victorian*, and *modern* pianos, respectively. These labels are general, referring to approximate periods rather than exact years.

The piano was invented and developed during the *antique* period. Many experimental designs were tried, various materials were used, and all sorts of short-lived, unusual pianos were made and then discontinued to make way for something better.

Illus. 1-2 A Victorian upright.

By the 1850's, or the *Victorian* period, piano design was approaching standardization. Most Victorian pianos have certain things in common and make use of mass produced parts. They may be categorized into three types: the *upright*, the *square grand*, and the *grand*. Most vertical pianos were called *uprights*, with the strings and soundboard positioned vertically. *Square grand* pianos were built in a rectangular shape with the strings positioned horizontally and approximately parallel to the keyboard. Although most square grand parts were mass produced, they are out of production and are not available. *Grand* pianos were made with

Illus. 1-3 A square grand.

the strings positioned horizontally, approximately at right angles to the keyboard. The best Victorian grands and uprights were excellent pianos, while square grands were valued more for their appearance than their musical qualities.

Illus. 1-6 A modern upright.

Illus. 1-4 A Victorian grand, made by Steinway in 1857.

Most *modern* pianos, made since 1900 or so, use conventional parts which are still available, except for certain experimental designs which have been discontinued. Modern pianos may be classified in two distinct types: *grands* and *verticals*. *Grands* have the soundboard and strings positioned horizontally over the floor, while *verticals* have the soundboard and strings positioned vertically.

There are three types of vertical pianos. The type is determined by the relative location of certain parts, which is governed in turn by the height of the cabinet. The *upright* piano has the mechanism or *action* located a distance *above* the keys, requiring extensions called *stickers* to connect the keys to the action. All modern uprights have stickers. The *console* piano, or *studio upright*, is of medium height, having the action mounted *directly over* the keys without stickers. The *spinet* piano (pronounced spin'et) is the least tall of the verticals, with the action partially or completely *below* the keys. Spinets have *drop stickers* extending downward from the keys to connect them to the action.

Illus. 1-7 The upright action is mounted above the keyboard.

In summary, a modern piano is either a grand or a vertical, and if a vertical, either an upright, console or spinet.

Other adjectives are often attached to piano names. These classify the piano according to size, wood finish, or cabinet design. The accompanying

Illus. 1-5 A modern Steinway concert grand.

Illus. 1-8 A modern console piano, with the action resting directly on the keys.

Illus. 1-9 A modern spinet, with the action partially below the keyboard.

illustrations show the usual names for various sizes and furniture styles of pianos.

Throughout the history of the piano, some makers and dealers have attempted to glorify their instruments by giving them misleading names which are usually associated with better pianos. Because most grands are better musical instruments than most verticals, one common trick is to call a vertical piano an *upright grand, studio grand* or *inverted grand*. This would lead the uninitiated to believe that the piano had qualities typical of grand pianos which are not found in ordinary verticals. Upon close examination, such pianos bear no more resemblance to a grand piano than any other vertical does.

Most of this book is directed to the servicing of modern pianos. Here and there in the text, however, specific repairs for Victorian pianos are included because many are still in use. No information is included on antique pianos because of the many varieties which were made and because they are so infrequently encountered.

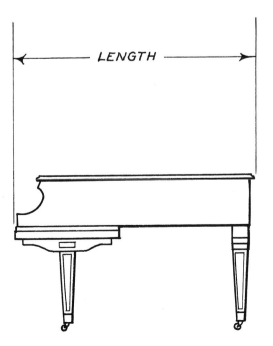

VERTICAL PIANO SIZES
(as measured from floor to top of piano)

Size	Typical Name
39" (99 cm) and smaller	Spinet
39"–51" (99–130 cm)	Console or Studio Upright
51" (130 cm) and larger	Upright

GRAND PIANO SIZES
(as measured from front to back of piano with lid closed)

Size	Typical Name
5'8" (173 cm) or smaller	Baby Grand
5'10" (178 cm)	Living Room Grand
6' (183 cm)	Professional Grand
6'4" (193 cm)	Drawing Room Grand
6'8"–6'10" (203–208 cm)	Parlour, Artist, Salon or Music Room Grand
7'4" (224 cm)	Half Concert or Semi Concert Grand
8'11" (272 cm) and larger	Concert or Orchestral Concert Grand

Illus. 1-10 Popular furniture styles for modern pianos.
Left, top to bottom:
Early American Pine   (Kimball)
Contemporary   (Kimball)
Italian Provincial   (Sohmer)
Traditional   (WurliTzer)
Right, top to bottom:
Spanish or Mediterranean   (Story & Clark)
French Provincial   (Sohmer)
Early American or Colonial   (Steinway)

Chapter Two
Construction of the Piano

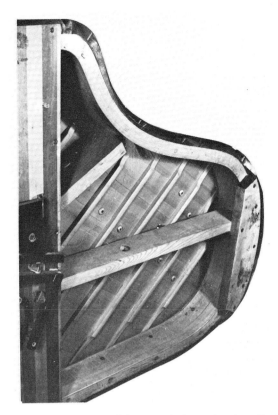

BASIC PARTS

A piano's foundation is its *frame*, usually made of oak timbers but sometimes made of a combination of timbers and steel or iron bars. The frame, visible from the back of a vertical piano and from the bottom of a grand, helps to support the tons of tension exerted by the stretched steel piano strings and also helps to hold the cabinet together.

Illus. 2-2 The wood frame of the grand piano after installation of the soundboard.

The *soundboard* is a large wooden diaphragm which is forced to vibrate by the strings, increasing their loudness. It is glued to the rim around its edges, leaving the middle free to vibrate. The front (or top, in a grand) of the soundboard is fitted with *bridges,* which connect it to the strings. Wooden *ribs* are glued to the back of the soundboard, adding strength and helping to maintain its proper shape.

Illus. 2-1 The wood frame of the vertical piano, prior to installation of the soundboard.

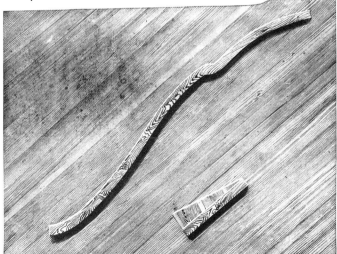

Illus. 2-3 Front view of upright soundboard, with long treble bridge and shorter bass bridge attached.

Illus. 2-4 Rear view of upright soundboard, with ribs glued in place.

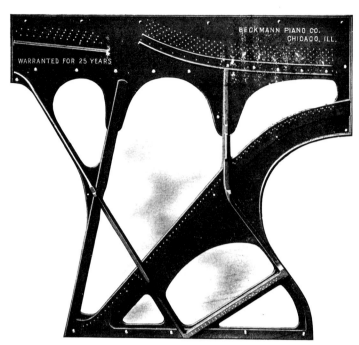

Illus. 2-5 A cast iron plate for a vertical piano.

Mounted above the soundboard in a vertical piano (and in front of it in a grand) is the *pinblock*. To the novice, this is one of the more mysterious parts of a piano, because it is usually hidden unless the piano is taken entirely apart. The cast iron *plate* covers the pinblock and soundboard, as illustrated. Anchored in holes in the pinblock, and protruding

through the plate are steel *tuning pins*. One end of each string is attached to a tuning pin; from there it passes under guide bars on the plate, over the soundboard bridges, to a steel *hitch pin* embedded firmly in the plate.

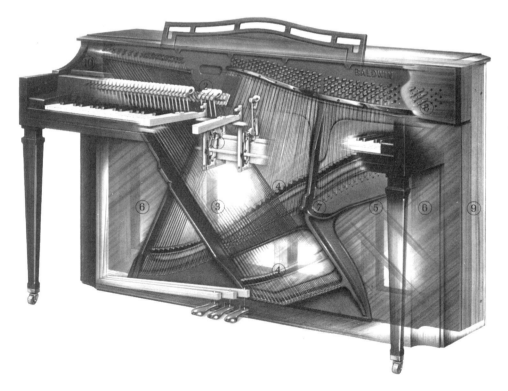

Illus. 2-6 Basic construction of the vertical piano.
1. Action
2. Hammers
3. Strings
4. Bridges
5. Ribs
6. Soundboard
7. Plate
8. Pinblock
9. Back
10. Cabinet

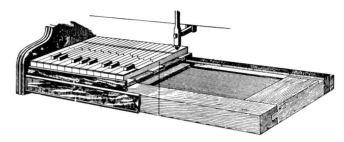

keybed, which provides firm support for the keyboard and action. It is made of thick planks solidly glued together, planed flat, screwed, and sometimes glued to the cabinet.

Illus. 2-8 The vertical piano keybed.

Illus. 2-7 Exploded view of a grand piano, showing basic construction. Copyright © 1965 by Scientific American, Inc.; from the article *The Physics of the Piano* by E. Donnell Blackham.

If all of the strings were of the same thickness and under the same tension, with high C the usual two inches or 51 mm long (approximately), low C would have to be about thirty feet (9.1 m) long. In order to build pianos of practical length, the bass strings are weighted with wrappings of copper or iron wire, wound around the core wire in a special lathe. The extra weight of the wrapping or *winding* slows the vibration of the wire to the correct rate without adding undue stiffness.

The lowest bass strings are so thick that one string is loud enough for each note. Higher bass strings are thinner, requiring two strings per note. In the treble, or upper range, each note has three strings, all tuned alike, which reinforce each other to produce the required loudness.

The frame, soundboard, bridges, pinblock, plate and strings form one integral unit in the piano. In the vertical this unit is called the *strung back,* around which the cabinet is built. In the grand, this unit is built into the *rim,* which forms the main part of the cabinet.

Securely fastened to the rim or cabinet is the

Upon the keybed rests the *action.* The action consists of a series of levers, starting with the *key,* (the link with the pianist's finger) and ending with the *hammer* (the felt-covered piece of wood which strikes the string and produces the tone). The action enables a pianist to play loudly or softly, repeating notes as quickly or slowly as the music dictates. If a piano hammer were attached directly to the back end of a key, when the key was depressed, the hammer would hit the string and stay there, damping out all vibration and sound. For this reason, all piano actions have some kind of escapement mechanism for each key, allowing the hammer to be released from the key *just before hitting the string.* After the hammer is released, it continues under its own inertia, hits the string, and rebounds. When the key is released, the action returns to its original position and resets itself for another cycle.

For each key and hammer in the piano, except in the high treble there is also a *damper.* When the key is up, the felt damper rests on the strings, preventing them from vibrating. When the key is depressed, the damper lifts from the strings,

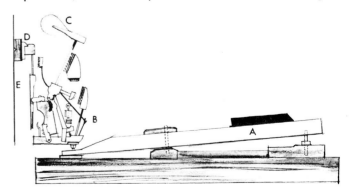

Illus. 2-9 Basic parts of the vertical piano action: A-Key; B-Escapement; C-Hammer; D-Damper; E-String.

allowing them to vibrate as long as the key is held down. When the key is released, the damper returns to the string, deadening the vibrations and stopping the sound. In the high treble, the tone dies away so quickly that no dampers are needed.

Most pianos have two or three pedals. The right pedal is always the *sustaining pedal*. It raises all of the dampers at once, allowing all notes which are played to continue sounding after the keys are released.

The left pedal is always some type of soft pedal. In vertical pianos and a few grands, it moves the hammers at rest closer to the strings, decreasing their travel and thus their striking force. In most grands, the soft pedal shifts the entire action sideways, causing the treble hammers to hit only two of their three strings. The shifting type of soft pedal is also called the *una corda* pedal.

Many pianos have only two pedals, soft and sustaining, but some also have a third pedal positioned between the other two. In most good quality grands and a few uprights, this is the *sostenuto* pedal. It sustains only those notes which are depressed *prior to and while* holding the pedal down, and does not sustain any notes depressed *after* holding it down. It enables the pianist to hold certain keys down with his fingers, sustain their sound with the pedal, release the keys and then play other notes without having *them* sustained and blurred together with the previous notes. The sostenuto is useful in rare musical instances where it takes the place of a "third hand."

In some pianos, the middle pedal is the *bass sustaining* pedal, which lifts only the bass dampers, allowing the pianist to play a bass note, sustain it with the pedal, and then use both hands elsewhere on the keyboard without blurring the sound of the treble notes. Musically speaking, this pedal is a cheap substitute for a sostenuto pedal.

In some uprights, the middle pedal is a *practice* pedal, which lowers a thick piece of felt between hammers and strings, muffling the tone.

Common names for the various parts of the piano cabinet are given in illustration 2-10.

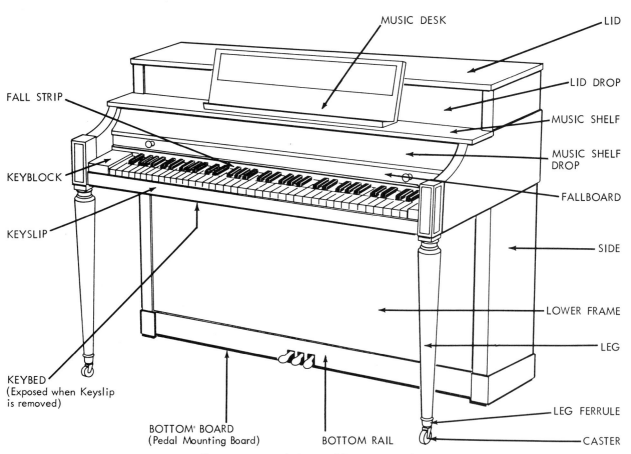

Illus. 2-10 Vertical piano cabinet nomenclature.

8

DETAILS OF CONSTRUCTION
The Soundboard

Soundboards are usually made of spruce about ⅜″ (1 cm) thick, which has the ideal amount of stiffness. Softer wood absorbs vibrations like a sponge, while harder wood is too stiff to vibrate properly. When a soundboard is made, spruce boards of about four to six inches (10–15 cm) in width are glued next to each other to gain the desired width; then the entire board is cut to the right shape and planed to the proper thickness.

The new, flat soundboard is placed face down on concave supports, where curved wooden ribs are glued to the back under pressure, at right angles to the grain, forcing the board to assume their curved shape. After the glue dries and the soundboard is installed in the piano, the ribs force the board to stay slightly curved. This curvature is called *crown.* Crown helps a soundboard to resist the downward pressure of the strings, keeping it from caving in, and making it more resilient and responsive to vibration.

Illus. 2-11 Richard Schoolmaster glues ribs to a new soundboard in the Aeolian-American piano factory.

Some soundboards are planed down to a thickness of about ¼″ (6.5 mm) around the edges, to provide a more flexible area where the board is glued down. Steinway's name for such a soundboard with thinner, more flexible edges, is the *diaphragmatic soundboard.*

When a spruce soundboard is subjected to extremes of humidity and dryness for a number of years, it tends to crack along the grain. Piano makers have experimented with laminated (plywood) soundboards, which are supposed to remain free of cracks, regardless of climate extremes. It is generally agreed, however, that a solid spruce soundboard vibrates better than a plywood soundboard does.

In some pianos, odd ringing sounds originate in a certain part of the soundboard. To suppress these objectionable sounds, a wooden strip is attached to the back of several ribs. This strip is called the *harmonic trap.*

Another device built into some pianos including the Mason & Hamlin is the *tension resonator,* invented by Richard Gertz in 1900. It consists of an assembly of rods and turnbuckles connected to the rim, to add dimensional stability. The turnbuckles are *not* to be adjusted by the technician.

Illus. 2-12 A Mason-Hamlin 9′ (274 cm) concert grand under construction, showing the tension resonator.

The Soundboard Bridges

Bridges are made of hardwood, and are glued and screwed to the soundboard. The screws go through wooden rings called *soundboard buttons* where they enter the back of the soundboard.

Sounding Board Button

9

Some bridges are made in one piece; others are laminated. The top layer of a laminated bridge is called the *cap*.

Illus. 2-15 A Broadwood grand piano with straight stringing.

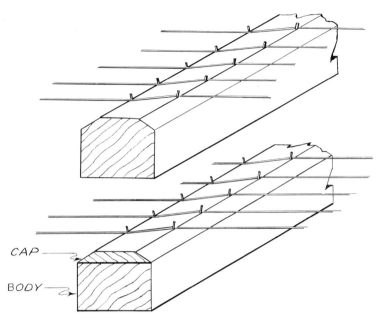

Illus. 2-13 One-piece and laminated treble bridges.

In order for piano strings to vibrate the soundboard efficiently, they must press down slightly on the bridges. This slight downward pressure is called *down bearing*. Tone quality is directly related to the amount of down bearing. Too little bearing causes a long-sustained but weak tone, while too much causes a loud, harsh tone that fades away quickly.

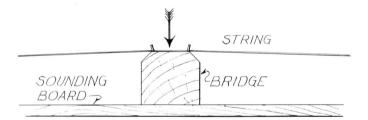

Illus. 2-14 Strings are mounted in such a way that the string tension produces a force on the bridge in the direction of the arrow. This force is called downbearing even in a vertical piano. Note that the string is not parallel to the soundboard.

In order to conserve space and fit the longest possible strings into a cabinet, modern pianos are *overstrung*, with the bass strings crossing over the treble strings for maximum length. Most overstrung pianos have separate bass and treble bridges, but some have one continuous bridge for all of the strings.

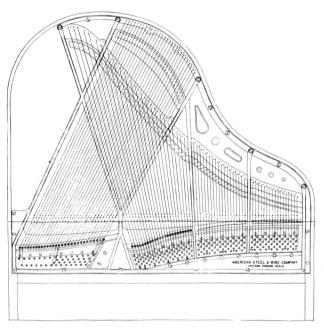

Illus. 2-16 Showing how the bass strings cross over the treble strings in an overstrung piano. This design permits the maximum possible string length in a given size cabinet.

In order for the strings to contact the bridge solidly and pass their vibrations efficiently through it into the soundboard, the top of the bridge is fitted with rows of copper-plated steel *bridge pins*. They are staggered and inserted at angles, giving the strings *side bearing*, and holding them firmly. In order to transmit string vibrations to the soundboard efficiently the bridge is made as small as possible, consistent with having enough strength to hold the bridge pins in place without cracking. The bridge edges are notched in line with the pins, to

10

prevent the strings from making extraneous contact.

Since the best bass tones are produced by the longest possible strings, the bass bridge must be positioned close to the edge of the soundboard, where the board vibrates poorly because it is glued down. To help overcome this problem, many pianos have an offset bass bridge, or *shelf bridge,* which allows the strings to have maximum length but transmits their vibrations to a more flexible part of the board. The connecting piece is called the *shelf* or *apron.*

Illus. 2-17 An offset or shelf bass bridge.

In high quality pianos, the plate braces are arranged to pass over the bridges. In other pianos, however, the treble bridge has a large notch to allow the brace to pass through it without touching. Notching the bridge reduces its ability to vibrate as one continuous piece, and in some pianos an extra piece of wood is glued behind the notch on the back of the soundboard, supposedly compensating for the notch.

Illus. 2-18 A continuous bridge.

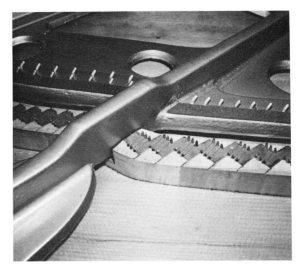

Illus. 2-19 Notching the bridge to allow a plate brace to pass through it reduces its ability to vibrate as one continuous piece.

The Pinblock

The pinblock is made of laminated hardwood with the grain running at different angles to support the tuning pins without cracking. It must simultaneously hold them *tight* enough to keep them from turning under string tension, and *loose* enough that they may be turned smoothly by the tuner.

Illus. 2-20 A piece cut from a pinblock to illustrate the cross-grain laminations of rock maple.

Illus. 2-21 Cross section of a Baldwin pinblock, showing the many thin layers of maple, and how the tuning pins fit into the block.

In all vertical pianos, the pinblock is glued to the top of the soundboard, and to the front of the top horizontal frame timber. It extends from the soundboard enough to accommodate a lip or *flange* cast into the plate. When the plate is mounted in the piano, large screws go through it, through the pinblock, and into the frame, forming a sandwich, with the pinblock supported by the plate, flange and frame but not by the soundboard. Everything must fit together perfectly, with the string tension distributed evenly over the entire pinblock into the frame and plate. If the pinblock does not make good contact all over, string tension is concentrated on several small points, which may eventually break down.

After the back is assembled and strung, the cabinet sides are glued on, adding a little more strength.

In some old uprights, including most Victorian uprights, the plate stops at the flange and does not cover the front of the pinblock. A piano with this type of plate is commonly called a *half plate* or *three quarter plate* piano. Although the flange bears a lot of tension, the pinblock is held in place by the frame. Three quarter plate pianos usually have extra large screws holding the pinblock and frame together, and sometimes have bolts, which do a better job. Some companies disguised the fact that their pianos had three quarter plates by fitting each one with a separate matching extension plate over the pinblock.

Due to the construction of the grand piano, the frame ends at the front edge of the soundboard, leaving a large cavity for the action. In most grands, the plate has the usual flange, and the pinblock is screwed to the bottom of the plate. Here, the fit of the pinblock to the plate is even more critical than in a vertical because the pinblock is not attached to the frame. It must make firm contact with the entire surface area and flange of the plate in order for the piano to stay in tune.

Illus. 2-23 Showing how a grand pinblock is fitted to the plate, as viewed from the bottom, with plate removed from piano.

Illus. 2-24 Showing the location of the pinblock in a grand piano as viewed from the area normally occupied by the action.

In some grands, the pinblock is mortised into notches in the rim, dowelled to the beam above the fallboard, and glued in place. This adds support and gives greater tuning stability. Many Victorian grands have a ¾ plate, with the pinblock mortised into the rim.

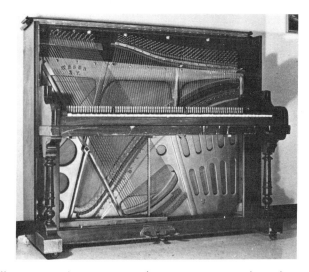

Illus. 2-22 A three-quarter plate Victorian upright with action removed to illustrate size of plate. Notice that the plate extends only to the bottom of the pinblock, and does not cover it.

The Plate

The plate is made of cast iron and is designed to support, with the help of the frame, many tons of string tension. The average medium size piano has about 230 strings, each string having about 160 (72.7 kg) pounds of tension, with the combined pull of all the strings equalling approximately eighteen tons (16,300 kg). The tension in a concert grand is close to thirty tons (27, 180 kg).

To hold the strings in the right place, the plate is fitted with various guide pins and other supports. The upright plate usually has an *upper plate bridge*, which supports the treble strings near the tuning pins. The *pressure bar* holds the strings against the plate bridge. Firm contact between the strings and plate is necessary for proper vibration. Since taut steel wire has a tendency to sink into the cast iron of the upper plate bridge, some pianos have the plate bridge fitted with a nickel-plated steel rod for the strings to rest on. The lower ends of the treble strings sometimes pass over a *lower plate bridge* and then go to the *hitch pins,* steel pins mounted in holes drilled in the plate. Sometimes the strings go directly from the treble soundboard bridge to the hitch pins without a lower plate bridge.

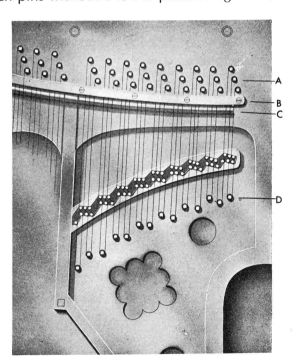

Illus. 2-25 Details of the vertical piano plate: A-Tuning pins; B-Pressure bar; C-Upper plate bridge; D-Hitch pins.

The hitch pins in Baldwin pianos made after the late 1960's are made of slotted tubular steel and are mounted at a 90° angle to the strings. They are called Acu-just hitch pins, and they allow the height of each string to be adjusted individually for correct down bearing.

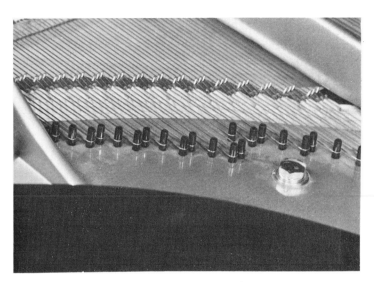

Illus. 2-26 The Baldwin Acu-just hitch pin.

Because the bass strings cross over the treble strings, they are supported by a larger and thicker plate bridge, which is fitted with spacer pins to keep the strings in place. The bass plate bridge has no pressure bar, since its height assures that the strings will make good contact with it. The bass strings pass over the bass soundboard bridge and are attached to hitch pins.

Some vertical pianos have individual fittings called *agraffes* which hold the treble strings in place. Each agraffe holds the strings for one note, is screwed into the plate, and takes the place of the plate bridge and pressure bar. Because the agraffe is screwed into the iron plate, instead of the wooden pinblock as the pressure bar is, there is less chance of having the string tension and the tuning altered by humidity-caused changes in the wood. Also, a pressure bar and upper plate bridge cause small bends in the string. When the string is tuned and the tension is changed, the friction at the two bends prevents the string from equalizing its tension easily down its entire length. A string slips more easily (in tiny amounts) through the single hole of an agraffe than past the bends caused by a pressure bar and upper bridge. Thus, a piano with agraffes is easier to tune and stays in tune longer than one having a pressure bar.

Illus. 2-27 Agraffes for single, double and three-string unisons.

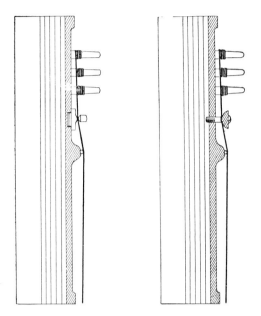

Illus. 2-28 This illustration compares vertical pianos using agraffes (at the left) and a pressure bar (at the right). Each drawing illustrates an upper plate bridge.

In the vertical piano, the hammers push the strings *toward* the plate, which is desirable. If the grand plate were made like the upright plate, the hammers would push the strings *away* from their plate bridge, since the hammers strike the strings from the bottom. This would disrupt the firm contact between strings and plate, to the detriment

of the tone quality. To eliminate this problem, some grand plates have agraffes throughout, while others have the *capo tasto* or *capo d'astro* bar in place of the agraffes. The capo bar, as it is usually called, holds the strings in place from above, so the hammers tend to push them *toward* it and seat them more firmly.

In any piano, the plate must hold everything together under enormous tension, but at the same time must permit the strings and soundboard to vibrate freely without absorbing and deadening too much vibration. To accomplish this double purpose, a plate is screwed down around its perimeter but does not touch the soundboard anywhere else.

The pinblock, frame and soundboard must be aligned precisely to support the plate all the way around without any high or low spots, so nothing is forced to bend when the plate is screwed into the piano. At the same time, the height of the plate over the soundboard must be adjustable, in order to adjust the downbearing of the strings on the bridge for optimum tone quality.

In the upright, the plate height is governed by wooden shims between the plate and soundboard. The shims are planed carefully to the correct thickness so the bearing will be correct, so the plate will touch them all around its edges, and so the plate will also rest firmly on the pinblock.

In a grand, the plate is usually supported by wooden dowel pins or bolts mounted in the rim; their height is adjusted until the plate makes contact with all of them, without rocking.

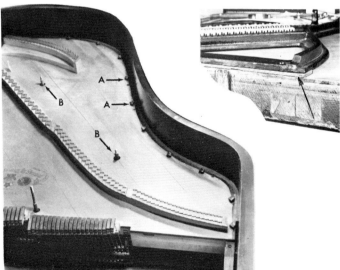

Illus. 2-29 The capo bar, an integral part of many grand plates.

Illus. 2-30 *Left:* Showing the plate support bolts (A) and nose bolts (B) in a Chickering grand. These support the plate in a way that it does not touch the soundboard; *Right:* in the vertical, wooden shims support the plate around its perimeter.

14

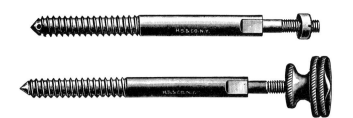

Illus. 2-31 Grand piano nose bolts, showing two styles of nuts.

Most piano plates also have one support somewhere in the middle, consisting of a *nose bolt* screwed into one of the members of the frame and passing through an oversize hole in the soundboard. The nose bolt has a shoulder, and a nut screws the plate down to the shoulder. The height of the bolt is usually set so the plate does not bend when the nut is tightened.

Some grands have a second nose bolt attached to an iron casting called a *bell,* under the high treble part of the soundboard. The bell has two functions. By screwing the nose bolt further into the frame, and by tightening the nut, the plate may be pulled down and flexed a little, in order to restore bearing to the high treble after the soundboard gets old and loses some of its crown; also, the hollow casting of the bell supposedly adds brilliance to the high treble notes by sympathetic vibration of the air chamber.

The main purpose of the usual nose bolt is to support the plate, not to give the tuner a means of bending the plate down to restore downbearing of the strings on the bridge. Bending a plate may cause it to crack; cast iron is very brittle.

Another feature found on some vertical piano plates is the *keybed support.* This is a shelf or small projection cast into the plate, to which the back of the keybed is fastened. The keybed support helps to keep the keybed from sagging or warping. There is sometimes a space between the keybed and support, which is filled with washers or shims before the screws are tightened.

Tuning Pins

Tuning pins are made in three basic types and in various sizes. Dimensions are given on page 140. They are finely threaded over the portion which is inserted in the pinblock, and have a hole called the eye to hold the end of the music wire, and a tapered square head to accommodate the tuning lever.

Most old pianos have blued-steel tuning pins which rust if exposed to high humidity. Nickel-plated pins do not rust as easily but these do not hold as tightly in the pinblock because the plating dulls the fine threads. Makers have overcome this problem by producing pins having the best attributes of both types: combination nickel-plated blued pins. The exposed end is plated, but the threads are blued, giving the durability and beauty of nickeled pins with the mechanical benefit of blued pins.

In some pianos, the plate has oversize holes for the tuning pins to pass through; in others, the holes are lined with wood *plate bushings.* Theoretically, the bushings give extra tightness and support to the pins, to keep them from flexing or bending.

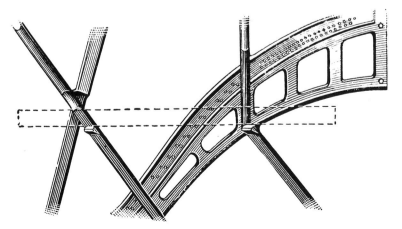

Illus. 2-32 The dotted lines show how the keybed is supported by projections which are cast into the plate.

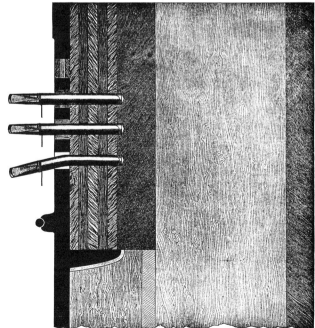

Illus. 2-33 A greatly exaggerated drawing showing the theoretical merits of plate bushings.

HITCH PIN   START OF WINDING   END OF WINDING

Illus. 2-34 A double wound bass string.

Strings

Piano strings may be categorized into two types: *treble strings,* made of steel wire, and *wound strings,* made of steel wire wrapped with a copper or iron winding, which adds weight and thickness without adding too much stiffness. In order to have the proper tension on each string, the wire length and diameter decrease from left to right, or from the lowest to the highest notes. All bass strings in most pianos are wound strings. Sometimes a few wound strings are used at the lower end of the tenor (low treble) section to smooth out the change in sound which occurs at the break between the highest bass string and the lowest treble string. The core wire of most wound strings is flattened under the ends of the winding, to give the winding a better grip. Higher bass notes having two strings per note have *single wound* strings; the lowest bass notes with one thick string per note have *double wound* strings, with two layers of winding. Wound strings are given a twist in the direction of the winding before they are placed on their hitch pins, to insure against the winding coming loose.

Illus. 2-35 Detail of bass string with hexagonal core wire.

All bass strings, and occasionally a few treble strings are tied to their hitch pins with a machine-made loop. Most treble strings start at one tuning pin, go around the hitch pin, and end at the next tuning pin, with one continuous piece of wire forming two treble strings. This saves the time and space involved in having a separate knot and hitch pin for every string, although some pianos are made this way.

Some high quality pianos have what is called a *duplex stringing scale* or simply *duplex scale.* Instead of muting off sections of the strings which are not struck by the hammers, these segments are allowed to vibrate sympathetically, to add to the brilliance of the tone. In some pianos, the plate is fitted with adjustable bars or plates called *aliquot bars* which may be moved to tune the duplex scale.

Illus. 2-36 Two types of duplex scales, illustrating Steinway aliquot plates (A) and Mason-Hamlin aliquot bars (B).

A more rarely encountered feature is *aliquot stringing.* Aliquot strings are extra strings which are tunable but are mounted above the line of the regular strings and are not struck by the hammers. They vibrate sympathetically whenever their corresponding note is struck, supposedly enhancing the tone.

Several types of felt and cloth are used in conjunction with the piano strings and plate. *Under string felt* is sometimes placed on the plate under the upper portions of the strings, to prevent them from vibrating sympathetically. *Stringing braid,* which comes in long strips, is woven in and out of certain string segments, also to prevent them from ringing sympathetically. Little washers, called *hitch pin punchings,* are placed on the hitch pins in some pianos prior to stringing to prevent the string loops from scratching the plate, and sometimes to decrease slightly the down bearing on the bass bridge.

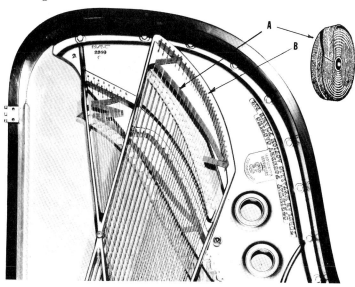

Illus. 2-37 Stringing braid (A) and understring felt (B).

Keybed

The keybed is heavily constructed to remain flat when exposed to humidity and temperature changes. If the keybed were to warp, it would change the relative positions of the action parts, throwing them out of the precise adjustment necessary for the action to work properly. Most

Illus. 2-38 Removing the keybed from a vertical piano.

vertical piano keybeds are screwed into the bottom of the cabinet arms, with three or four large screws at each end. In many vertical pianos, the keybed is also screwed to keybed supports cast into the plate. In most grands, the keybed is similarly screwed, and sometimes glued, to the rim.

Key Frame

Upon the keybed is positioned the assembly which holds the keys and action in place; this is called the *key frame*. It usually consists of a *balance rail* or *center rail* upon which the keys pivot; the *back rail* upon which the rear ends of the keys rest when they are not being played, and the *front rail,* which supports the fronts of the keys when they are pushed down. The three rails are securely fastened together so the whole key frame may be removed from the piano in one piece.

The grand key frame has regulating screws or *glides* on the bottom, which may be adjusted up and down until it rests perfectly flat on the keybed.

Illus. 2-39 The grand key frame viewed from below, showing adjustable glides.

The vertical key frame is screwed down to the keybed, and is leveled by means of paper shims. Some verticals also have key frame leveling screws.

The key frame is fitted with steel pins which hold the keys in their proper positions: *balance rail pins* and *front rail pins*. The pins are positioned so the fronts and centers of all the keys are evenly spaced. The back ends of the keys have no guide pins, and fan out at angles to leave spaces where the plate braces interrupt the spacing of the strings and hammers.

Each key rests on a cloth washer called the *center rail punching*. To make all the keys perfectly level with each other, paper punchings of various thicknesses are inserted under the cloth punchings. Steinway uses half-round wooden bearings under the keys on the balance rail instead of cloth punchings. Key height is adjusted with paper punchings under the wooden bearings. Steinway's name for this system is the *accelerated action*.

Each front rail pin has a cloth *front rail punching* with its paper punchings for fine regulation of how far each key can be depressed. The back rail has a strip of *back rail cloth,* on which the rear ends of the keys rest when not being played.

Action and key cloths serve two purposes: to prevent various pieces of wood from clicking against each other, and to give the action the proper feel to a musician.

Keys

The keyboard is made by gluing a number of softwood boards together side by side, forming one large piece which is then sawn into eighty-eight individual keys. The wood is light weight and has little inertia, allowing quick response. White key tops are covered with ivory or plastic, and black key tops or *sharps* are made of ebony or molded plastic. Each key has two cloth-bushed holes, one for each guide pin. In a good quality piano, each key has a wooden block called the *key button* glued over the balance rail hole and containing the cloth bushing. In cheaper pianos with no key buttons, the balance rail bushings are glued in the keys.

Illus. 2-41 At left, two types of capstan screws. Above, a key button.

The front rail pin is flat on the sides, to fit into the bushed front rail hole in the key. The extra surface area provided by the flat sides spreads the amount of wear over a larger surface of cloth, helping the cloth to last longer.

The rear end of the key usually has a *capstan screw* or *capstan,* a screw with holes or square sides to accept a wrench for adjustment, with a highly polished head to minimize friction between key and action. Some pianos have other types of capstans, which are discussed on pp. 24-25.

The Hammers

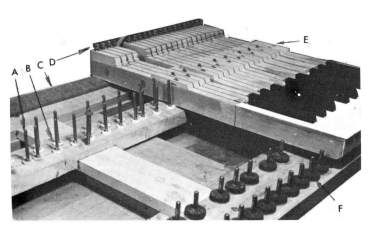

Illus. 2-40 Detail of key frame and keys: A-Balance rail pin; B-Balance rail punching; C-Back rail cloth; D-Capstan screw; E-Key button; F-Front rail punching.

A piano hammer consists of a wood *molding* and the surrounding felt. Hammers gradually decrease in size from bass to treble, along with the size of their respective strings. Good quality hammer felt is of such density and resilience that it is neither too firm, which causes a tinny sound, not too soft, which causes a dull, lifeless sound. All hammers in each section, treble and bass, are made from one long piece of laminated felt which is thicker down the middle than the edges, and one continuous piece of wood. The felt is wrapped around and glued to the molding under tremendous pressure in a large hydraulic or mechanical press. After the glue dries, the long strip is sliced into individual hammers. In some treble hammers, the felt is stapled to the molding for additional strength. A colored reinforcing liquid is sometimes applied to the felt. This stiffens the felt and helps to hold the hammer in its proper shape.

THE UPRIGHT ACTION

The upright action is built around a framework of four cast iron *action brackets* and several hardwood *rails* on which all the other parts are mounted. The action brackets typically have a socket at the lower end to rest on the bottom *action bolt* which is screwed into the keybed, and a fork at the top to slip over the top action bolt, which is screwed into the pinblock. Each top action bolt has a shoulder and a nut to hold the action in place. The entire piano action is removed from the piano in one piece by removing the four nuts, disconnecting the pushrods connecting it to the pedals, and lifting it out of the piano.

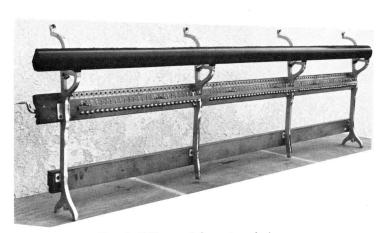

Illus. 2-42 The upright action skeleton.

The names of the various rails reflect their functions. Most of the movable parts for each individual note are attached to the *main rail*. Wherever these parts are screwed to the rail, it has a tongue which mates with grooves in the action parts, keeping them aligned. The *sticker rail* supports the stickers. The *regulating rail* holds one adjustable *regulating screw* for each note, and is fastened to the main rail with *regulating rail posts*. The *hammer rail* serves as a rest for the hammers and is padded with felt. It is movable, and is attached to the action brackets with *hammer rail hooks* or *hammer rail swings*. The hammer rail swing holes in the action brackets are bushed (or lined) with cloth.

The *spring rail* holds one spring for each hammer, and is padded with felt to keep the dampers from clicking against it. One other part, the *damper lift rod*, is not a rail, but affects all of the dampers so is considered part of the main body of the action. It swings from *damper lift rod hooks* or *swings*. The swings pivot from felt-lined metal clips which are screwed to the main rail.

The rest of the action is made of identical pieces, one of each type for each note in the piano, or 88 of each type altogether.

Most of the moving parts of the action are mounted on little hinges called *flanges*.

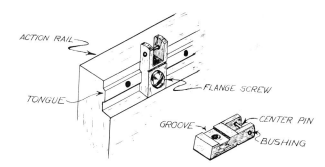

Illus. 2-43 Detail of flange with center pin and cloth bushings. Note the tongue and groove which keep the flange in alignment.

The flange and action part are pinned together with a *center pin* which fits tightly in the wood of the movable part, and rotates in the cloth-bushed holes of the flange. The center pin must fit perfectly to allow free movement of the action part without any wobble. Some flanges, such as the jack flange, are glued in place instead of being screwed down. Other parts are pinned together without a flange. Various types of flanges are illustrated on p. 24.

The movable action parts, of which there is one

complete set for each key in the piano, may be broken down into four main assemblies per note: the *sticker, whippen, hammer,* and *damper* assemblies.

The sticker assembly conveys motion from the key to the whippen. The whippen conveys motion from the sticker through the jack to the hammer butt, and the hammer hits the strings. The whippen also operates the damper, which is lifted away from the strings, allowing them to ring as long as the key is depressed.

UPRIGHT ACTION DRAWING

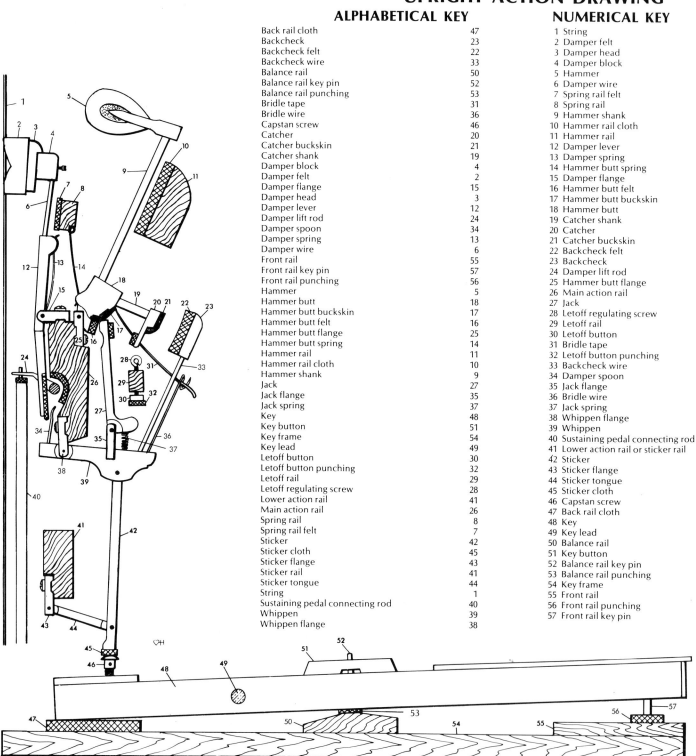

ALPHABETICAL KEY		NUMERICAL KEY	
Back rail cloth	47	1 String	
Backcheck	23	2 Damper felt	
Backcheck felt	22	3 Damper head	
Backcheck wire	33	4 Damper block	
Balance rail	50	5 Hammer	
Balance rail key pin	52	6 Damper wire	
Balance rail punching	53	7 Spring rail felt	
Bridle tape	31	8 Spring rail	
Bridle wire	36	9 Hammer shank	
Capstan screw	46	10 Hammer rail cloth	
Catcher	20	11 Hammer rail	
Catcher buckskin	21	12 Damper lever	
Catcher shank	19	13 Damper spring	
Damper block	4	14 Hammer butt spring	
Damper felt	2	15 Damper flange	
Damper flange	15	16 Hammer butt felt	
Damper head	3	17 Hammer butt buckskin	
Damper lever	12	18 Hammer butt	
Damper lift rod	24	19 Catcher shank	
Damper spoon	34	20 Catcher	
Damper spring	13	21 Catcher buckskin	
Damper wire	6	22 Backcheck felt	
Front rail	55	23 Backcheck	
Front rail key pin	57	24 Damper lift rod	
Front rail punching	56	25 Hammer butt flange	
Hammer	5	26 Main action rail	
Hammer butt	18	27 Jack	
Hammer butt buckskin	17	28 Letoff regulating screw	
Hammer butt felt	16	29 Letoff rail	
Hammer butt flange	25	30 Letoff button	
Hammer butt spring	14	31 Bridle tape	
Hammer rail	11	32 Letoff button punching	
Hammer rail cloth	10	33 Backcheck wire	
Hammer shank	9	34 Damper spoon	
Jack	27	35 Jack flange	
Jack flange	35	36 Bridle wire	
Jack spring	37	37 Jack spring	
Key	48	38 Whippen flange	
Key button	51	39 Whippen	
Key frame	54	40 Sustaining pedal connecting rod	
Key lead	49	41 Lower action rail or sticker rail	
Letoff button	30	42 Sticker	
Letoff button punching	32	43 Sticker flange	
Letoff rail	29	44 Sticker tongue	
Letoff regulating screw	28	45 Sticker cloth	
Lower action rail	41	46 Capstan screw	
Main action rail	26	47 Back rail cloth	
Spring rail	8	48 Key	
Spring rail felt	7	49 Key lead	
Sticker	42	50 Balance rail	
Sticker cloth	45	51 Key button	
Sticker flange	43	52 Balance rail key pin	
Sticker rail	41	53 Balance rail punching	
Sticker tongue	44	54 Key frame	
String	1	55 Front rail	
Sustaining pedal connecting rod	40	56 Front rail punching	
Whippen	39	57 Front rail key pin	
Whippen flange	38		

Illus. 2-44 The upright action.

FRONT VIEW OF THE ACTION

How does the Upright Action Work?

When a key is depressed slowly, it rocks on the center rail and goes up in back. The key raises the sticker and whippen. The whippen pushes the jack, which pushes the hammer butt. The hammer butt pivots on its flange and moves the hammer toward the string. When the key is half way down, the spoon engages with the damper lever, lifting the damper off the strings. When the hammer is almost to the strings, the jack heel bumps into the regulating button, and as the whippen keeps going up, the jack pivots and slips out from under the hammer butt. The hammer continues under its own inertia to the string, instantly rebounding. The catcher is caught by the backcheck and held in this position as long as the key is depressed.

When the key is released, the whippen drops, the backcheck releases the catcher, the bridle tape gives a little tug on the hammer butt, and with the help of the butt spring, the hammer returns to the hammer rail. The damper spring returns the damper to the strings, and the jack spring returns the jack under the butt, ready for the next repetition. This entire sequence occurs in a fraction of a second, allowing the pianist to repeat notes rapidly.

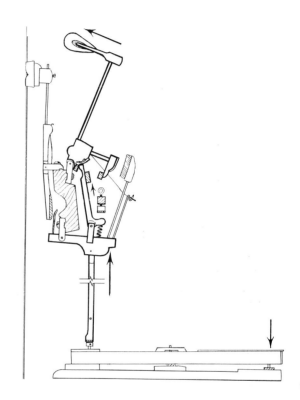

Illus. 2-45 Operation of the upright action: Key goes down, raising sticker, whippen, jack and hammer butt.

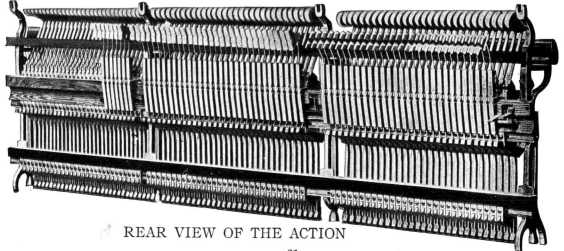

REAR VIEW OF THE ACTION

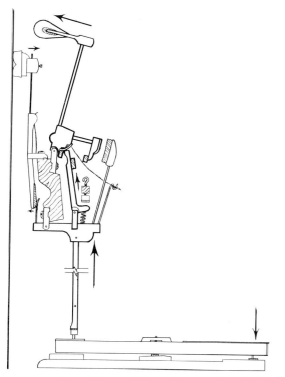

Illus. 2-46 Operation of the upright action, continued: Damper spoon begins to move damper lever.

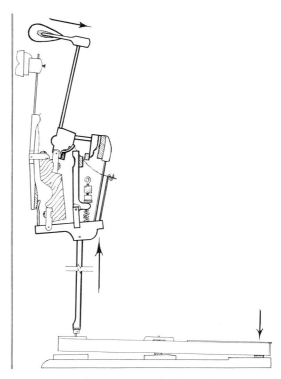

Illus. 2-48 Hammer hits string and rebounds. Butt catcher is caught by backcheck.

The Dampers

The lower a note is, the more vigorously the wire moves when it vibrates, and the more firm the damper must be. Bass dampers usually have felt wedges, while treble dampers usually have flat felt pads, as illustrated.

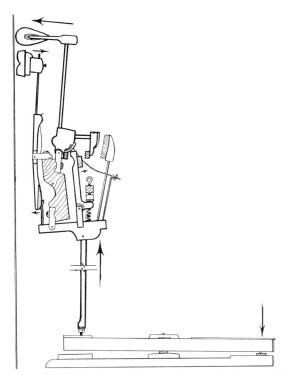

Illus. 2-47 Jack disengages from hammer butt when jack heel engages with letoff button.

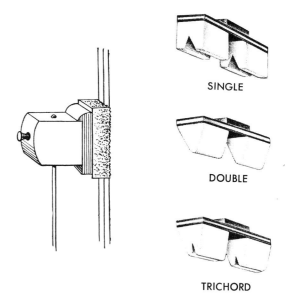

SINGLE

DOUBLE

TRICHORD

Illus. 2-49 Illustrating various types of vertical piano dampers: treble damper, left; bass wedges, right.

The Upright Pedals

Upright pedals are mounted on the bottom of the piano by means of various levers and pivots called the *trapwork.* Connecting the trapwork to the action are *pedal dowels.* Some dowels fit into sockets, while others have steel pins which fit into holes in the trapwork and action.

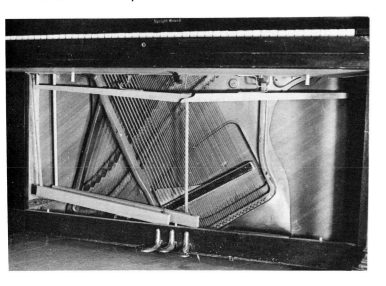

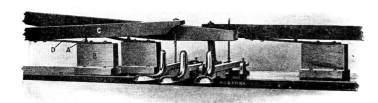

Illus. 2-50 Typical upright pedal trapwork.

The *soft pedal,* always on the left, is connected to the hammer rail. When depressed, it pushes the hammer rail and hammers about half way to the strings. In this position, the hammers have less distance to travel, so the pianist cannot put as much energy into them, resulting in softer playing.

The *sustaining pedal,* always on the right, connects to the damper lift rod. When depressed, the damper lift rod engages with all of the damper levers regardless of which keys are depressed, lifting the dampers away from their strings.

Some pianos have a *dummy damper,* a regular damper lever having a spring but no wire or head, and mounted over a whippen having no spoon. Its purpose is to return the damper lift rod to the rest position away from the damper levers when the sustaining pedal is released. The dummy damper spring pushes the dummy lever against the lift rod,

and thus acts as a lift rod return spring. In pianos having no dummy damper, the damper lift rod either returns to its rest position by its own weight or rests lightly against all the damper levers when the pedal is released.

The *bass sustain* pedal, in the middle if present, operates a second damper lift rod, the length of the bass section and mounted above or below the full sustain lift rod.

The *practice pedal,* in the middle if present, connects to a wood or aluminum rail. A piece of thick, soft felt is attached to the rail and hangs down from it about 1½ inches (3.9 cm). When the pedal is depressed, the felt is lowered between the hammers and strings, muffling the tone. In some pianos, the practice pedal has a special notch in the cabinet, allowing it to be locked down. After depressing the pedal, it may be pushed sideways into the notch, holding the felt muffler in place between hammers and strings, so the pianist may use both feet for the other pedals.

Illus. 2-51 Felt muffler rail in place between hammers and strings.

The *sostenuto pedal* is so rarely encountered in vertical pianos that its operation is not described here. It is similar to the grand sostenuto pedal, which is described on pages 33-34.

Upright Action Variations

The most common variations found in vertical pianos are various styles of hammer butt flanges, including the *Billings,* the *brass flange rail,* the *Kimball brass flange rail,* and the *double flange.*

The Billings flange is made of brass. The two prongs fit into a groove in the main rail, keeping the flange in proper alignment. The center pin fits tightly in the flange, and the hammer butt is bushed and rotates around the pin.

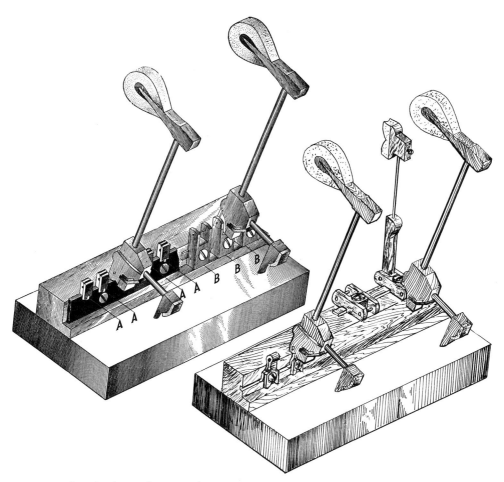

Illus. 2-52 From left to right, the brass flange rail, conventional flange, Billings flange and double flange.

The brass flange rail is a continuous piece of brass screwed to the main rail. For each hammer, a screw goes through a hole in the rail into a threaded hole in the brass butt plate.

The Kimball brass flange rail is similar to the regular brass rail, but the rail holes rather than the butt plates are threaded, so the screws go in from the opposite side.

The purpose behind all three metal flange systems was to hold the center pin solidly in a piece of metal, which does not get loose like a piece of wood does when the humidity goes down. Unfortunately, old brass which has been stressed and relaxed many times (such as the brass in a flange rail) breaks more easily than old wood usually does.

The fourth type of odd flange is the double flange, which holds both the damper lever and hammer butt.

The capstan is another part of the action which has been made in several different styles, including the *dowel capstan, regulating screw capstan,* and *rocker capstan.*

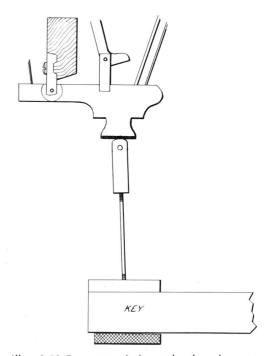

Illus. 2-53 Capstan variations: the dowel capstan.

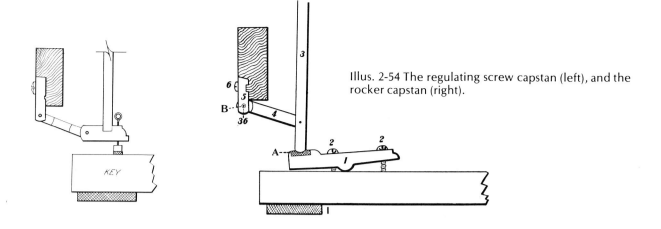

Illus. 2-54 The regulating screw capstan (left), and the rocker capstan (right).

Most European and Japanese, and some American verticals use the *Schwander* hammer butt. The *spring loop* is attached to the flange, and the butt spring is mounted in the butt. There is no spring rail.

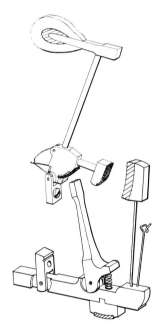

Illus. 2-55 A Schwander hammer butt and whippen, encountered in European, Japanese and some American pianos. Note that the jack is pinned directly to the whippen.

Lost motion compensators were sometimes used on the stickers. In the regular vertical action, when the soft pedal is depressed, pushing the hammer rail and hammers halfway toward the strings, a space or *lost motion* is introduced between the jack and the hammer butt. Soft playing thus accomplished is accompanied by decreased control over the hammer, since the key has to go part way down before it does anything. The lost motion compensator, one for each key, makes use of leverage to eliminate lost motion when the hammer rail goes up, allowing the pianist to play more softly by decreasing hammer travel distance, while at the same time giving the keys control over the hammers through their full stroke. The compensator mechanism was used only on expensive uprights made in the early 1900's, and it greatly enhanced the soft playing capabilities of the upright piano. Unfortunately, as manufacturers sought to reduce their costs, this complicated device was the first to go.

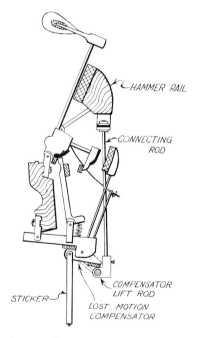

Illus. 2-56 The lost motion compensator action. As the pianist depresses the soft pedal, the hammer rail moves the hammers closer to the strings. In an ordinary action, this introduces a gap between the jack and the butt. In this mechanism, the connecting rod raises the compensator lift rod, which in turn raises the jack, eliminating lost motion.

25

An extra rail called the *touch rail* is found in some actions. In normal vertical actions, each jack and each catcher have mating pieces of felt to prevent a clicking noise when the jack slips out from under the hammer butt. The touch rail takes the place of the catcher felt.

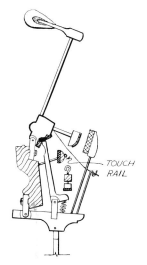

Illus. 2-57 Touch rail, sometimes used in place of hammer catcher felt to silence operation of jacks.

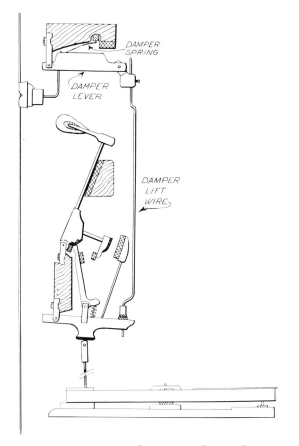

Illus. 2-58 Victorian upright action with over dampers.

Some old uprights have dampers mounted on long wires and resting on the strings above the hammers. These are called *over dampers;* actions having them are commonly referred to as *squirrel cage* or *bird cage* actions. Since the early 1900's, their use has been confined to the lowest two or three treble notes where the normal dampers must be cut off at an angle where the bass strings cross over. Most pianos made since about 1915 have the stringing scale designed so that no over dampers are necessary, allowing enough room between the hammers and the bass strings near the break for normal dampers of adequate length.

In some old uprights, the middle pedal controls an attachment which changes the tone of the piano. Typically called the *mandolin, zither,* or *harp* attachment, this usually consists of a rail similar to the practice pedal muffler rail, but having metal-studded tabs in place of the felt in the treble section. When keys are played with the attachment lowered between hammers and strings, the hammers bump the tabs against the strings, causing a tinny honky-tonk sound.

THE CONSOLE ACTION

A console piano, or studio upright, is basically a short upright *without stickers.* The action is identical to the upright action, except the whippens have cloth pads instead of stickers, and rest directly on the capstans. Some taller consoles and studio uprights have dowel capstans, while shorter consoles have regular capstans. Many medium size Victorian uprights have long dowel capstans instead of stickers.

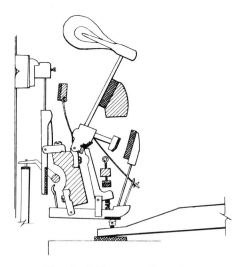

Illus. 2-59 The console action.

A few small consoles have the rarely-encountered Wood & Brooks 90° *inverted direct blow* action. Despite its different shape, this action works exactly like the regular console action.

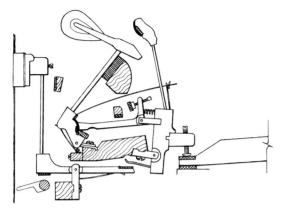

Illus. 2-60 The Wood & Brooks 90° inverted direct blow action.

THE SPINET ACTION

In order to build a piano under 38" (.965 m) in height, with the keyboard the proper height above the floor, the action must be located *below* the keyboard. This arrangement is called the *drop action,* and the whippens are connected to the keys with *lifter elbows* and *inverted stickers* or *drop stickers.* Except for the inverted sticker, the drop action works exactly like the upright action.

Some spinet action brackets are screwed directly to the plate without the usual upper action posts. With this type of bracket, there is no danger of

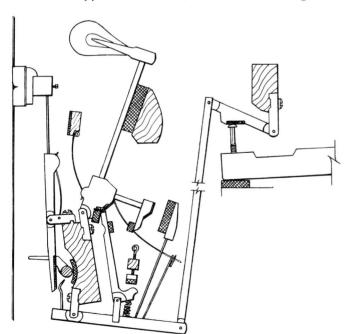

Illus. 2-61 The spinet action.

damaging the dampers by bumping them into the action posts when removing the action from the piano.

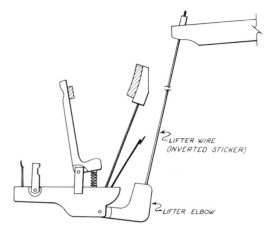

Illus. 2-62 A spinet action with lifter elbow connecting the inverted sticker to the whippen.

THE GRAND ACTION

Like the vertical, the grand action is built around a framework of four cast iron action brackets and several hardwood rails, as illustrated. In the Steinway action, the wooden rails are encased in metal tubing. The grand action is screwed directly to the key frame, so the action, keys and key frame all come out of the grand in one piece.

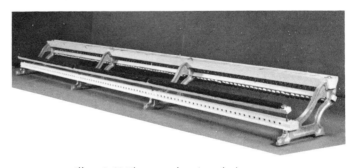

Illus. 2-63 The grand action skeleton.

The grand action has certain things in common with the vertical, including keys, capstans, whippens, jacks, hammer shanks, hammers and dampers. As in the upright, the key pushes on the whippen, the whippen on the jack, and the jack on the hammer. From here on, the resemblance ends, however, because the grand action has an additional assembly on each whippen called the *repetition lever.* The repetition lever is so named because it enables the pianist to repeat notes faster than is possible on a vertical piano.

GRAND ACTION DRAWING
NUMERICAL KEY

1 String
2 Damper head
3 Damper felt
4 Damper guide rail
5 Damper wire
6 Hammer
7 Hammer shank
8 Drop screw
9 Hammer flange
10 Main action rail
11 Damper stop rail
12 Damper lifter flange
13 Damper wire screw
14 Sostenuto rod
15 Backcheck
16 Hammer rest*
17 Repetition lever screw
18 Repetition lever flange
19 Repetition lever
20 Hammer knuckle
21 Repetition lever button
22 Whippen spoon

23 Combination jack spring and
    Repetition lever spring**
24 Whippen
25 Jack regulating button
26 Jack regulating screw
27 Letoff regulating screw
28 Letoff rail
29 Letoff button
30 Letoff button punching
31 Jack
32 Action bracket
33 Damper lever flange
34 Damper lift rail spring
35 Sostenuto tab or lip
36 Damper lever
37 Damper lever key cushion
38 Backcheck wire
39 Whippen flange
40 Whippen rail
41 Whippen cushion
42 Capstan screw
43 Key button
44 Balance rail key pin
45 Key

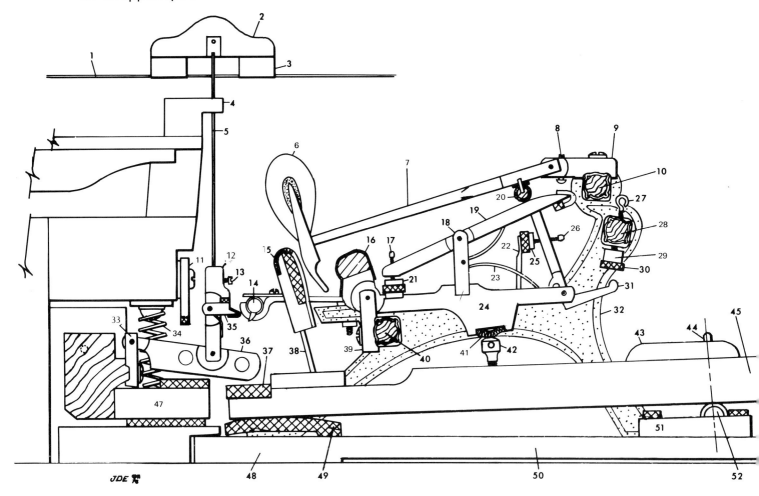

JDE

GRAND ACTION DRAWING
ALPHABETICAL KEY

*The hammer rest is built into the Steinway-style whippen. Other actions have a separate hammer rail located in the same position.

**These are two separate springs in many actions.

***The Steinway balance rail bearings take the place of the usual cloth punchings.

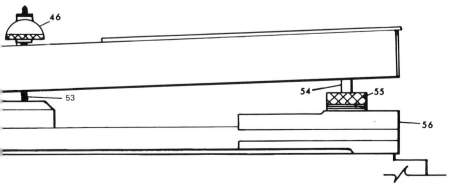

How does the Grand Action Work?

When the key is depressed slowly, the capstan pushes on the whippen, which pushes on the jack, which pushes on the hammer knuckle and moves the hammer. When the key is half way down, the back end of the key begins to raise the damper from the strings. As the key continues, and the hammer is almost to the strings, the jack bumps into the letoff button, and slips out from under the knuckle. The hammer continues by inertia, hits the strings and rebounds. When the hammer rebounds, the jack has already been tripped and is no longer under the knuckle, so the knuckle lands on the repetition lever instead. The downward force of the hammer is stronger than the repetition lever spring, so the hammer knuckle pushes the repetition lever down, pivoting it on its flange. The downward motion continues until the hammer tail catches on the backcheck, and the hammer remains in this checked position as long as the key is depressed.

For a moment, pause to consider the positions of the various parts. The key is depressed. The damper is up. The hammer has bounced against the strings and is now being held in place by the backcheck. The jack is out from under the hammer knuckle, having been tripped by the letoff button. The repetition lever with its spring, however, is trying to push the knuckle upwards but can not move it because the hammer tail is being held by the backcheck. Now, back to the operation when the key is released.

When the key is released *slowly*, the backcheck releases the hammer tail, allowing the repetition lever to support the hammer just enough for the jack to slip back under the knuckle, *as soon as the jack clears the letoff button*. Because the jack clears the letoff button when the key is less than halfway up, the action is ready for another complete cycle *without the need for the key to return to its rest position*. Remember that in the vertical, the pianist must release the key and let it come almost all the way up before the jack slips under the butt, allowing the cycle to be repeated. In the grand, the pianist can repeat notes without letting the keys come all the way up. Because less time is spent waiting for the keys to return, and less finger motion is used, the grand is capable of more rapid repetition than the vertical, particularly when played softly.

When the key is released fully, it lowers the damper to the strings, muting the sound.

This sequence occurs much faster than the eye can follow, let alone the time it takes to be described in writing. From the above slow-motion description, it would seem that the repetition lever always pushes the hammer upward to allow the jack to return under the knuckle. During louder playing, however, the pianist releases the key faster than in the above description; the pull of gravity on the key and the inertia of the hammer cause the repetition lever spring to push the whippen *downward*, rather than the hammer *upward*, in the first moment that the key is released. When a note is to be repeated softly, the pianist repeats the cycle before the hammer has time to drop all the way to the rest position. The more loudly the pianist repeats the note, the farther he allows the key to come up, and the farther the hammer drops away from the strings toward its rest position between repetitions.

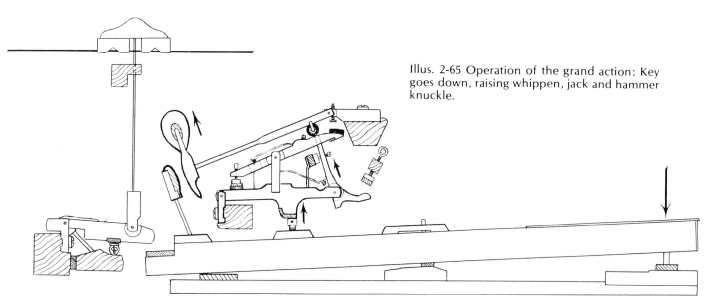

Illus. 2-65 Operation of the grand action: Key goes down, raising whippen, jack and hammer knuckle.

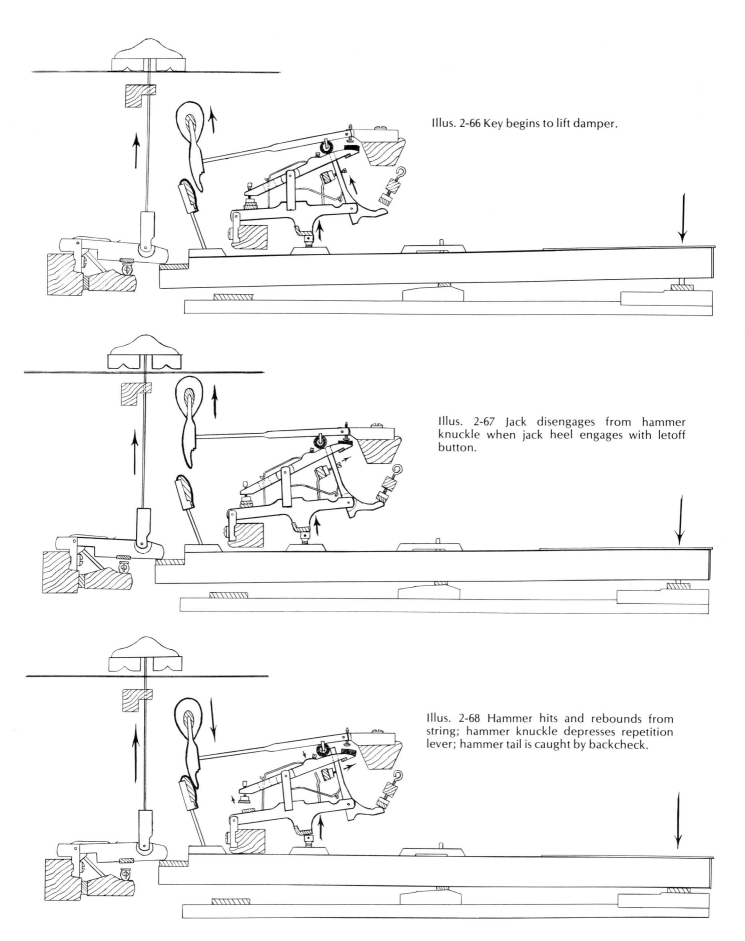

Illus. 2-66 Key begins to lift damper.

Illus. 2-67 Jack disengages from hammer knuckle when jack heel engages with letoff button.

Illus. 2-68 Hammer hits and rebounds from string; hammer knuckle depresses repetition lever; hammer tail is caught by backcheck.

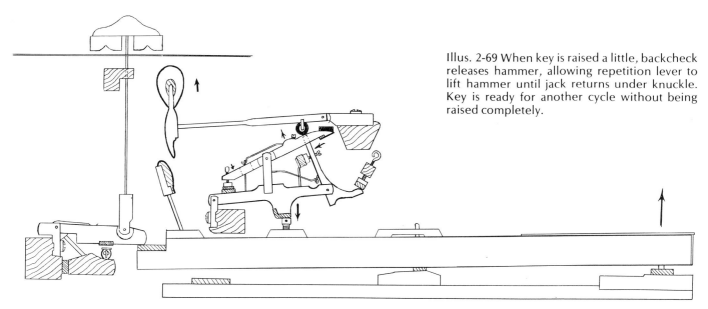

Illus. 2-69 When key is raised a little, backcheck releases hammer, allowing repetition lever to lift hammer until jack returns under knuckle. Key is ready for another cycle without being raised completely.

The Grand Hammer Rail

With the grand hammer knuckle normally resting on the repetition lever when the key is at rest, why is a hammer rail necessary? When a pianist plays a loud stacatto (extremely short) note just once without repeating it, the hammer rebounds forcefully from the strings, but the backcheck is down because the key has been released. The entire returning force of the hammer would be too much for the jack and knuckle to support, so the hammer rail does most of the job of stopping the hammer. The rail is set slightly below the line of the hammers at rest so it normally provides no support, but adds the extra needed cushion when the hammers vigorously rebound from the strings to their rest position.

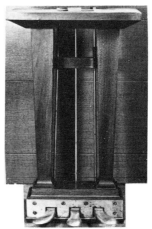

The Grand Pedals

Grand pedals are suspended from the bottom of the keybed by the *pedal lyre*. To withstand the heavy pressure exerted on the pedals, the lyre is attached with large screws or bolts, and braces.

The grand soft pedal, to the left, is usually a shifter or *una corda* pedal. By means of a lever which fits into a notch in the bottom of the key frame, the pedal shifts the entire action sideways, usually to the right, just far enough so the treble hammers hit only two of their three strings, reducing the volume of sound. A spring returns the action to its normal position when the pedal is released.

Illus. 2-70 Pedal lyre assemblies: Steinway (above) and Chickering (below).

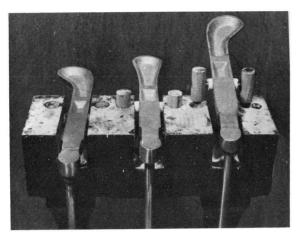

Illus. 2-71 A frequently encountered method of mounting the pedals in the pedal lyre, shown in an inverted view.

In some grands, the soft pedal lifts the hammer rail, moving the hammers closer to the strings and decreasing their striking distance, as in the upright. This type is not as desirable to the pianist, because it changes the feel or touch of the action. It is often used in self-playing grand pianos, however, because less power is needed to move a hammer rail up and down rapidly than to shift the weight of the entire action back and forth.

The sustaining pedal, to the right, lifts all of the dampers at once with the damper lift rail.

Illus. 2-72 Details of grand damper action located directly behind piano action: A-Lifter flange and damper wire screw; B-Sostenuto rod; C-Damper lever and damper wire screw; D-Damper lift rail.

The middle pedal usually operates the sostenuto mechanism. When a key is depressed, and then the sostenuto pedal is depressed, the sostenuto rod lip engages with the lip on the damper assembly, holding the damper up off the strings after the key is released. In other words, any notes played and held down while depressing the sostenuto

pedal are sustained after their keys are released, as long as the sostenuto is held down. Any keys depressed *after* the sostenuto pedal is depressed are not affected, because *their* damper sostenuto lips remain *under* the lip on the rod, allowing the dampers to drop when the keys are released. The sostenuto allows the pianist to play certain notes, sustain only those notes with the pedal (which acts like an extra hand) and then use both hands to play other non-sustained notes.

In some grands, the middle pedal operates a bass sustain device which is either a separate damper lift rail in the bass, or a separate section of the main damper lift rail.

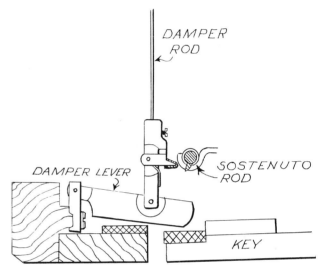

Illus. 2-73 Operation of the sostenuto mechanism: key and sostenuto rod at rest.

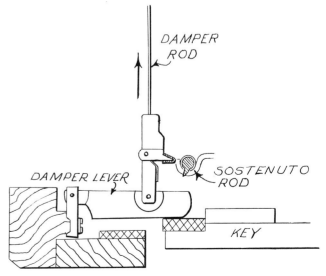

Illus. 2-74 Key is depressed, raising damper lever and sostenuto lip above rod.

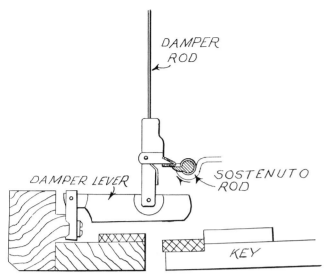

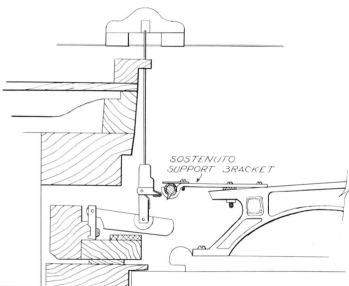

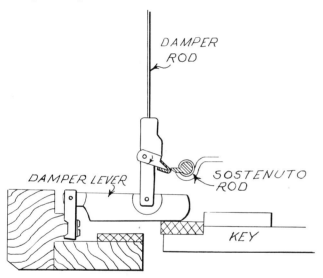

Illus. 2-75 Operation of sostenuto mechanism, continued: Sostenuto pedal is depressed, catching lips of dampers which were up, leaving other dampers down.

Illus. 2-76 With sostenuto still engaged, another key lifts its damper. Its damper lip remains below the sostenuto rod allowing damper to fall when key is released.

Illus. 2-78 Two ways of mounting the sostenuto assembly.

Grand Action Variations

Most grand actions are similar, with minor variations occuring at the capstans, letoff screws, whippens, or knuckles, as illustrated.

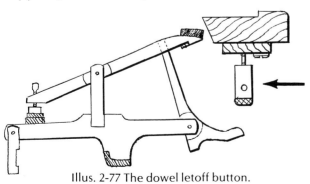

Illus. 2-77 The dowel letoff button.

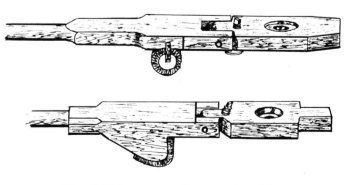

Illus. 2-79 Two types of hammer knuckles.

VICTORIAN PIANOS

As explained in Chapter One, the name *Victorian piano* is used here to denote any piano made between about 1850 and 1900 which has standardized, mass-produced parts. The Victorian upright or grand is similar to its modern counterpart, but usually has a ¾ plate. The action brackets are sometimes made entirely of wood instead of cast iron, and most Victorian uprights have dowel capstans instead of stickers.

THE SQUARE GRAND

The square grand is a completely different type of piano. The strings are arranged in a fan-shaped pattern, with the pinblock and tuning pins toward the back of the cabinet. The soundboard is suspended between the keybed and strings, with an opening for the hammers running parallel to the plate bridge toward the rear of the piano. Square grand keys are very long, and the action parts and hammers are arranged in an arc conforming to the pattern of the strings. The hammers are much smaller and lighter than in the modern piano. The jack flanges are attached to the keys, eliminating

the need for whippens. The dampers are mounted on levers, and are lifted by damper lifter wires which rest on the back ends of the keys.

Illus. 2-81 Top view of square grand with lid open. Note radial pattern of strings.

Operation of the Square Grand Action

When the key is depressed slowly, the jack goes up, lifting the hammer. When the key is half way down, it begins to lift the damper. When the jack bumps into the letoff button and slips out from the butt, the hammer continues toward the strings, rebounds from them and is caught by the backcheck. When the key is released, the key, whippen, damper and hammer fall back to their normal positions, and the jack spring returns the jack under the hammer butt. Because there are no repetition levers, the hammers rest on a hammer rail as in the upright. The sustaining pedal lifts all of the damper levers. The soft pedal slides a felt strip between hammers and strings.

Illus. 2-80 The square grand action. Note curve of hammer line.

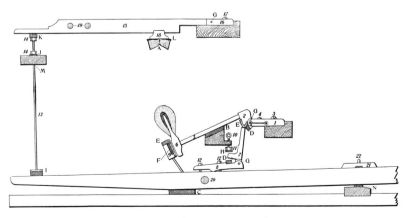

Illus. 2-82 Cross section of the square grand action.

Chapter Three
What is Piano Servicing?

Piano servicing may be separated into six areas: tuning, regulating, tone regulating (or voicing), repairing, rebuilding, and refinishing.

Tuning is the art of adjusting the tension of each string to make it sound the most pleasant when played with other strings. This is accomplished by turning the tuning pins slightly one way or the other.

Regulating consists of adjusting the action to make everything work properly.

Voicing or *tone regulating* consists of changing the tone quality, usually by making the hammers softer or harder.

Repairing involves fixing broken parts, usually "on location." Replacing a broken string, regluing several loose hammers or keytops, and fixing a sticking key, are typical repair jobs.

Rebuilding involves major reconditioning procedures, normally undertaken only in a workshop equipped with a workbench, and for some jobs, non-portable tools. Rebuilding usually involves the installation of entire sets of new parts or complete reconditioning of original parts. Replacing a set of hammers, recovering the keytops with new plastic, restringing an entire piano and restoring a broken and cracked soundboard are rebuilding jobs.

Refinishing is making all of the parts of a piano look like new. This book explains how to refinish the soundboard, (which is accessible only to a piano technician who has the piano taken apart), and leaves cabinet refinishing to one of the books listed in the bibliography.

The person who has his own piano servicing business is usually called a *piano tuner, technician, tuner-technician,* or *rebuilder.* The typical tuner knows how to make minor repairs, and possibly how to voice a piano, in addition to tuning. The tuner-technician knows all aspects of piano servicing, with the possible exception of cabinet refinishing. The rebuilder usually spends most of his time in the workshop completely overhauling pianos; his rebuilding skills enable him to make all types of repairs, and many rebuilders also specialize in cabinet refinishing.

Player pianos require specialized repair techniques. Extensive experience is usually necessary before the technician can repair them profitably, so most player piano technicians spend most of their time on them. Literature concerning this branch of the field is listed in the bibliography.

Quality of Workmanship

Whenever any type of repair is made, the technician should try to make the part function and look just like it did when the piano was new. An exception is when repairs are made on battered old pianos, where it may not be worth the trouble to make the broken parts look like new, providing that they do their job and look at least as good as the other old parts in the piano. The technician's continuing goal, however, should be to improve the quality of his work until he can put any part of any piano into brand new condition.

Chapter Four
Tuning

Acoustic Theory

A piano sounds *in tune* when its strings vibrate at certain frequencies, according to musical and acoustical rules. For clarity, these rules are explained in the following sequence: musical tone versus noise; how wire vibrates; what happens when two or more wires vibrate simultaneously; how the vibrations are organized into the tuning scale of the piano; how to identify the notes by name; and how the vibrations are related mathematically to each other.

Musical Tone Vs. Noise

When something vibrates, it causes the surrounding air to imitate its movement. For example, when a gasoline engine runs, it transmits its scrambled collection of vibrations to the surrounding air, which in turn vibrates the eardrums and gives the sensation of *noise*. Any unorganized collection of vibrations is heard as noise. On the other hand, when an object vibrates at a certain speed and causes peoples' eardrums to vibrate at the same regular rate, *musical tone* is heard, as long as the vibration is within the range of human hearing. If the vibration is too slow, each cycle is heard individually like the clicks of a ratchet; if the rate is too fast, it is not heard at all. The speed at which the object vibrates is its *frequency,* measured in *cycles per second,* or *hertz (hz).* The faster the vibration, the higher the frequency and the higher the audible tone; the slower the vibration, the lower the frequency and the lower the tone. The frequency of vibration in hz is also called *pitch;* the higher the pitch, the faster the vibration.

The Vibration of Wire

Three factors influence the pitch of a vibrating wire:
1. The *length:* other factors being the same, the shorter a wire, the higher its pitch.

2. The *thickness:* other factors being the same, the thinner a wire, the higher its pitch.

3. The *tension:* other factors being the same, the tighter a wire, the higher its pitch.

Illus. 4-1 In each of the three illustrations above, the string on the right will have the higher pitch.

Another factor, the *stiffness,* is a result of the other factors. If two wires of different lengths have the same thickness, the shorter wire is shorter *in proportion to its thickness* than the longer wire, so the shorter wire is stiffer. Other factors being the same, the stiffer a wire, the higher its pitch.

Wire vibrates in a complex way. Not only does an entire string vibrate, producing the *fundamental pitch;* it also divides itself into two vibrating halves, three thirds, four quarters and so on, all at the same time. Each portion produces its own pitch, called a *partial.* Whenever a string vibrates, it produces a whole series of *partials* (or *partial series*) along with the fundamental pitch.

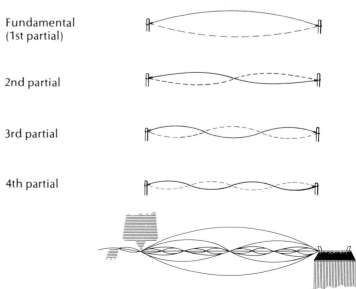

Illus. 4-2 A vibrating wire subdivides itself into many simultaneously vibrating fractions. Each fraction produces an audible pitch of its own, called a *partial.*

The partials are usually much softer than the fundamental, but it is possible to force a partial to predominate by touching a string lightly at a half, a third or various other fractions of its length, and then playing it. The partial produced by the isolated segment will sound louder than the fundamental.

Illus. 4-3 Touching a string lightly at its midpoint forces the second partial to predominate. Touching it at various other fractions of its length allows the listener to pick out other partials.

Musicians have used the words *partial* and *harmonic* interchangeably to describe vibrating string segments, but the words do not have the same exact meaning. A *partial* is the pitch produced by any vibrating string segment, whether or not its frequency is an exact multiple of the fundamental pitch. A *harmonic* is an exact multiple of the fundamental. Thus, every harmonic is a partial, but not every partial is a harmonic. In this book, *partial* refers to any vibrating string segment, while *harmonic* refers only to a partial which is a multiple of the fundamental pitch. String stiffness causes the vibrating segments to produce partials which are not true harmonics. The deviation of partials from the harmonic series is called *inharmonicity* and is described on pp. 53-54.

Simultaneously Vibrating Wires

If two wires are adjusted, or *tuned*, to the same pitch and are struck, the sound produced by one reinforces the other, and the two produce a louder combined tone. This is called "constructive interference."

If one wire vibrates out of synchronization with the other, they subtract from each other and produce a softer tone, by "destructive interference." If in a laboratory, two strings are forced to vibrate out of synchronization with each other, so that each one travels toward the eardrum while the other travels away from it, the combined tone is softer than when they are vibrating together.

If one string is tuned to 440 hz and the other to 442 hz, the vibration of the faster string will catch up to and overtake the slower string twice per second, and the tone will get louder and softer twice per second. Each time the tone gets louder and softer is called one *beat*. Two strings vibrating at 440 produce no beats; two strings vibrating at 442 produce no beats. Strings tuned to 440 and 441 beat once per second; strings tuned to 440 and 445 beat five times per second. If strings beat much faster than fifteen times per second individual beats are not heard. Instead of sounding like one tone with beats (or fluctuations), the tone sounds like two pitches played at once.

Partials, as well as fundamental pitches, can cause beats. Thus, if one vibrating string has a partial in its series vibrating at 100 hz, and the fundamental (or a partial) of another string is tuned to 102 hz, two beats per second will be heard.

How Are Pitches Organized in the Musical Scale?

The musical scale, or tuning scale, of a piano is the collection of pitches to which the strings are tuned, and which can be played by pushing the keys down one after the other. The musical scale is played whenever a practicing pianist runs his fingers up and down the keys of a well-tuned piano. The word *scale* has several meanings. Do not confuse it with the *stringing scale*, which refers to the physical dimensions of the plate, bridges and strings.

Of the infinite number of different pitches it is possible to produce, only certain ones sound good when played at the same time, and it is these pitches which make up our musical scale. Which pitches are they?

Every culture has had its own musical scale or scales, and they do not all sound alike. The collection of pitches that African tribes call their scale sounds entirely different from the scale used by the ancient Chinese, and neither one resembles *our* scale, which has been used by the Western world for the past three centuries. This Western scale sounds good to us because it is familiar, and that is why old Oriental music sounds odd to untrained Western ears; it is unfamiliar.

Music theorists had decided how to tune the contemporary Western scale by the late seventeenth century, and had set down some basic rules, including the following:

1. One pitch, or a *unison*, sounds better than anything else. This is logical, since a single vibrating string theoretically produces no beats.

SIXTH PARTIAL	1320	2640
FIFTH PARTIAL	1100	2200
FOURTH PARTIAL	880	1760
THIRD PARTIAL	660	1320
SECOND PARTIAL	440	880
FUNDAMENTAL		
(1st Partial)	220 hz	440 hz

Illus. 4-4 The partial series of two theoretically perfect strings, one tuned to 220 and the other to 440, produce no audible beats because all partials either coincide or are too far apart.

2. The best sounding combination of two pitches is when one is twice the frequency of the other. If the partial series of two theoretically perfect strings are compared, one tuned to 220 and the other to 440, no beats are produced between any of the partials, because no two numbers are close enough to produce beats. These two pitches sound better, or more beatless, than any other combination. In fact, two pitches, one of which is twice the frequency of the other, sound so much alike that they have the same letter name in the scale.

Note that every so often on illustration 4-5 another "A" comes along, and that each A is twice the frequency of the previous A.

If the scale were made up of only one basic pitch and those pitches obtained by doubling its frequency over and over, they sound so much alike that there are not enough pitches to play melodies. For example, a pretty tune can not be played using only the "A"'s on the keyboard. This leads to the next rule:

3. Going up the scale, there are twelve pitches between any two notes of the same name, or between a pitch of one frequency and the pitch of double or half that frequency. Look at the keyboard again, and count the keys between one A and the next. Every time the frequency doubles, twelve steps have gone by.

To review what has already been covered, random vibrations produce *noise*, while organized vibrations produce *musical tone*. A vibrating wire produces a whole series of *partials* by subdividing itself into many vibrating parts, in addition to its *fundamental* tone. Pitches of nearly coincident frequencies produce *beats*, or pulsations in the loudness of the tone. The speed of the beats is determined by the mathematical difference between the two pitches. From these principles some logical conclusions may be drawn, to arrive at the basis for the Western tuning scale.

A vibrating string has a fundamental and a series of partials. No beats are produced. A single vibrating string is the most pleasant sound in a piano. Therefore, a tone having no beats is the most pleasant, and the more beats which a combination of pitches produces, the less pleasant is the sound. The most pure combination of two pitches is when one has double the hz of the other, because, theoretically, no beats are produced. Given the fact that the musicians who developed our scale decided on twelve steps every time the frequency doubles, then the twelve basic pitches should be those which produce the fewest beats when played together in any combination. This, indeed, is the basis of the tuning system.

Musical Terminology

Before a complete understanding of the tuning system is possible, the names of the pitches as they are represented by the keyboard, and names of certain combinations of pitches, or *intervals*, must be learned.

An interval is *the distance between any two keys on the keyboard.* For musical reasons, the distance between any two *adjacent* keys is called a *half step.* Remember that two white keys having a black key between them are not adjacent.

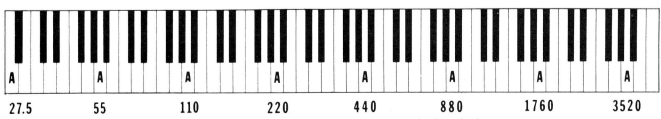

Illus. 4-5 A piano keyboard with the hz of all A's identified.

39

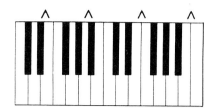

Illus. 4-6 The smallest *interval* on the keyboard is the *half step*. Any two adjacent notes form a half step. The two legs of each carat point to notes which are a half step apart.

Each white key has its own letter name. Memorize them.

Each black key borrows the name of *either* adjacent white key and therefore has two names. The *sharp* symbol (♯) indicates the pitch a half step higher than the letter name; the *flat* symbol (♭) indicates the pitch a half step lower.

Illus. 4-7 Names of all white and black keys.

Notice that the key marked with an asterisk in illustration 4-7 is a half step higher than F and a half step lower than G. This key may be called F♯ or G♭. In music, the adjacent white keys may also borrow each others' names, such as C♭ or B♯, but the tuner need not worry about them as long as he is aware that these names exist. The interchangeable names are necessary in order for musicians to be logical about composing melody and harmony, but the tuner need memorize only what the names are. Notice also that there are *seven* letter names from one letter to the next key of the same letter, but there are *twelve* half steps. The remaining five keys are the sharps (or flats), which borrow their letter names.

To go *up* the musical scale means to go higher in pitch, to the right on the keyboard; to go *down* is to go lower in pitch, farther to the left. A note *above* another is higher in pitch and farther to the right; a note *below* another is lower in pitch and farther to the left.

In the following discussion, when the pitches in an interval are named, the first letter is the lower pitch. Thus the interval C-G refers to C and the next

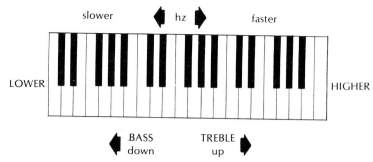

Illus. 4-8 The higher the pitch, the farther to the right the note is on the keyboard.

higher G. G-F♯ refers to G and the next higher F♯. G-G is G and the next higher G.

As stated earlier, the smallest interval is the half step, which consists of any two adjacent notes. The names of larger intervals tell how many *letter names* the two notes are apart. To figure out an interval, count the *letter* of the starting note as "one", and keep counting each letter until the desired note is reached. Counting C as "one", and going up the scale, C-D is a *second*, C-E a *third*, C-F a *fourth*, C-G a *fifth*, and so on up to C-C, the *octave*. The octave is a very important interval because it identifies a given note and the next higher or lower note of the same letter name, which is double or half its frequency. To identify intervals larger than an octave, the same sequence may be continued (ninth, tenth, etc.) or they may be broken down into two parts (octave and a second, octave and a third, etc.). Sharps and flats are not considered when figuring the size of an interval. Thus C-E♭, and C-E and C♯-E are all thirds.

Another term used when discussing tuning is the *unison*. A unison is any one single pitch. The term is needed because in the treble or upper range of a piano there are three strings per key to augment the loudness. Tuning these strings to each other is

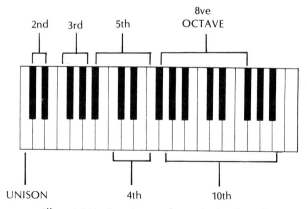

Illus. 4-9 Various intervals on the keyboard.

40

called "tuning the unisons", or getting all three strings tuned together so they reinforce each other and produce one loud pitch.

Mathematics of the Scale

The octave interval consists of two notes of the same name; one pitch is double the frequency of the other, and there are twelve pitches in between.

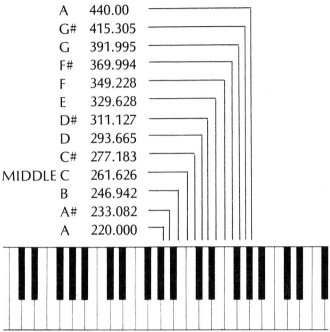

A	440.00
G#	415.305
G	391.995
F#	369.994
F	349.228
E	329.628
D#	311.127
D	293.665
C#	277.183
MIDDLE C	261.626
B	246.942
A#	233.082
A	220.000

Illus. 4-10 Theoretical pitches of the twelve basic notes near the middle of the keyboard. The frequency of each pitch is found by multiplying the adjacent lower pitch by the twelfth root of 2, or 1.0594631.

Given the pitch of the middle A on the keyboard (A440), the pitches of all the higher A's may be found by doubling 440 over and over, and the pitches of the lower A's may be found by halving it over and over (see Illus. 4-5).

Given the pitches in hz of all of the A's, how are the frequencies of the other eleven pitches found?

The frequencies of all twelve pitches are related according to a mathematical law. This law states that starting with any pitch (say A220, for example), and multiplying it by a *constant number* twelve times in a row, the result is double the frequency of the starting pitch (or ˙A440). For the mathematically inclined, the number is 1.0594631, the twelfth root of two. In 1925, musicians decided that the international pitch standard, or tuning standard, would be A440. Starting with A an octave lower (A220) and multiplying it by 1.0594631 twelve times in a row gives the frequencies for the twelve pitches near the middle of the keyboard, and ends up on A440. Given these twelve pitches, it is a simple matter to find the frequencies of the remaining keys on the piano, by halving each basic pitch over and over to get the lower octaves, and by doubling them over and over to get the higher octaves. The results are in illustration 4-11.

At this point, do not proceed until everything which has been covered is mastered, including how wire vibrates, partials, harmonics, beats, the names of all notes, the definition of an *interval,* sharps and flats, determining the size of an interval given the names of the two notes, and how to determine the

OCTAVE

PITCH	1	2	3	4	5	6	7	8
G#	51.913	103.826	207.652	415.305	830.609	1661.219	3322.437	
G	48.999	97.999	195.998	391.995	783.991	1567.982	3135.963	
F#	46.249	92.499	184.997	369.994	739.989	1479.978	2959.955	
F	43.654	87.307	174.614	349.228	698.456	1396.913	2793.826	
E	41.203	82.407	164.814	329.628	659.255	1318.510	2637.020	
D#	38.891	77.782	155.563	311.127	622.254	1244.508	2489.016	
D	36.708	73.416	146.832	293.665	587.330	1174.659	2349.318	
C#	34.648	69.296	138.591	277.183	554.365	1108.731	2217.461	
C	32.703	65.406	130.813	261.626	523.251	1046.502	2093.004	4186.009
B	30.868	61.735	123.471	246.942	493.883	987.767	1975.533	3951.066
A#	29.135	58.270	116.541	233.082	466.164	932.328	1864.655	3729.310
A	27.500	55.000	110.000	220.000	440.000	880.000	1760.000	3520.000

Illus. 4-11 Theoretical fundamental pitches of all eighty-eight notes. The box includes the twelve pitches of the temperament octave. This table was computed with a model 25 Hewlett-Packard electronic calculator by multiplying each successive half step by 1.0594631 (the twelfth root of two). Although the above pitches are rounded off to three places, computations were carried out to six places (five places, from C6 up).

frequencies of all pitches, given the starting pitch (A440).

Tuning Theory

To tune a piano, the tuner adjusts the tension of the strings so they sound pleasant when played in combinations, by listening, comparing and adjusting. When comparing one pitch to another, the tuner listens for beats, and either eliminates them or adjusts their speed.

To begin, the starting pitch, near the middle of the keyboard where beats are heard most easily, is compared to a pitch standard such as a tuning fork, tuning bar, or electronic pitch-generating device. This first note is tuned beatless to the pitch reference.

Next, the twelve notes surrounding the starting pitch are tuned. These twelve notes include one pitch of each letter name, and form the *temperament octave*. The initial tuning octave is called the temperament octave, or simply the *temperament* because the various intervals within this octave are adjusted, or tempered. Prior to the adoption of the equally tempered scale, the scale was tuned so that certain intervals were beatless, while other intervals had such rapid beats that they were unusable for music. In our equally tempered scale, all of the intervals within the temperament octave, except the octave itself, are tuned so that each interval has a slow beat; none is pure (beatless) but none is so bad that it is unusable in music.

Tuning the temperament involves setting each interval within the temperament octave to the correct beat rate. For a moment, refer to illustration 4-11 showing the fundamental pitches of each note within the temperament octave. The difference in hz between the fundamental pitch of any two notes is such a large mathematical difference that no beats are produced. Each pitch, however, also has a series of partials. To tune the temperament, *nearly-coincident partials* between each two notes are compared. That is, in any temperament tuning interval, each pitch has a partial somewhere in its series which nearly coincides with a partial of the other pitch, and the partials are mathematically close enough to produce beats. To illustrate the nearly coincident partials, illustration 4-12 gives the first six partials of each pitch within the temperament octave.

To find the beat rate between any two notes in the temperament octave, find the partials which are closest. For example, find the beat rate between C and G. The third partial of C (784.878) is closest to the fourth partial of G (783.992). Subtracting gives the beat rate for C-G in the temperament octave: .886 per second, or 4.43 beats per 5 seconds.

Illustration 4-13, giving the beat rates per second of all intervals within the temperament octave, was derived from illustration 4-12. To find the beat rate of a certain interval, follow the line of numbers to the right of the *lower* note over to the column below the *upper* note. That number is the correct rate. For example, find the beat rate between G and

HARMONICS
(THEORETICALLY PERFECT PARTIALS)

	Fundamental or 1st	2nd	3rd	4th	5th	6th
F	349.228	698.456	1047.684	1396.912	1746.140	2095.368
E	329.628	659.256	988.884	1318.512	1648.140	1977.768
D#	311.127	622.254	933.381	1244.508	1555.635	1866.762
D	293.665	587.330	880.995	1174.660	1468.325	1761.990
C#	277.183	554.366	831.549	1108.732	1385.915	1663.098
C	261.626	523.252	784.878	1046.504	1308.13	1569.756
B	246.942	493.884	740.826	987.768	1234.710	1481.652
A#	233.082	466.164	699.246	932.328	1165.410	1398.492
A	220.000	440.000	660.000	880.000	1100.000	1320.000
G#	207.652	415.304	622.956	830.608	1038.260	1245.912
G	195.998	391.996	587.994	783.992	979.990	1175.988
F#	184.997	369.994	554.991	739.988	924.985	1109.982
F	174.614	349.228	523.842	698.456	873.070	1047.684

Illus. 4-12 Frequencies of the first six partials of each note in the temperament octave. (The fundamental is the first partial.)

42

Illus. 4-13 Beat rates per second of all temperament octave intervals.

(lower note)	F#/Gb	G	G#/Ab	A	A#/Bb	B	C	C#/D	D	D#/Eb	E	F
E												*
D#/Eb											*	*
D										*	*	15.850
C#/D									*	*	14.958	10.997
C								*	*	14.121	10.382	1.180
B							*	*	13.327	9.798	1.116	*
A#/Bb						*	*	12.577	9.250	1.053	*	.790
A					*	*	11.870	8.732	.995	*	.744	*
G#/Ab				*	*	11.202	8.244	.941	*	.702	*	9.424
G			*	*	10.578	7.778	.886	*	.664	*	8.894	*
F#/Gb		*	*	9.982	7.343	.838	*	.625	*	8.396	*	*
F	*	*	9.424	6.930	.790	*	.590	*	7.925	*	*	0

* The beat rates of these intervals are too fast to be useful.

C. G is the lower note. Following the line to the right of G over to the C column, the beat rate is .886 The asterisks on the chart indicate intervals having beat rates which are too fast to be useful in tuning.

In illustration 4-14, all useful tuning intervals from illus. 4-13 are listed in order of speed of beat rate. The left portion includes intervals which are used for tuning; their beat rates are given per five seconds. The right portion includes the test intervals, which are used for checking the accuracy of the tuning intervals. Because it is impossible to count beats in hundredths or tenths of a second, all beat rates are rounded off to the nearest half beat per second.

Tuning Interval		Theoretical Beat Rate Per Five Seconds	Rounded Off Beat Rate
Fifths	F-C	2.95	3 –
	F#-C#	3.125	3 +
	G-D	3.32	3.5 –
	G#-D#	3.51	3.5
	A-E	3.72	3.5 +
	Bb-F	3.95	4 –
Fourths	F-Bb	3.95	4 –
	F#-B	4.19	4 +
	G-C	4.43	4.5 –
	G#-C#	4.71	4.5 +
	A-D	4.98	5
	A#-D#	5.27	5.5 –
	B-E	5.58	5.5 +
	C-F	5.90	6 –

Test Interval	Theoretical Beat Rate Per Second			Rounded Off Beat Rate
	Maj. Thirds (4 Half Steps)	Sixths	Min. Thirds (3 Half Steps)	
F-A	6.93			7 –
F#-A#	7.34			7 +
G-B	7.78			8 –
F-D		7.93		8
Ab-C	8.24			8 +
F#-D#		8.40		8.5 –
A-C#	8.73			8.5 +
G-E		8.89		9 –
Bb-D	9.25			9 +
Ab-F		9.42		9.5 –
F-Ab			9.42	9.5 –
B-D#	9.80			10 –
F#-A			9.98	10
C-E	10.38			10 +
G-Bb			10.58	10.5 +
Db-F	11.00			11
G#-B			11.20	11 +
A-C			11.87	12 –
A#-C#			12.58	12.5
B-D			13.33	13 +
C-Eb			14.12	14 +
C#-E			14.96	15
D-F			15.85	16

Illus. 4-14 Beat rates of intervals used in *tuning* the temperament (left hand column, beats per five seconds) and for *verifying its accuracy* (right hand column, beats per second).

The temperament octave is tuned by adjusting the intervals to the correct beat rates in a certain sequence. This sequence is explained later, under "tuning procedure".

After the temperament is tuned, the rest of the piano is tuned one note at a time. Every new note is compared to a previously tuned note by listening for beats.

TUNING TOOLS

To tune a piano, the following tools are needed:
A tuning lever, used for turning the tuning pins.

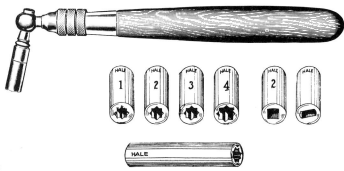

Illus. 4-15 An extension tuning lever with interchangeable heads and tips. The long head is used for grands, the short head for verticals. The tips accommodate various sizes of tuning pins including oblong pins which were used in some Victorian pianos.

A tuning fork or bar, which produces a standardized reference pitch.

A felt temperament strip. There are three strings per note in the temperament octave of most pianos. The temperament strip is inserted to silence all but one string per note. After the twelve pitches are tuned to each other, the temperament strip is removed one string at a time, and the unisons are tuned.

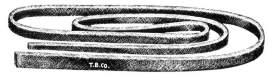

Used to mute two octaves at once by pushing between the groups of strings with a screw-driver or flattened hammer shank.

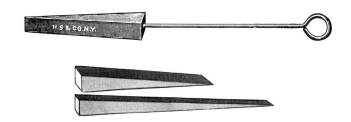

Rubber or felt mutes. After the temperament is tuned, the remaining unisons are muted so one string may be tuned at a time. For tuning three-string unisons in the middle of the keyboard, two regular mutes are used. Narrow mutes are used in the upper treble, where mutes of regular width get in the way of the hammers. In the bass of an upright, the long, slender, flexible tip of the regular mute is inconvenient to slip into place. Here, a stubby mute, made by cutting the end off of a regular mute, is used.

One other tool is needed in order to learn to judge the speed of beats: a metronome. A metronome is a mechanical or electrical device which ticks or beeps at a certain speed, set on a dial or a sliding scale. A metronome may be purchased at any music store or piano parts supplier. The use of the metronome is discussed in tuning exercise #4.

BEGINNING EXERCISES

It is impossible to learn tuning by practicing on a piano with hammers that click, wobble and miss some of the strings, an action so badly regulated that the hammers do not have enough power to produce good solid tones, strings so rusty that they break, single strings that produce beats, tuning pins that jump or are so loose that they do not stay in place, and so forth. Repair any such defects before practicing the following tuning exercises.

If you have had no previous musical experience, or if you are unsure of what a beat sounds like, locate a good piano tuner and have him tune your piano. Watch his posture and the way he holds the tuning lever; listen to what he does. When he is finished, you might not understand everything he did, but your piano should be in tune, giving you an example of what it *should* sound like.

The Use of the Tuning Lever

The first skill to learn is the correct use of the tuning lever. The student must acquire a feel for the right amount of pressure on it; without this feel it is impossible to control the way the pins turn and make them stay in the right position. Unless a piano is drastically out of tune, the lever is moved only a fraction of an inch at the most, so acquiring this feel is a must.

Although the tuning pins are made of steel and are embedded as deep as 1¼" in the pinblock and plate bushings, they have internal torsion, and they bend enough to affect the pitch of a string. The tuner must learn to *rotate* the pin, feeling the amount of flexing as pressure is applied to the lever. Any bending or flexing of the pin is only temporary, and a string which is tuned by flexing the tuning pin goes out of tune as soon as the pin bends itself back to its natural position. Because of the tight grip of the pinblock, and the slight flexing of the pins, each pin must be turned a little too far and then eased back to the position where it will stay. Tuners call this procedure *setting the pins.*

Another factor involved in tuning is applying the same amount of tension along the entire length of each string. Each string passes from the tuning pin across several bearing points. Each bearing point has a slight amount of friction. If a string is below pitch, tension is added to *one end* as the pitch is raised. Imagine stretching a rubber band over a cigar box and pulling on one end. That end has more tension than the center section, because of the friction at the edge of the box, or bearing point. The friction in the rubber band example is greatly exaggerated, but it does occur to some extent in a piano. If the pitch of a string is *raised* by turning the tuning pin in only one motion, the string segment nearest the tuning pin will have more tension than the speaking segment. When the string is played, the hammer blow will equalize the tension, causing the string to go *sharp.* Conversely, if string tension is *lowered* by turning the pin in one motion, the segment nearest the tuning pin will have less

tension, and the string will go *flat*. For this reason, each note must be played loudly after each motion of the tuning lever to equalize string tension. Alternately tune and play until the string remains in tune after it is played. This procedure is called *setting the strings.*

The head of the tuning lever is star shaped, but the tuning pins are square. This is so the lever may be placed on each pin with the handle extending away from the piano, in line with the string, or as close to this position as possible, regardless of the position of the pin. Always put the lever on the pin in this position. In doing so, tuning pressure is least apt to be applied in a direction which will bend the pin.

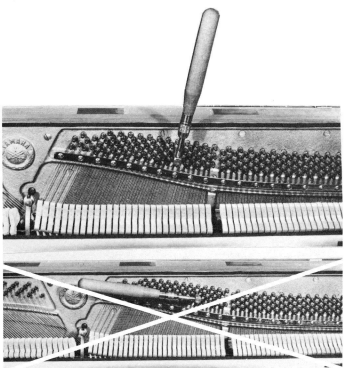

Illus. 4-16 Showing correct (upper) and incorrect (lower) positions of tuning lever on pin. Always place the lever on the pin in as nearly a vertical position as possible, for minimum bending of the pin.

Good tuning posture is very important. In order to remain comfortable and to maintain the correct grip on the tuning lever, assume the position shown in the appropriate photograph. The strings are wound onto the left side of the tuning pins in vertical pianos and onto the right side in grands. If the same hand is used for tuning all pianos, the tuner *pushes* on the lever to raise the pitch in one type and *pulls* to raise the pitch in the other type. It is the opinion of most tuners that the same hand should always be used, even though the motions are opposite in verticals and grands.

Illus. 4-17 Correct tuning posture. The pictures at the left illustrate a left handed technician; those at the right, a right handed technician.

For the best control of the lever, rest the elbow firmly on some part of the piano, as illustrated. With the elbow resting on the piano, the wrist and elbow are pivot points for the hand. With the elbow in midair, the shoulder is also a pivot point, decreasing control.

Illus. 4-18 Poor posture inevitably leads to discomfort and poor results.

In the following exercises, the directions apply to a right handed tuner tuning a grand, or a lefty tuning an upright. If you are the opposite, exchange the words "push" and "pull" wherever they occur.

Tuning Exercise #1

PURPOSE: *To gain a feel for the tuning lever; to learn to hear beats.*

Play middle C. Find the three strings for this note. Mute the right string, leaving the center and left strings unmuted. Put the tuning lever on the pin for the left string, in the proper position. Double check to be sure that the lever is on the unmuted string. Many strings have been broken by beginning tuners who were "tuning" a muted string, could not hear any difference in the sound, and kept turning until the string broke.

Grasp the lever, and play middle C firmly, once every two seconds. Listen carefully for pulsations of loudness. Gradually pull the lever in a counter-clockwise direction, to feel the grip of the pinblock on the pin. With a little pull, the pin does not turn, but flexes enough to change the sound. Keep playing and listening. As you pull harder, the pin will turn, and you will hear beats. As you keep lowering the pitch, the beats will get faster and faster, until the note is so out of tune that the beats become inaudible. Now, gradually push on the lever in a clockwise direction, as slowly as possible, until the strings are almost in tune and you can hear beats again. As you apply more pressure, listen for the beats to get slower until they disappear and the note is in tune. If you make the unison beatless and release your push on the lever, the note will go slightly out of tune again. If the string you are tuning is flat, you have to raise it slowly until it is slightly *above* beatless, and as you relax your push, the pin will settle back in tune. If the pin is extremely tight, you may have to move the lever back and forth, a little less each time, until the pin is centered at the same time the string is in tune.

If you flatten the string, gradually raise it until the tone is beatless, and keep pushing, it starts beating again. The beats increase as you get sharper and sharper. Now the string is too sharp, and it must be lowered to the correct pitch. Untune and tune middle C until you can make it beatless.

Remember:

1. Play firmly to settle the string tension.
2. Untune the string to the flat side.

3. Raise it slowly until it is slightly sharp.
4. Release your push; pull slightly to set the pin.
5. Never jerk the lever; always move it smoothly.
After tuning the left string, mute it and practice on the right string, again using the center string for a reference. Do not adjust the center string, which will be a pitch reference until you get through the next few exercises. When you can tune the middle C unison accurately, proceed to exercise #2.

Tuning Exercise #2

PURPOSE: *to tune any unison beatless.*

Now that you can tune middle C to itself, practice the same exercise on the F below middle C. Then proceed toward the treble, one note at a time. The higher the pitch, the more difficult it is to tune the unisons, for two reasons: it takes a smaller movement of the lever to eliminate beats, and the sound fades away faster. Repeat each note as rapidly as necessary to sustain the tone, up to about twice per second in the highest treble octave.

While you practice, *do not* adjust any of the center strings of the unisons, as explained in exercise #1.

After practicing on treble unisons, start with the E below middle C and work your way toward the bottom of the scale. In the bass, most of the notes are two-string unisons, so you will not need any mutes for this exercise in the bass. Practice untuning and tuning the left string of each two-string unison, leaving the right hand strings alone. When you can tune any unison in the piano, proceed to Exercise #3.

Tuning Exercise #3

PURPOSE: *to learn to tune octaves.*

As stated earlier, the octave (*any* octave) is the best sounding interval in the piano. It is also the easiest interval to tune. Tune each unison in the temperament octave beatless. Leave the center strings of each unison in the temperament octave alone for now, tuning the outside strings only.

Mute off the two outside strings for F above middle C. Play F below middle C and the F above at the same time. Flatten the upper note, listening for beats, and raise it gradually into tune. Set the pin by raising the string slightly above pitch and easing it back down into tune. When you can tune the F-F octave beatless, proceed up to the top of the piano and then from E to the bottom.

As you get progressively higher, the octaves become harder to tune. In some cases, it may be helpful to play the new note a fraction of a second after playing the reference note. Turning the head at a different angle sometimes helps. Assuming that you can tune the high *unisons* beatless, it will just take practice to tune the high *octaves*. This is covered more fully in the section on tuning difficulties, p. 54.

In the bass, each octave has two prominent beats of different speeds occuring simultaneously. If one beat is eliminated, the other is offensive, so the place to tune the string is between these two points. Both beats should be slow, but neither is as bad as it is when the other is eliminated. This problem is discussed in more detail on pp. 54-55.

By this time you should be proficient at hearing and eliminating beats in unisons and octaves in all registers of the piano. You are now capable of all skills used in piano tuning except one: setting the temperament. All intervals within the temperament octave have a slow beat; no interval is beatless, except the octave, but none of the beats is fast enough to be offensive. To set the temperament, you must be able to judge the speed of beats, and tune each interval to the correct beat rate.

Tuning Exercise #4

PURPOSE: *to learn to judge the speed of beats.*

Beat rate is measured in *beats per second.* To measure the beat rate of an interval accurately, you must be able to count seconds accurately. Although it may be possible to learn to count seconds and other intervals of time by practicing with a wristwatch, the use of a metronome makes learning easier. Set the metronome at 60 mm, and tap your finger along with it. Stop the metronome, keep tapping, and start it again. Practice this until you have a good mental idea of what a second is. For a test, have someone adjust a metronome behind your back until you think it is set at 60. When you can do this accurately, proceed.

The slowest beat rate, 3 per 5 seconds (36 per minute) is hard to set accurately on a mechanical metronome, so set it at twice that speed, 72 beats per minute, and ignore every other tick. Tap your finger at the rate of 3 per 5 seconds. Stop the metronome, keep tapping, and after 10 or 15 seconds, check your speed with the metronome again. Keep doing this until you have a mental concept of 3 beats in 5 seconds.

Other beat rates used in tuning are given in illustration 4-19, along with their equivalent metronome settings. Practice them until you can recognize each rate by memory. For a test, have someone set the metronome to various beat rates and tell him the correct rate without looking. Check yourself against the second hand of your wristwatch.

BEAT RATE	METRONOME SPEED
3 per 5 seconds	72 (count every other tick)
3.5 per 5 seconds	84 (count every other tick)
4 per 5 seconds	96 (count every other tick)
4.5 per 5 seconds	108 (count every other tick)
5 per 5 seconds	60 (count every tick)
5.5 per 5 seconds	66 (count every tick)
6 per 5 seconds	72 (count every tick)

Illus. 4-19

Certain intervals called *tuning intervals* are adjusted during the tuning process. They are tuned to beat at the rates given in illustration 4-19. As more notes are tuned in the temperament, additional combinations of notes become available for testing the job. These are called *test intervals*. For example, the first three intervals to be tuned are C-F, G-C and then D-G. Three intervals have been tuned, but now there is an additional combination of notes, F-D. This is a test interval. *Test intervals are never adjusted.* They are only used for checking the accuracy of the tuning intervals, as tuning of the temperament progresses. If a test interval beats at the wrong speed, something is wrong with one or more of the tuning intervals already tuned, and the tuner must go back and readjust them until the test intervals are also correct.

Test intervals beat at speeds from six to ten per second. To learn these speeds, set the metronome at 120, or two ticks per second, and count according to illustration 4-20.

BEAT RATE	BEATS PER TICK
6 per second	3 beats per tick
7 per second	7 beats per 2 ticks (between 6 and 8 per second)
8 per second	4 beats per tick
9 per second	9 beats per 2 ticks (between 8 and 10 per second)
10 per second	5 beats per tick

Illus. 4-20

49

Tuning Exercise #5

PURPOSE: *to learn to set beats at certain speeds.*

When tuning the temperament, you must judge and set the beat rate between two different pitches. Learning this skill is easier if you first practice setting the beat rate of a *unison*, to get accustomed to hearing the very slow beat rates which are involved. During actual tuning, beats are never purposely introduced into unisons, but if you learn to gauge beat rate this way, it will be easier to learn to set the rate of two different notes.

Mute the right string of the middle C unison, and put the lever on the left pin. Set this unison to beat at each of the slow beat rates in exercise #4, from three per five seconds to six per five seconds. After setting each speed, check it with the metronome and then with your wristwatch. When you can set the unison to beat at any of these speeds, using only your wristwatch, you are ready to tune your first temperament.

TUNING PROCEDURE

Step 1: Mute all outside strings of the unisons in the temperament octave, F below middle C to F above, with the felt temperament strip.

Step 2: Tune C above middle C to a C tuning fork or Deagan C tuning bar. A tuning bar is easier to use, because it does not need to be hand held, and it produces a louder, longer sustained tone than a tuning fork does. If a fork is used, hold it near the base, and strike one tine against the kneecap. Then press the base of the fork against the little flap in front of the ear canal, and press the flap shut against the ear opening. This eliminates outside noise and, at the same time, amplifies the audible tone by conducting it directly to the ear canal. Play the piano with one hand and hold the fork with the other, comparing the two tones. Tune the string, and then compare it to the fork again until it is in tune.

Step 3: Tune middle C to the C above, beatless.

Step 4: Tune the lower F to middle C, a little less than 3 beats per 5 seconds *sharp*.

Step 5: Tune F above middle C to the lower F, beatless.

Step 6: Test the F-C interval by comparing it to C-F. C-F should beat at exactly twice as fast as F-C, with the octave F-F beatless.

Step 7: Continue tuning the temperament octave, according to illustration 4-21. The symbols are defined at the right:

> *faster than;* G-E F-D means the G-D interval.

< *slower than;* opposite of above.

TUNING INTERVAL AND BEAT RATE PER 5 SEC. Note being tuned is in bold face (see text).		COMPARED TO BEAT RATES OF PREVIOUS TUNING INTERVALS	TEST INTERVALS AND BEAT RATES PER SEC.
F-C	3 –	F-C = ½C-F (6 –)	
G-C	4.5 –	G-C > F-C (3 –)	
G-**D**	3.5 –	G-D > F-C (3 –) G-D < G-C (4.5 –)	F-D (8)
A-D	5	A-D > G-C (4.5 –)	F-A (7 –) < F-D (8)
A-**E**	3.5 +	A-E > G-D (3.5 –) A-E < G-C (4.5 –)	G-E (9 –) > F-D (8) G-E < C-E (10 +)
B-E	5.5 +	B-E > A-D (5)	G-B (8 –) > F-A (7 –) G-B < F-D (8)
F#-**B**	4 +	F#-B > A-E (3.5 +) F#-B < G-C (4.5 –)	F#-A (10) > G-E (9 –) F#-A < C-E (10 +)
F#-**C#**	3 +	F#-C# > F-C (3 –) F#-C# < G-D (3.5 –)	A-C# (8.5 +) > ´F-D (8) A-C# < G-E (9 –)
G#-C#	4.5 +	G#-C# > G-C (4.5 –) G#-C# < A-D (5)	A♭-C (8 +) < F-D (8) A♭-C < A-C# (8.5 +) F-A♭ (9.5 –) = A♭-F (9.5 –) F-A♭ > G-E (9 –) F-A♭ < F#-A (10)
G#-**D#**	3.5	G#-D# > G-D (3.5 –) G#-D# < A-E (3.5 +)	F#-D# (8.5 –) > A♭-C (8 +) F#-D# < A-C# (8.5 +) B-D# (10 –) > F-A♭ (9.5 –) B-D# < F#-A (10)
A#-D#	5.5 –	A#-D# > A-D (5) A#-D# < B-E (5.5 +)	F#-A# (7 +) > F-A (7 –) F#-A# < G-B (8 –) B♭-D (9 +) > G-E (9 –) B♭-D < A♭-F (9.5 –)
B♭-F 4 – Test interval only, since F is already tuned.		B♭-F = F-B♭ B♭-F > A-E (3.5 +) B♭-F < F#-B (4 +)	

Illus. 4-21 Temperament tuning sequence.

Following illustration 4-21, tune G to middle C, 4.5 (-) per 5 seconds flat. Compare it to the previous tuning interval, F-C. G-C should beat faster than F-C, which is 3 (-) per 5 seconds.

The next interval is G-D. Tune D to G, 3.5 (-) beats per 5 seconds flat. As shown in the second column, it should beat faster than C-F and slower than G-C. The third column shows one test interval which is now available: F-D. It should beat 8 per second. If it does not, go back and correct the tuning intervals until everything is right. Then proceed in the same way until the entire temperament is tuned.

When every interval is tuned to your satisfaction, there are several final tests to check the accuracy. Refer to illustration 4-14 on p.43 and notice that the intervals are grouped according to size: fourths, fifths, major thirds (four half steps), minor thirds (three half steps), and sixths. Within each group of like intervals, (all fourths, for example), the beat rate increases from the lowest interval to the highest. When the temperament is tuned properly, the beat rate should gradually increase from the lowest fourth to the highest, and the lowest of each other kind of interval to the highest. Play the sequence of fourths from F-B♭ up to C-F and listen for a smoothly increasing beat rate from the lowest to the highest. Then do the same with all of the fifths, sixths, minor thirds and major thirds. If each interval beats a little faster in each sequence, you may be congratulated on a good temperament.

As proficiency in setting the temperament is gained, you will be able to omit the extra test intervals for G♯, D♯, and A♯. While you are learning, however, check your work thoroughly with all tests given.

Step 8: Remove the felt temperament strip one string at a time, tuning each unison in the temperament octave beatless.

Step 9: Tune the treble, as outlined in exercise #3, starting with F♯ above the temperament octave. Mute the outside strings of the upper note, tune the middle string to the octave below, and then tune the upper note unison.

Step 10: Tune the bass, as outlined in exercise #3, starting with E below the temperament octave.

Professional Quality Tuning

In addition to octave tuning, the professional tuner tests other intervals as he progresses into the treble and bass. Because of inharmonicity, which is discussed on p. 53, it is sometimes necessary to compromise the tuning of octaves in order for the other intervals to be in tune.

One of the final tests in tuning the temperament is to see that in each series of like intervals (all fourths, for example), each progressively higher interval beats a little faster. This same test is employed by professional tuners throughout most of the piano, to be sure that the beat rate of like intervals increases smoothly from one interval to the next. Other fine-tuning tests are described in Treble and Bass Tuning Hints, on pp. 54-55.

WHY DOES A PIANO GO OUT OF TUNE?

Piano strings are under a great deal of tension which is supported by the frame, plate, pinblock, tuning pins, bridges and soundboard. Anything which affects the position of these parts will cause a change in tension and make the piano go out of tune.

Humidity

Even though a soundboard is varnished, moisture from the air can seep into and out of the wood, causing the crown to increase and diminish. For a discussion of crown and downbearing, see pp. 9-10. This is the most important factor causing a good piano to go out of tune. A typical piano goes sharp in the spring when rain increases the humidity and thus the crown, and flat again in the early winter when the dry heat of the furnace removes moisture from the soundboard, diminishing the crown. This seasonal pitch change is noticeably absent from pianos which are kept in climate-controlled (temperature *and* humidity controlled) environments.

Temperature Changes

When the temperature rises, the soundboard expands and increases its push on the strings. Since the room temperature surrounding a typical piano usually stays within 10° or so, this factor does not affect the tuning as much as humidity does. Temperature changes also have a slight effect on the strings, frame and plate, but this factor is even less important.

Stretching of the Strings

New music wire is very elastic; it begins to stretch as soon as it is pulled up to pitch. New strings stretch the most during their first few years in a piano. Because of this stretching, many new pianos sink a quarter step flat within a few months after each tuning, for two or three years; then the stretching decreases, and the pitch becomes stable for longer periods of time. Some piano makers and rebuilders stretch their new strings with a small roller immediately after a piano is pulled up to pitch. This procedure can be effective, but if overdone it may cause objectionable false beats in the treble.

Slipping Tuning Pins

This factor does not enter into the tuning of a good quality new piano. The pins in a new piano should be so tight that the string tension does not cause them to turn. In an older piano, however, which has been exposed to regular seasonal humidity changes for many years, the pinblock loses its tight grip on the pins, from continual expansion and contraction. When the pins get loose enough, the strings rotate them slowly in the pinblock and the pitch gradually goes down.

Playing

The louder and more often a piano is played, the faster it goes out of tune. A piano with tight tuning pins is not "knocked" out of tune as fast, of course, as one with loose pins, but playing is a factor even in fine quality pianos.

Summary

Any piano has one or more factors at work to make it go out of tune. In addition, a poor tuner can leave a piano in tune but in a state in which it will not stay that way very long; see *setting the pin* and *setting the string* on p. 45. Some of these factors may be controlled by skill of the tuner; others may be corrected only by restringing or by controlling the climate. Humidity and temperature changes and hard use normally affect even a fine piano; that is why pianos must be tuned regularly. How often should a piano be tuned? This depends upon the condition of the piano and the musical demands of the owner. A piano which is used mainly for a piece of furniture probably will not "need" tuning more than once a year. A piano which is given regular use and is in good condition may get by with being tuned twice a year, each time the seasonal humidity changes. A piano given a daily workout by a professional musician or serious student might need monthly or even more frequent tunings.

TUNING PROBLEMS

If all pianos were theoretically perfect, and followed the acoustical laws cited in previous chapters, tuning would be much easier than it really is. Unfortunately, very few pianos come close to acoustical perfection, and most of them have various faults which cause problems for the tuner. Some problems are built into pianos and cannot easily be changed; others crop up with age or certain circumstances, and may be corrected. The following discussion omits obvious mechanical problems (loose tuning pins, wobbly hammers, etc.) which are covered in the repair and rebuilding chapters.

False Beats

The false beat is the worst single enemy of most tuners. It is a beat within one single string which can not be eliminated by tuning. A string with a false beat sounds like two strings which are out of tune with each other. False beats occur most commonly in the upper middle register of the piano, from the treble break, where the plate brace comes between two notes, up to the middle of the top octave.

The only way to "tune" a string having false beats is to untune it to the flat side until the real beats may be distinguished from the false beats. Then, slowly raise the pitch, concentrating on the real beats and ignoring the false ones, until it is as close to being beatless as possible. It may take several tries, but with patience, the place will be found where the two strings sound the least out of tune. In a piano having many false beats in the treble, it is impossible to do a good job of tuning unless the cause of the false beats is eliminated. Professional tuners have various theories regarding the causes of false beats, including improper contact between string and bridge or capo bar, rust specks, kinks or twists in the wire, and stretching a wire too far above the correct pitch when stringing or tuning. For further discussion on false beats and how to eliminate them, see pp. 100 and 101.

Sympathetic Beats

The tuner will sometimes notice a very soft, confusing beat which is not in the string being tuned. These *sympathetic beats* usually are caused by depressing the sustaining pedal or a few extra keys accidentally, allowing a completely different note or notes to vibrate sympathetically. Sometimes during pitch raising, the strings in the high treble which have no dampers resonate along with the strings being tuned. This problem disappears when the high treble is tuned more closely. Sometimes a rubber mute fails to dampen its string completely, allowing the muted string to ring, adding beats. When this occurs, insert the mute farther up or down the length of the string. Rarely, a segment of string in the duplex scale beats with one being tuned. This is corrected by tuning the duplex scale. See pp. 56-57.

Tuning Instability

The tuner occasionally encounters a piano with tight tuning pins, which is close to A440, in which one end goes out of tune as soon as the other end is tuned. Repeated tunings make no improvement. This condition is usually caused by a loose pinblock. As the tension is changed, the pinblock shifts a little, throwing everything out again. Tightening the plate screws around the pinblock often helps this situation. In more extreme cases, in grand pianos, the space between the pinblock and plate must be filled, as described on p. 92.

Inharmonicity

A theoretically perfect vibrating wire would follow the three vibrational laws given on p. 37. (The frequency in hz is directly proportional to the square root of the tension, and inversely proportional to the thickness and length.) Thus, if a perfect wire vibrated at 110, each half of the wire would vibrate at 220, each third at 330, each quarter at 440, and so forth up the harmonic series.

There is another law to consider, however, and it is this factor which causes strings to deviate from theoretically perfect vibration. The law states that the shorter a wire is, *in proportion to its thickness*, the stiffer it is. The stiffer a wire is, the faster it vibrates.

ILLUSTRATION: Take two steel wires, both identical in all respects except length.

WIRE A   .05" thick
             10" long

WIRE B   .05" thick
             2" long

Reducing these fractions, the thickness of the 10" wire is 1/200 of its length, while the thickness of the 2" wire is 1/40 of its length. The 2" wire is thicker in proportion to its length; it is also stiffer.

For an elementary demonstration of stiffness, flex a stiff plastic ruler and see how much it bends. Then break it in half, and notice how much less the half bends due to its greater stiffness. Nothing is different but the length.

The stiffer a wire is, the faster it vibrates. When a typically *imperfect* piano string vibrates, the fundamental and all partials are produced by the same piece of wire, of uniform thickness. The higher a partial is, the shorter and stiffer the segment of wire is. The stiffer the segment is, the faster it vibrates, and the sharper the partial is. The result? The higher the partial, the more it deviates,

to the *sharp* side, from its theoretical harmonic.

Large pianos have relatively longer strings and less inharmonicity. Small pianos have short, stiff strings with a great deal of inharmonicity. The inharmonicity, along with the relative loudness of the various partials, determine the tone quality of a piano, to a large extent. This is the cause of the tinny, strange sounding bass tone of a typical spinet, and the rich powerful bass of a concert grand.

Inharmonicity is the cause of several tuning problems: octave stretching, and treble and bass tuning difficulties.

Octave Stretching

The meaning of *octave stretching* and its causes and effects must be understood in order for the tuner to do a professional job.

Most strings have inharmonicity, meaning that each progressively higher partial is a little sharper than its respective harmonic, and sharper to a greater extent than the previous partial. Any string with inharmonicity sounds in tune with itself, if it has no false beats, even though the partials are sharp, because no two partials are close enough together to create beats. For example, the 2nd partial of A880 may be 1765 cps instead of 1760, but the string sounds in tune with itself because no beats are produced. (All identical segments of a string having no false beats produce the same pitch.) However, when the next higher A (theoretically, A1760) is tuned, its fundamental pitch must be raised or *stretched* to 1765 in order for it to be beatless. Since the fundamental of the higher A (1765) is compared with the second partial of the lower A (also 1765), the interval is in tune at 1765. The higher a note is in a piano, the more stretching is involved, because the wire is stiffer in proportion to its length, and the partials are sharper.

Octave stretching is automatically accomplished by tuning the upper octaves *beatless*. The partial series of the lower note is *stretched* due to the stiffness of the wire, and when the upper note is tuned beatless it is also stretched the proper amount.

It is a characteristic of the human ear to hear upper notes flatter than they really are. For example, if middle C is played and then the highest C is played, high C tends to sound flat even if it is in tune. To compensate for this peculiarity, some tuners artificially stretch the upper octaves to the point that they have rapid beats. In the opinion of

	Theoretically perfect harmonic series of low C.	Actual series of partials.
6th Partial	196.218	198.435
5th Partial	163.515	164.779
4th Partial	130.812	131.434
3rd Partial	98.109	98.401
2nd Partial	65.406	65.523
Fundamental Pitch	32.703	32.703

Illus. 4-22 Because of stiffness of piano strings, among other factors, the actual partial series deviates from the theoretical harmonic series. This table illustrates the inharmonicity in hz of a low C bass string in a fine quality upright piano, as measured in a laboratory.

Treble Tuning Hints

As discussed earlier, learning to tune the high treble is one of the hardest areas for the beginner. It takes very little movement of the tuning lever to change the pitch the correct amount, and the tone dies out quickly in this area, making the beats hard to hear. If those reasons are not enough, false beats are the most prevalent in this register, complicating matters.

Each note should be played loudly and repeated rapidly enough to prevent the tone from dying away. If the student is uncertain about whether a treble string is in tune, it should be untuned to the flat side until it is obviously flat, and then slowly brought up to pitch again, without raising it too far. Repeated practice should improve the student's skill. It is sometimes helpful to pluck high treble strings to distinguish their pitch.

If the string is untuned to the flat side so far that the pitch is considerably flat and no difference can be heard, the student might need the help of another tuner to learn high treble tuning, or the student's hearing simply might not be accurate enough to hear the high frequencies involved. If no progress is made after considerable practice,

the student should not aspire to be a professional tuner.

For fine treble tuning, other intervals in addition to octaves should be tested. These tests comprise intervals in which the fundamental of the upper note is the same as the third, fourth, or fifth partial of the lower note. For example, the third partial of middle C is G an octave and a half higher. After the treble octaves are tuned, a series of tests should be made using this interval, starting with low F of the temperament and C above middle C, then F♯-C♯, G-D, etc., making minor corrections to make each interval sound pleasant without making any octaves offensive. Then a series based on the double octave, (the fourth partial) should be tested, followed by the series of two-octaves-and-a-third (the fifth partial).

Bass Tuning Hints

The partials produced by the vibration of any given string are approximately multiples of the fundamental frequency of that string, but are not necessarily equally tempered. Upper partials of bass strings are low enough that they correspond to the fundamentals of notes near the middle of the piano keyboard. The partials also are loud enough that they are quite easily heard when a bass note is played along with these corresponding higher notes. Because the piano is equally tempered, but the partials of the bass strings are not, bass strings produce prominent beats when played with certain other notes. For example, compare the partial series of C2 with corresponding higher notes on the keyboard (see illustration 4-23). Although the octave, double octave, etc., are theoretically in tune, the other partials are not. Therefore, when C2 is played simultaneously with any of these other notes, a distinct beat is heard. If C2 is tuned beatless to any of these notes, the other intervals are offensive.

Because of the weakness of the first two partials of low bass strings, particularly in small pianos, these strings must be tuned to tempered intervals which beat against the lower strings, such as the twelfth (octave and a fifth) and seventeenth (double octave and a third). (These two intervals form the most prominent beats.) Because each bass string has several prominent partials which have different beat rates when compared to their corresponding pitches in the scale (see illustration 4-23), each bass note must be tuned to compromise

Theoretical partial series of C2		Name of note whose fundamental pitch is closest to harmonic of C2	Theoretical frequency of fundamental pitch of note in column 2
6th Partial	392.436	G4	391.995
5th Partial	327.030	E4	329.628
4th Partial	261.624	C4	same
3rd Partial	196.218	G3	195.998
2nd Partial	130.812	C3	same
Fundamental	65.406	—	—

Illus. 4-23 Comparing the partial series of C2 to various other notes. See text for details.

Note Being Tuned	Comparison Chord Notes
C3	G3-C4-E4
B3	F#3-B4-D#4
A#3	F3-A#4-D4
A3	E3-A4-C#4
G#2	D#3-G#3-C4
G2	D3-G3-B4
F#2	C#3-F#3-A#4
F2	C3-F3-A4-C4
E2	B3-E3-G#3-B4
D#2	A#3-D#3-G3-A#4
D2	A3-D3-F#3-A4
C#2	G#2-C#3-F3-G#3
C2	G2-C3-E3-G3
B2	F#2-B3-D#3-F#3
A#2	F2-A#3-D3-F3
A2	E3-A4-C#4
G#1	D#3-G#3-C4
G1	D3-G3-B4
F#1	C#3-F#3-A#4
F1	C3-F3-A4
E1	B3-E3-G#3
D#1	A#3-D#3-G3
D1	A3-D3-F#3
C#1	G#2-C#3-F3
C1	G2-C3-E3
B1	F#2-B3-D#3
A#1	F2-A#3-D3
A1	E2-A3-C#3

Illus. 4-24 Helpful bass tuning chords.

the beat rates with no interval sounding more offensive than the others.

If the non-equally-tempered harmonic phenomenon did not cause enough problems, bass strings also have the most inharmonicity of any strings in a piano. The greater inharmonicity makes it harder to tune bass strings because of the many simultaneous beats. Inharmonicity in bass strings varies from one piano to the next, not only because of scale design (length, tension, diameter of strings and striking point of the hammers) but also because of minute variations in diameter and tightness of the windings. Therefore, it is impossible to formulate a table illustrating beat rates of intervals which include low bass strings. Instead of tuning bass strings to an arbitrary table of beat rates, they must be tuned to sound their best when compared to various upper notes, without having one beating interval sound worse than the others.

In most pianos, the tenor register may be tuned by octaves down to the third A from the bottom. At this point, the double beats begin to get confusing, so from the third A down to the second A, tune by the above procedure. The intervals *from the lower note up* are one octave and a fifth, and two octaves and a third. For the last octave in the bass, tune to two octaves and a third, and two octaves and a fifth, setting the note between the places where either beat stops.

Other combinations of notes are also helpful for testing the accuracy of the bass. These are *major chords*. A *chord* is a combination of three or more notes; a *major* chord is the cheerful-sounding combination of an octave, and the fifth and third contained within the octave. Bass tests using major chords are summarized in illustration 4-24.

55

The longer bass strings are, the easier they are to tune. It would be helpful if every beginning tuner could practice his first tuning exercises on a concert grand piano. Small spinet pianos have wild inharmonicity in the bass, making them the hardest pianos to tune in that register.

Pitch Raising

Many pianos which are not tuned for a long time go a quarter step, half step, or even farther flat. Some tuners leave such pianos at whatever pitch they were, tuning the temperament, unisons and octaves, using A-420 or whatever it happened to be, for the pitch standard. A piano with its string tension too low sounds dull, lifeless, and lacks brilliance. It is impossible to play along with certain other instruments, and hampers the musical ability of any student who regularly practices on it. To tune such a piano to the wrong pitch is hardly better than not tuning it at all!

If a piano is flat and the tuner tunes it to A-440 in the usual way, raising the pitch as he proceeds, by the time the entire piano is tuned, the first strings tuned will be somewhat flat again. This results from the added tension on the frame and plate. (In raising a piano one half step flat to the correct pitch, the additional tension amounts to over two tons.) To compensate for this effect, raise the middle octaves slightly above A-440 pitch, tapering off on the amount of sharpness toward the treble end, until the last half octave is tuned to the correct pitch. Then tune the bass to the correct pitch. By the time the first pitch raising is completed, the piano will have settled to somewhere near the correct pitch. If it is still flat, go through the procedure again, but do not raise the pitch as far above the correct pitch as the first time. With practice, a good tuner can get a piano which was a quarter step flat close enough to A-440 the first time, to tune it the second, and can tune almost any tunable piano in three tunings.

To avoid damaging a very old piano which is a half step or more flat, raise all the A's first, then all the A#'s, and so on, until all notes have been tuned. Repeat the procedure until the piano is within a quarter step of the correct pitch. Then use the procedure in the above paragraph once, and it should be ready to tune.

Certain conditions prevent a piano from being raised to the correct pitch. If either bridge is cracked, do not raise the pitch. If the tuning pins are extremely loose, the strings will go flat as soon as the tuning lever is released. In this condition, it is doubtful that the piano can be tuned at all. If the plate is cracked or broken, do not attempt anything (except to lower the string tension) unless the bad spot is repaired. Many tuners are afraid of breaking the plate by raising the pitch. While it is true that a cracked plate will get worse, or break completely apart if the tension is raised, a good plate was made to withstand the correct tension, and it is unlikely that it will crack unless the piano has been dropped.

If the plate is good and the pins are tight, the worst thing likely to happen is for a few rusty strings to break. To avoid breaking rusty strings, let the tension of each string down just enough to break the rust bond between the string, pressure bar and plate bridge. If the strings are badly rusted, warn the owner that no responsibility is assumed for broken strings, and be ready to replace some of them. Never raise a rusted or corroded string above the correct pitch.

Pitch Lowering

When a piano is tuned to the correct pitch during a dry season and is then exposed to high humidity, it goes sharp. In this condition, there is too much stress on the frame and plate, and other instrumentalists have a hard time tuning to the high pitch. Any such piano should be lowered to A-440 pitch.

When a piano is sharp and the tuner tunes it to A-440 in the usual way, lowering the pitch as he proceeds, by the time the entire piano is tuned, the first strings tuned will be somewhat sharp again. This is the reverse of what happens when raising the pitch. In order to lower the pitch, begin in the middle by setting the temperament lower than usual; in fact, set it as far *below A-440* pitch as it was *above*. Taper off the amount of flatness toward the treble end, until the last half of the treble octave is tuned to the correct pitch. Tune the bass to 440 pitch. By the time the entire piano is gone through once, the pitch should be close enough to A-440 to allow the piano to be fine-tuned in one tuning.

Tuning the Duplex Scale

The *duplex scale* is the name for the nonspeaking segments of the strings in some pianos. While most pianos have this section of each string muted with a piece of stringing braid or felt, fine quality pianos have this section unmuted, so these string segments may ring sympathetically with the speaking portions, adding to the brilliance of the tone.

The aliquot bars in some pianos have pins which fit into holes in the plate. These can not be adjusted without grinding the pins off, but they rarely need tuning anyway. Other aliquot bars merely are held in place by the string tension. Tuning the duplex scale is a delicate matter, accomplished by tapping each aliquot bar with a punch and mallet until the string segment speaks the desired note when plucked. If the correct pitches are unknown, write to the factory for instructions for that particular piano.

Illus. 4-25 Tuning a Mason & Hamlin duplex scale aliquot bar by tapping gently.

Difficulty in Equalizing String Tension

If the tuning lever must be moved exceptionally far before a string begins to change pitch, and then the pitch suddenly changes too much, the pressure bar is probably screwed in too far. This causes it to exert too much pressure and friction on the strings, making them difficult to tune. If the strings are bent at an unusually large angle by the pressure bar, raise it a little. This will help the string tension to equalize along the entire length of the strings, making tuning easier. Do not raise the pressure bar so high that any of the strings slip sideways.

Tuning Two Pianos Together

If all pianos were acoustically perfect, any two pianos which were tuned to A-440 would be perfectly in tune with each other. Because of string stiffness, however, a piano with short strings has a different degree of inharmonicity than does a piano with longer strings. The more inharmonicity, the more octave stretching is required for a piano to be in tune with itself. This means that if a spinet and a concert grand are each carefully tuned to A-440, the upper and lower notes of the two pianos will be out of tune with each other because of the different amounts of octave stretching required in each piano. For further discussion of inharmonicity, see pp. 53-55. The extremes of a smaller piano must be stretched more than the extremes of a larger piano, with the result that the smaller piano bass will be flat and treble will be sharp to the larger piano. Therefore, it is impossible for two pianos of different sizes to be perfectly in tune with themselves and each other simultaneously.

When two pianos are used in concert together, they should be of identical stringing scale (i.e., identical brand and model), when possible. Tune each piano separately. Then, with the help of an assistant, compare the pianos one note at a time, correcting any discrepancies.

If two identical pianos are not obtainable, two pianos having strings of as nearly the same length as possible should be used. Tune each piano separately, and do not make one piano out of tune with itself in order to make certain notes more in tune with the other piano.

Tuning a Piano to an Organ

Most organs, and particularly pipe organs, change pitch drastically with temperature and humidity changes. This is because warmer or wetter air is thinner and vibrates faster in the organ pipes, producing a higher pitch. The pitch of some electronic organ circuits also changes with temperature or humidity variations. Therefore, it is essential that the temperature in the room during tuning is the same as it will be during the performance. Select an 8' *diapason* or *string* stop on the organ. Do not use a stop marked *tremolo* or *celeste*; these purposely introduce pitches which waver, or are slightly out of tune for chorus effects. Use F below middle C on the organ for a pitch reference, and then tune the piano to itself in the usual way. Do not tune a piano one note at a time to an organ, for this will result in the piano being out of tune with itself.

Tuning a Piano
on a Bandstand

If a snare drum is near a piano, the snares vibrate sympathetically when the piano is played, causing an annoying buzzing sound and making it difficult to tune the piano. Most snare drums have a lever to release the snare away from its head, which eliminates sympathetic vibration.

Illus. 4-26 Releasing a snare.

Tuning Victorian Pianos

Most pianos made prior to the 1920's were designed to be tuned to A-435. A Victorian or an early twentieth century piano having a three-quarter plate should be tuned to A-435 to avoid possible damage. To tune a piano to A-435, obtain a C-517.3 tuning fork. The pitch of C above middle C is 517.3 when A is 435. Tune the piano in the usual way, using the low-pitch fork as a pitch standard. If an electronic tuning aid is used, calibrate it twenty cents flat. One cent equals one hundredth of a half step; A-435 is twenty cents flat of A-440.

If an old piano is heavily constructed, with heavy wooden bracing and a full iron plate, and is in good condition, it probably may be tuned to A-440. When the pitch standard was changed from 435 to 440 in the early twentieth century, some factories continued to build the same identical pianos, tuning them to the new higher pitch. This indicates that many well-built pianos are sturdy enough to withstand the additional strain.

Some Victorian grands have oblong tuning pins which require a special tuning lever tip or adapter. These are available from piano supply companies.

GAINING PROFICIENCY

As the student becomes more proficient in tuning pianos he will undoubtedly want to learn ways of speeding up his work without sacrificing quality.

One way to improve is to learn to raise the pitch without using any mutes. For this skill, the tuner must learn to tune two strings of a unison beatless while the third string vibrates a quarter-step or half-step out of tune. This can be quite difficult at first, but becomes easier with practice. An incidental benefit of learning this skill is the improved ability to tune strings with false beats, as the tuner learns to distinguish the right beats from the wrong ones.

Learn to set the pin and string with as few back-and-forth movements of the tuning lever as possible, for less wasted motion.

Learning to read music and to play the piano are valuable skills which make the tuning job more interesting to the technician even if they do not contribute directly to tuning proficiency. Being able to demonstrate a piano after tuning it helps the technician to establish a professional image.

Join an active chapter of the Piano Technicians Guild, and attend meetings and seminars to pick up many useful ideas for improvement.

Above all, tune a lot of pianos! There is no better way to improve tuning skill than to tune pianos daily.

ELECTRONIC TUNING AIDS

An electronic tuning aid is a device which converts musical tone into a visual pattern. All electronic tuners have several features in common: a knob which may be set to the desired pitch, a microphone, and a visual display which shows whether the pitch is sharp, flat, or in tune. (An exception is the StroboConn, which has twelve visual displays, one for each pitch.) The visual displays incorporated into various brands of tuners include stroboscope discs (Conn and Peterson), circular patterns of blinking lights (Hale Sight-O-Tuner), cathode ray tubes (Yamaha), and electronic meters (Tunemaster). When the pitch is out of tune, the strobe wheel, pattern of blinking lights, meter needle, etc., moves in one direction or the other. When the pitch is in tune, the visual indicator stands still. Although all electronic tuning aids are fairly accurate, the newest solid state instruments are more accurate than some of their vacuum tube predecessors, due to the greater stability of solid state electronic circuits.

Using an Electronic Tuner

If pianos were acoustically perfect, it would be possible to calibrate an electronic tuning aid to A440, tune each note on the piano to the tuner, and end up with perfectly beatless octaves throughout. Because of inharmonicity, however, the octaves must be stretched in order to be beatless, with the treble notes sharp of their theoretical pitches and the bass notes flat. If a piano is tuned to an electronic aid without compensating for inharmonicity, the treble will be flat and the bass will be sharp. It is therefore necessary to determine the amount of inharmonicity of each note and compensate for it when using an electronic aid. Many beginning technicians have used electronic tuners as shortcuts to good tuning, without understanding inharmonicity. Their poor results have lead many piano owners to the false belief that it is impossible to tune a piano correctly with an electronic tuner. It is possible to tune a piano with an electronic aid if the proper procedure is followed. The electronic aid is also a valuable learning tool, providing that it does not become a crutch.

In order to tune a piano competently with an electronic device, the technician must be able to tune any unison beatless. He must also have the same dexterity with the tuning lever as he would if he were tuning by ear, in order to set the pins and set the strings, so the piano will remain in tune for a reasonable length of time.

The first step in electronic tuning is to tune the temperament. Calibrate the electronic aid to A440 following the instruction manual. If the piano has non-wrapped three-string unisons at least all the way down to the F below middle C, mute the two outside strings of that note and tune the center string so the tuner indicates *in tune*. Unmute the outside strings one at a time, and tune them beatless by ear. Follow the same procedure for each note up to the E above middle C. At this time, the temperament will be in tune.

To tune the treble, the following procedure must be used to compensate for inharmonicity. After tuning the temperament, the next note to be tuned is F above middle C. The fundamental of this F is the same as the second partial of F below middle C. Set the tuner to F *above* middle C (or watch the

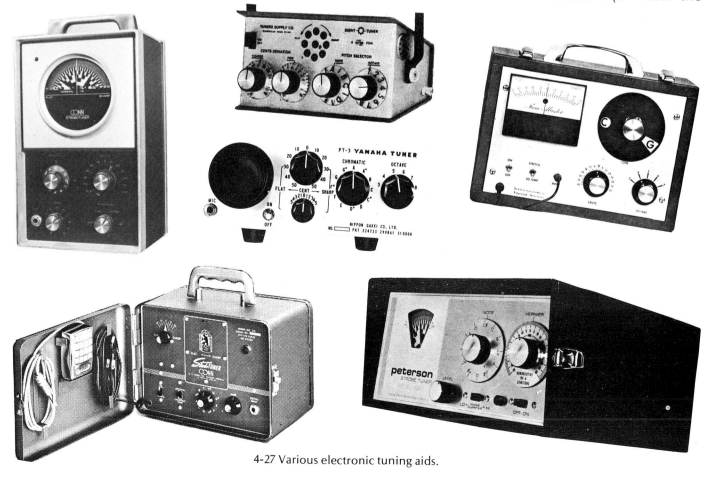

4-27 Various electronic tuning aids.

appropriate band on the disc of a stroboscopic tuner), and play F *below* middle C. You are now reading the 2nd partial of F below middle C to see if it is in tune or stretched. If it is in tune with its fundamental, tune F above middle C to the tuner. If the second partial of the lower F registers *sharp* on the tuner, keep playing that F, and recalibrate the tuner until its second partial registers *in tune*. Then tune F above middle C to the tuner. The fundamental of the upper F is now in tune with the second partial of the lower F, and the octave is beatless. This procedure appears lengthy and complicated on paper, but once the compensation method is grasped it is fairly quick.

The same procedure is followed for every note in the treble of the piano, calibrating the tuner to compensate for the inharmonicity of the lower note, and then recalibrating it for each next pitch.

To tune the bass, the opposite calibrating procedure is used. The first note below the temperament octave to be tuned is E below middle C. Calibrate the tuner so it is in tune with the fundamental of E above middle C. Play E below middle C, and read its second partial on the tuner. The second partial of the lower E is the same pitch as the fundamental of the upper E. Tune the lower E so the second partial is in tune. The fundamental is then stretched properly. To tune the next note, E♭ below middle C, recalibrate the tuner so it is in tune with the fundamental of E♭ above middle C, and repeat the same procedure. Remember to recalibrate the tuner to the upper octave of each new note to be tuned.

Many small spinets have wrapped strings or heavy non-wrapped two-string unisons in the lower part of the conventional temperament octave. Because of the pronounced inharmonicity of these strings, it is difficult to set an accurate temperament with them electronically. Instead, set the temperament from Middle C to the B above, tuning the rest of the piano by the compensation procedure.

Precautions

The instruction manuals for some electronic tuning aids include octave stretching tables which arbitrarily show how to recalibrate the tuner, to compensate for the inharmonicity in an "average" piano. Recalibrating the tuner according to a table may produce better results than not stretching the octaves at all, and produces excellent results when used with certain pianos on which the tables are based, but the best tuning is accomplished by following the above procedure.

Some electronic aids, particularly those of the stroboscopic type, do not show the tuning of the lowest and highest notes clearly, so a combination of aural and visual tuning must be used. As the student progresses, he may find that it becomes easier to tune the octaves by ear than to use the visual inharmonicity-compensating procedure for each note. At that point, the student may use the tuning aid for the temperament, tuning the octaves by ear. After more progress is made in hearing and timing slow beat rates, the student may find that it is faster to tune the entire piano by ear.

Chapter Five
Regulating

Precautions

Piano actions are heavy but fragile. Pick up a vertical action only by the action brackets, or by the hammer rail if securely attached to the brackets; carry a grand action only by the key frame.

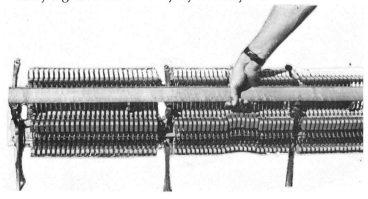

Illus. 5-1 Carrying the vertical action.

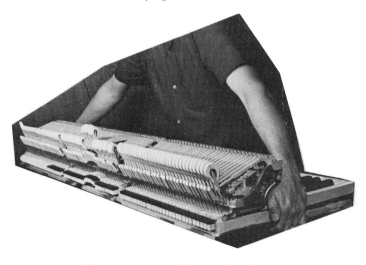

Illus. 5-2 Carrying the grand action.

Before removing any parts, always number them, starting with #1 in the bass, so they can be replaced in the proper order. Identical looking parts are not necessarily interchangeable.

A number of specialized tools are illustrated in this and following chapters. Some of these may be made by modifying regular tools; others should be purchased. Many of these fit in a standard *combination handle*, to eliminate the bulk and expense of having a separate handle for each tool. Each tool has a special purpose. Whether action regulating tools are purchased or homemade, the right tool should always be used for each job.

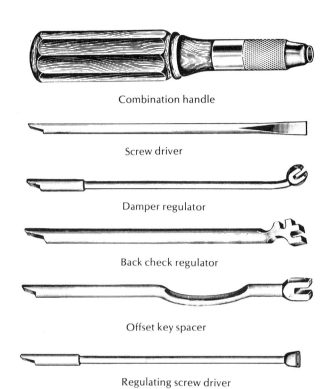

Combination handle

Screw driver

Damper regulator

Back check regulator

Offset key spacer

Regulating screw driver

Illus. 5-3 A combination handle and some of the many tools which may be inserted in it, reducing the expense and bulk of individual tools.

VERTICAL ACTION REGULATING

1. *Remove the action.* To remove an upright or console action, first remove the music rack and fallboard. Then remove the four round nuts from the upper action support bolts. Grasp the two outside brackets, and pull them forward just enough to come off the bolts. Balance the action in place with the right hand, and disengage the pedal dowels from the action with the left. Grasp the end brackets again, and pull the top of the action out just enough for the dampers to clear the upper action support posts. Lift the action straight up and out of the piano. To replace the action, reverse the procedure, being careful that the dampers clear the upper support bolts, and that the action brackets come to rest on the lower support bolts with the lower ends of all stickers resting on top of the capstans.

Illus. 5-4 Removing the upright action. Notice the nuts have been removed from the four action support bolts, the action has been tilted forward, and is ready to be lifted out of the piano.

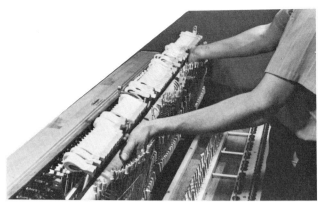

Illus. 5-5 Lifting action out of spinet piano.

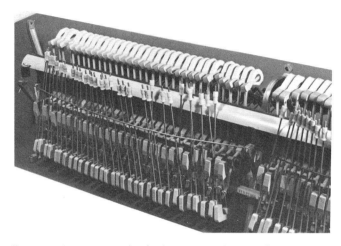

Illus. 5-6 Showing method of securing drop stickers to spinet action with coat hanger wire prior to removal of action from piano.

To remove a spinet action with flanged drop sticker extensions, unscrew the sticker extension rail support brackets from the keybed. Leave this rail attached to the action brackets. Remove the whole action, stickers and all, following the instructions for the upright.

To remove a Baldwin action having a drop sticker guide rail attached to the keybed, lift each end sticker up to the guide rail and tie them to the rail. Unscrew the rail from the brackets, move it toward the hammer rail, and tie it to the action brackets. The action is then ready for removal.

In a spinet with the stickers supported entirely by the keys, disengage all stickers from the keys and secure them to the action. Some spinets have a hook on each action bracket; a long rod may be inserted behind the hooks to hold the stickers in place. In other spinets, the rod should be tied to the brackets. When the stickers are secured, remove the action. Be sure the dampers clear the upper support brackets. Some spinets have long screws with spacers instead of bolts, or action brackets which reach to the plate; when the screws are removed there is nothing in the way to snag the dampers.

2. *Tighten all action screws,* with the action resting on a bench or sturdy table. Tighten all cabinet and plate screws which are accessible.

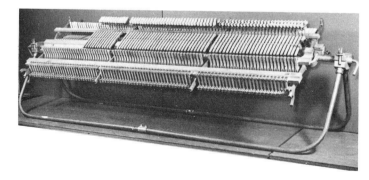

Illus. 5-7 A portable action cradle provides sturdy support for the action at any angle.

Illus. 5-8 The shape of the flange screwdriver enables it to be inserted between action parts and turned without damaging them. (Refer to illus. 5-3).

3. *Reshape the hammers* if they are grooved. (See pp. 113-115.) This not only improves the tone quality, but also enables the hammers to be aligned with the strings. If a grooved hammer is realigned without being reshaped, the old grooves will try to mate with the strings, throwing the hammer into its old alignment and putting a strain on the hammer, shank and butt.

4. *Clean* the piano and action. Blow out as much dirt as possible with the forced air end of a vacuum cleaner, a toothbrush, or better yet, an air compressor. (To clean pianos in the home, see pp. 120-121.) Tighten all screws before blowing dirt out of the action, to prevent dirt from being blown under loose flanges. Clean the damper springs and hammer butt springs with metal polish on a rag, and clean the spring punchings with a toothbrush or compressed air. Replace any badly rusted springs. Number and remove the keys; clean the keys and key frame.

5. *Correct or replace* all squeaky, sluggish, loose, wobbly, rusty or broken parts, as described in the repair chapter. Replace broken bridle tapes. Broken tapes allow the whippens to drop, letting the jacks slip under the bottoms of the hammer butts. If the action is replaced in the piano in this condition, the jacks will force the hammers against the strings, jamming them in that position.

6. Move the *regulating rail* in or out to align the buttons with the heels of the jacks, if necessary. Tighten the screws which attach the rail to its support brackets.

7. Both ends of the *damper lift rod* should lift at the same time, lifting all dampers at once. If one end lifts the dampers sooner, one of the support hangers is bent and should be straightened.

8. *Travel the hammers.* Each hammer should move in a straight line perpendicular to the hammer rail. If it swings to one side during its stroke, insert a bit of paper under one side of the flange, to change the direction of travel.

Replace the keys and action in the piano. In some spinets the keys must be weighted in back with a long slat or rod to get the action back in.

9. *Space the hammers.* Move each hammer up to its strings, and check its alignment. If it is off to one side, and if the action has wood flanges, loosen the flange screw, insert a small, thin screwdriver between that flange and the adjacent one, and twist gently in the desired direction. Hold the hammer head in the correct place while tightening the flange screw. If the hammer is still out of line when

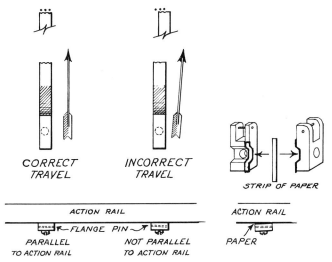

Illus. 5-9 Showing paper shim method of correcting hammer travel, as viewed from above.

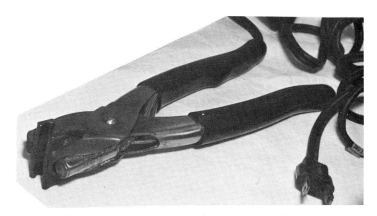

Illus. 5-10 Aligning a hammer to the strings. Position the hammer with one hand and tighten the screw with the other.

Illus. 5-11 An electric hammer shank bender.

Illus. 5-12 Using the shank bender. The hammer rail has been removed for this illustration.

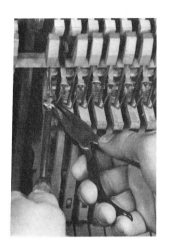 

Illus. 5-13 Spacing and squaring a backcheck.

the flange is turned as far as possible, the shank is warped and must be straightened. This also applies to brass flange actions, where no flange adjustment is possible. Heat the shank with an alcohol lamp or cigarette lighter. Move the flame up and down the length of the shank, making it as warm as possible without charring the wood. When the wood is warm, bend the shank in the required direction, and hold it there until cool; it should stay bent in the new direction. Do not apply excessive pressure to the flange. An electric shank bender is more expensive but easier to use, and poses less danger of overheating the shanks.

Align the hammers up and down, if necessary. Apply heat to the shank or the heel of the hammer where it is glued to the shank. Press the hammer head up or down until it cools, to align it with its neighbors.

10. *Space the backchecks* sideways to meet the catchers squarely. To keep from breaking the whippens, hold them securely whenever bending the stiff backcheck wires. The backcheck should first be spaced by bending the wire where it enters the whippen, and then squared by bending where the wire enters the backcheck. Never bend a backcheck wire in the middle.

11. *Square and space the keys.* If a key is tilted to one side, bend the balance rail pin by holding a screwdriver against the top of the pin and tapping it with the palm of the hand.

The front end of each key should be centered between its neighbors. If a key is off center, bend the front rail pin sideways. Never turn a front rail pin; the flat sides should be parallel to the cloth bushings. Ease any binding keys. (See pp. 102-103.)

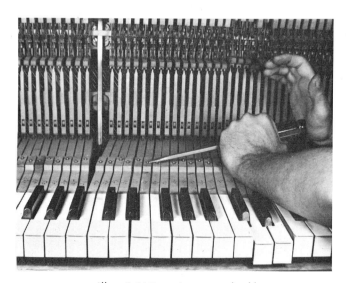

Illus. 5-14 Squaring a crooked key.

Illus. 5-15 Spacing a key by bending front rail pin.

Illus. 5-16 Measuring the hammer stroke.

12. Set the *hammer stroke,* or the distance between the hammers at rest and the strings. Hammer stroke is 1¾" (45 mm) in most old uprights, and it varies from 1½ to 1¾ (39–45 mm) in spinets and consoles. For exact measurements, see the "Piano Action Handbook", listed in the bibliography. When hammers wear, the blow distance is increased. To correct, glue blocking felt of the proper thickness under the felt spacers between the hammer rail and action brackets, using hide glue, white glue or a hot glue gun. Add the same amount of felt to each spacer; if the hammer rail is held up by one spacer, it will bounce when the soft pedal is released.

13. Regulate *lost motion* between jacks and hammer butts. The height of each jack in relation to its hammer butt is regulated by the capstan. If the jack is too high, the hammer rests on the jack instead of the hammer rail, preventing the jack from slipping under the butt when the key is released. If the jack is low, with excess space, or lost motion, between the jack and butt, the key will go down part way before engaging with the hammer, resulting in poor control and excessive wear of the butt buckskin.

Alternately press and release each key just enough to feel for lost motion. Eliminate any play between the jack and butt by turning the capstan counterclockwise with a capstan wrench until the key just barely moves before moving the hammer. To regulate rocker capstans, loosen one screw and tighten the other to elevate or lower the working end. In pianos having regulating screws mounted on the stickers, turn the screw down to reduce lost motion.

Illus. 5-20 Universal capstan wrench which fits both common styles of capstan screws.

Illus. 5-17 Gluing blocking felt under hammer rail to correct excessive hammer stroke.

Illus. 5-18 Regulating capstan to eliminate excess lost motion between jack and hammer butt.

Illus. 5-19 Testing for excess lost motion; there should be minimal movement of key and backcheck before hammer begins to move.

The jack should be as close to the butt as possible without raising it. There should be no play when the key is depressed lightly, but if the jack is tripped and released with the hammer at rest, the jack should return itself under the butt without rubbing on the buckskin. Another test is to pull back lightly on the hammer rail. All hammers should move with the rail a tiny amount, showing that they are resting on the rail and not on their jacks.

Illus. 5-21 Two methods of testing for proper regulation of capstan screws. *Left:* All hammers should move back slightly when hammer rail is gently pulled. *Right:* Each jack should return under its butt when released.

In a piano with badly worn hammers, when the hammer rail is shimmed up far enough to provide the correct hammer stroke, a great deal of lost motion is introduced between the jacks and hammer butts. To remove the lost motion, the capstans must be unscrewed so far that they become loose. To prevent this from happening, shim the back rail of the key frame up first to remove most of the lost motion, and then regulate the capstans.

14. Set the *key height.* The bottom of the front end of each white key should be about ⅛" (3 mm) below the top edge of the keyslip. To adjust all of the keys at once, insert paper shims under the balance rail. Adding shims uniformly under the front and back of the rail changes the height of all keys; shimming the front has more effect on the whites, and shimming the back has more effect on the sharps. Add the same thickness of shims under both sides of each screw, to prevent warpage when the screw is tightened. Key heights for specific pianos are listed in the Piano Action Handbook.

15. *Level the white keys.* Keys are leveled, or adjusted to exactly the same height, by adding or subtracting thin paper or cardboard punchings under the center rail cloth punchings. These are available in thicknesses ranging from .001" to .045". There are two methods of leveling keys.

Illus. 5-22 Measuring key height.

Illus. 5-23 Adjusting average height of keys with shims cut from index or business card.

Using a Key Leveling Tool

The most common version of this tool, the *Davis key leveler,* has a floating brass button which rides on the keytops as the tool is slid across the keybed with the keyslip removed. This tool is accurate, providing that the keybed is level. Slide the leveler from one end of the keybed to the other, noting which key is the highest. If the key height is adjusted properly in step #14, no keys should be too high. Set the leveler so the button is flush with its surrounding housing, when positioned over the center of the highest key. Then, starting at one end, position the leveler over the center of each white key, adding or subtracting paper punchings under the cloth center rail punching until the button is flush with the housing. With practice, it is possible to tell what thickness of punching is needed by looking at the button.

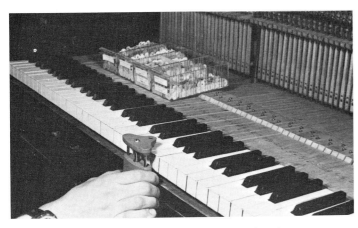

Illus. 5-24 Using the Davis white key leveler.

Illus. 5-25 To adjust individual key height, change paper punchings under cloth balance rail punching.

Cloth Front Rail Punchings—made in ¾" and ⅞" diameters
  .125" Thin
  .145" Medium Thin
  .165" Medium
  .185" Medium Thick
  .215" Thick

Cloth Balance Rail Punchings—½" diameter
  .050" Thin
  .065" Medium Thin
  .080" Medium
  .095" Medium Thick
  .110" Thick

Paper and Card Front Rail Punchings—⅞" diameter
  .003" Thinnest Paper
  .005" Thin Paper
  .007" Medium Paper
  .010" Thick Paper
  .015-.060" Card Punchings—specific thicknesses available; vary among suppliers

Paper Balance Rail Punchings—½" diameter
  .001" Tissue Paper
  .003" Thinnest Paper
  .005" Thin Paper
  .007" Medium Paper
  .010" Thick Paper
  .014-.045" Card Punchings—specific thicknesses available; vary among suppliers

Illus. 5-26 Table of key frame punching dimensions.

Using a Straightedge

In the absence of a key leveler, or if the keybed is warped, a straightedge may be used. An aluminum yardstick from an office supply or hardware store is handy for this purpose. Set the height of each end key, and the E above middle C, so they are as high as the highest white key, and block them up to this height with paper punchings. Then level each half of the keyboard separately.

Whichever leveling method is used, it is sometimes inconvenient to remove and replace keys with the action in place. If so, and if the keys are balanced to the front so they go down when the weight of the action is removed, obtain a set of small lead clip-on weights from a piano supply house. Clip them to the back ends of the keys to prevent the keys from dropping when the action is removed.

Do not bend paper punchings; a bent punching

will alter the key height until it flattens out later, making the keybed uneven again. If necessary, handle the punchings with tweezers to keep from bending them.

16. *Level the sharp keys.* The wooden part of the key behind the sharp should be flush with the adjacent white keys. The front of each sharp should be high enough that it is not "buried" between the whites when it is depressed, but not so high that the wood on the front surface shows.

An easy way to level sharps is with a Jaras sharp leveler. This is similar to the Davis device, but it straddles the sharp, resting on the adjacent white keys. Level a few sample sharps by leveling the wood with the adjacent white keys, and set the sharp leveling device to the average height of the samples. Then level the rest of the sharps with the leveler, adding or subtracting punchings until the floating button is flush.

Illus. 5-27 Using the Jaras sharp leveler.

In the absence of a Jaras regulating tool, a straightedge may be used. Block one sharp at each end and one sharp in the middle of the keyboard up to the proper height, with punchings, and use the straightedge to level all the sharps in between.

Illus. 5-28 Regulating letoff (left); showing the use of a wooden letoff strip as explained in the text (right).

17. Regulate *hammer letoff*. When each key is depressed slowly, the hammer should move to within ⅛" (3 mm) of the strings and then release when the jack slips out from under the butt. To adjust the letoff point, turn the letoff regulating screw up or down.

For uniform letoff, make a strip of wood exactly ⅛" (3 mm) thick, ¾" (or 2 cm) wide and 12" (or 30 cm) long, and wedge it in place, as illustrated. Turn each regulating screw up (counterclockwise) just high enough so the jack does not trip when the key is depressed. Hold each key down, pressing the hammer against the wood strip, and slowly turn the regulating screw down until the jack slips out from under the butt and the hammer lets off. Use the same pressure on each key for uniform letoff.

18. Regulate *white key dip*. Dip is the distance the key moves down until it stops on the front rail punching. It is usually ⅜" or ⁷⁄₁₆" (10–11.5 mm), and is regulated by adding or subtracting paper punchings under the cloth front rail punchings.

A key must have enough dip to go down a little further after the jack trips and the hammer lets off. This additional travel of the key in the vertical piano is called "after touch" and is necessary in order for the back checks to work properly.

Key dip is usually regulated with a ⅜" (10 mm) thick *key dip block*. Lay it on top of each white key and depress. Add or subtract punchings until the block is flush with the adjacent keys. Check a few sample keys to be sure that when the key dip is ⅜" (10 mm), there is adequate after touch. If not, use a ⁷⁄₁₆" (11.5 mm) block, made by gluing a ¹⁄₁₆" (1.5 mm) thick piece of cardboard on a regular dip block.

Illus. 5-29 Measuring white key dip with a ⅜" (10 mm) dip block.

19. Regulate *hammer checking*. Adjust the backcheck for the end white keys in each section so when the key is played moderately hard, the hammer will check, or come to rest, ⅝" (16 mm) from the strings. The closer the backcheck is to the hammer, the closer to the strings the hammer will check. Set the spacing by bending the wire where it enters the whippen, and then set the angle for good contact with the hammer catcher by bending where the wire enters the backcheck. Never bend the wire in the middle. After the end backchecks in each section are regulated, align the intermediate ones with an 18" straightedge.

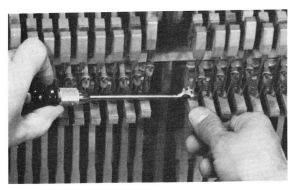

Illus. 5-30 Spacing the backcheck to sample white key hammer catcher so hammer checks ⅝" (16 mm) from strings.

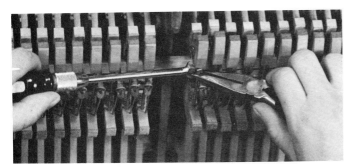

Illus. 5-31 Setting backcheck angle for maximum contact between backcheck and catcher.

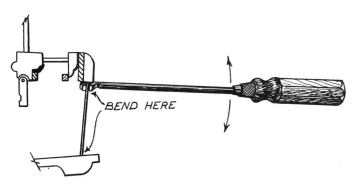

Illus. 5-32 Showing proper use of the backcheck regulating tool.

Illus. 5-33 Checking alignment of backchecks with straight-edge.

20. Regulate the *sharp key dip*. The point at which the hammer checks is determined by the setting of the backcheck *and* the key dip. If a backcheck is regulated properly but the key dip is wrong, the hammer will check at the wrong place. Conversely, if the backcheck is regulated properly, the hammer checking point may be used as a guideline to regulate the key dip. The white key dip and all backchecks have already been regulated. To regulate sharp key dip, play each sharp key with the two adjacent white keys, and add or subtract paper punchings under the sharp until the hammer checks at ⅝" (16 mm) from the strings, the same as the neighboring hammers.

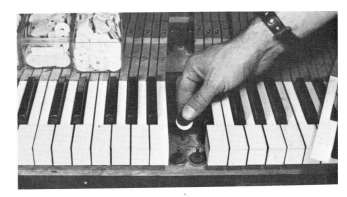

Illus. 5-34 Regulate sharp key dip by changing paper front rail punchings until hammer checks at ⅝" (16 mm) from strings.

21. Regulate the *dampers*. The sustaining pedal should lift all dampers at the same time. If any damper lifts too soon or too late, bend the wire where it enters the lever. When the dampers are regulated to lift uniformly with the pedal, be sure they mute the strings properly. If not, change the angle of the damper head by bending the wire where it enters the head.

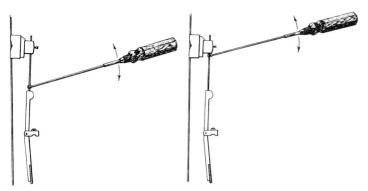

Illus. 5-35 *Left:* Regulating dampers to lift rod by bending wire where it enters lever. *Right:* Seating damper on strings by bending wire where it enters damper head.

23. Regulate the *damper spoons.* Each damper should lift when its key is pushed halfway down, or when the hammer is half way to the strings. The spoons are regulated by bending them with a *spoon bender,* with the action in the piano. Since they are on the back side of the action, they must be found with the tool by feel. Insert the bender between the whippen to be regulated and the adjacent one, and hook the end of the tool over the spoon, as illustrated. Hold the whippen with one hand, and use the tool in the other to bend the spoon in or out. Bending it toward the keyboard will cause the damper to lift later in the hammer stroke. Remove the tool, test the key, and repeat the procedure until the damper lifts properly.

Illus. 5-36 Showing how to reach damper wire with bending tool.

22. Regulate the *sustaining pedal.* Push the trap lever down, hold the pull wire up with one hand, and adjust the nut with the other, so there is a little lost motion between the sustaining pedal and dampers. The dampers should rest on the strings, not on the damper lift rod. If the piano has a bass sustaining pedal, regulate it the same way.

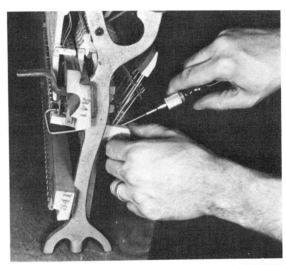

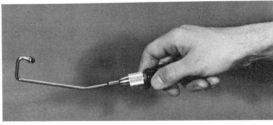

Illus. 5-38 *Top:* Showing use of the damper spoon bender. *Bottom:* Closeup of the tool.

Spoon regulating is one of the most difficult regulating procedures. To learn the proper feel for finding the spoon without being able to see it, remove the action and set it on a bench. Insert the spoon bender, and hook it around a spoon, watching where it goes and noticing what it feels like at the same time. With practice it is possible to find the spoon by feel, without looking.

24. Regulate the *soft pedal.* Adjust the nut, or change cloth punchings between trap lever and hammer rail dowel. When the soft pedal is

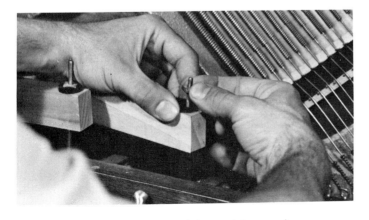

Illus. 5-37 Regulating sustaining pedal to trap lever.

depressed fully, the hammer rail should move the hammers half way to the strings.

25. Regulate the *bridle tapes*. Bend each bridle wire so the tape is taut, but does not move the whippen, when the soft pedal is depressed. All slack should be removed from the bridle tapes when the hammers are moved half way toward the strings, but the keys should not wink, or move down slightly. Space each bridle wire sideways so it does not touch the backcheck wire or the head of a regulating screw, to prevent clicking noises.

Spinet Regulating

The procedure is identical to upright regulating, with the following exceptions:

Lost motion regulation: some spinets have capstans at the rear ends of the keys. The keys must usually be removed to regulate these capstans. Some spinets have short dowels screwed onto the ends of the lifter wires, which are turned up or down for lost motion regulation. After regulating the dowel, press it into the key socket, and play the key firmly a few times. Then recheck the regulation. Some spinets have hex head screws which are turned with a 7/32″ nut driver. Remove the tool from the adjustment screw when testing accuracy of regulation.

Aligning the backchecks: this is done by sight, because there is not enough space to use a straightedge.

Regulating the damper spoons: the spoon bender is inserted underneath the keybed.

Regulating the Wood and Brooks 90° Action

Standard upright regulating procedure is followed, substituting the following measurements: 1⅞″ (48 mm) hammer stroke, 7/32″ (6 mm) letoff, 13/32″ (10.5 mm) key dip, 11/16″ (17.5 mm) hammer check, dampers lift when hammers are ½″ (13 mm) from strings.

Vertical Regulating Checklist for Quick Reference

1. Remove action.
2. Tighten all screws.
3. Reshape hammers.
4. Clean piano and action.
5. Make necessary repairs.
6. Align and tighten regulating rail.
7. Align damper lift rod.
8. Travel hammers.
9. Space hammers to strings.
10. Space and square backchecks.
11. Space and square keys.
12. Set hammer stroke.
13. Regulate key capstans.
14. Regulate key height.
15. Level white keys.
16. Level sharp keys.
17. Regulate hammer letoff.
18. Regulate white key dip.
19. Regulate hammer checking.
20. Regulate sharp key dip.
21. Regulate dampers to damper lift rod.
22. Regulate sustaining pedal to damper lift rod.
23. Regulate damper spoons.
24. Regulate soft pedal.
25. Regulate bridle tapes.

Partial Vertical Regulating

If a complete regulating job is not desired, it often is possible to improve the action by performing an abbreviated regulating job, providing that the keys are level, all moving parts work freely, and the dampers are regulated to the lift rod. For a partial regulating job, use steps 1, 2, 12, 13, 14, 17, 19, 22-24.

Changing the Touch of a Vertical Piano

A customer sometimes complains that the "touch" of a piano is too light, and requests that the technician make it heavier or stiffer. Regulating the action usually solves the problem, but if the customer still complains, one of the following procedures should help. Try each suggestion in the order listed, and have the customer practice on the instrument after each change is made, before proceeding to the next one. Swedge or rebush loose keys. Increase the tension of hammer butt springs and damper springs. Regulate the damper spoons so the dampers begin to lift when the hammers have moved ½″ (13 mm) instead of half way toward the strings. Finally, raise the height of the sharps by 1/16″ (1.5 mm). The pianist will have to raise his fingers higher to play the sharps, and after practicing strenuous exercises, he will be under the illusion that the piano is stiffer.

GRAND REGULATING

The grand action is inaccessible in the piano, so most adjustments are made with the action on the bench. A perfectly flat, sturdy bench is necessary for grand regulating. If the bench is not flat, the action will be out of regulation when replaced in the piano. The back of the bench is fitted with a grand *letoff rack*, as illustrated. The letoff rack target takes the place of the strings, and is adjustable to simulate string height for any piano.

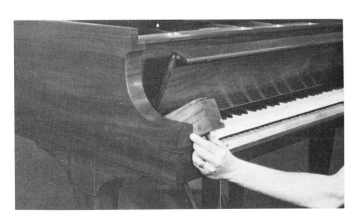

Illus. 5-39 A sturdy, flat bench is necessary for grand action regulating. This handy bench is equipped with a built-in letoff rack.

1. Tighten all accessible plate and cabinet screws.
2. Remove the action. First, remove the key slip, fallboard and cheek blocks, which are usually screwed in from the bottom. Most grands have a pin mounted in each side of the key frame. Remove the blocks which hold these pins down. Grasp the key frame and slide the action straight out of the piano. *Do not depress any keys;* hammers which are raised will catch on the pinblock and break off.

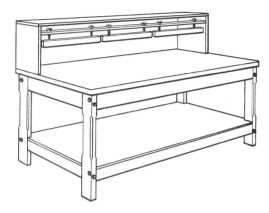

Illus. 5-40 Removing the fallboard and key blocks from a Steinway grand.

The action in some grands is held in place by the cheek blocks; removing them, along with the fallboard and key slip, allows the action to be removed. Grands having no una corda pedal usually have the front of the key frame screwed down to the keybed. The screws are exposed by removing the key slip.

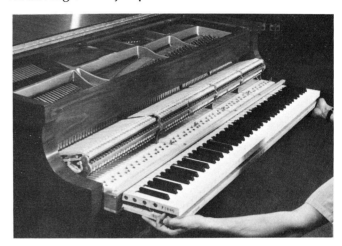

Illus. 5-41 Sliding the action out of the piano.

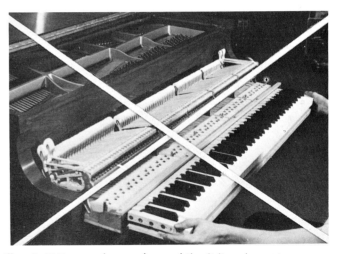

Illus. 5-42 *Do not depress keys while sliding the action out, or the hammers will break off!*

3. Tighten the damper lever flange screws. Check the operation of the dampers and damper levers, and repair as necessary.
4. Clean the piano, as described on pp. 120-121. Clean the keybed by rubbing lightly with 6/0 steel wool, with the grain; vacuum thoroughly, or blow out with compressed air.
5. Tighten all flange and rail screws.
6. Reshape the hammers, if necessary. If the hammers are grooved, they must be reshaped before the action may be regulated. See pp. 113-115.

7. *Clean the action.* Rub the key frame bottom with 6/0 steel wool, with the grain. Blow out the action with compressed air or the pressure end of a vacuum cleaner.

8. *Remove the action and keys* from the key frame.

Illus. 5-43 Lifting the action from the key frame.

9. *Repair* all loose, wobbly, tight, binding or broken parts. Action centers should be free but not loose. Each jack should be centered sideways in the hole in the repetition lever, so the side of the jack does not rub on the repetition lever. If a jack is off center, heat the repetition lever support flange with an alcohol lamp to soften the glue, and press it in the right position until cool. Reglue if necessary. If the repetition lever springs ride in slots in the levers, clean the slots. Number and remove the whippens, release the springs from the slots, and clean the slots by rubbing with a hammer shank sharpened to a blunt point in a pencil sharpener.

Apply a little graphite-alcohol mixture to the slots with another pointed hammer shank. Clean the spring ends with silver polish, carefully reposition the springs, and replace the whippens on the action. Ease the keys, if necessary. (See pp. 102-103). Polish the capstans, balance rail pins and front rail pins with silver polish. Do not use steel wool, which leaves tiny scratches in metal. Clean the hammer knuckles if necessary. (See p. 117). Lubricate the buckskin with graphite. File the sides of any swollen knuckles which rub against adjacent knuckles.

10. *Bed the key frame.* In a grand piano having a una corda pedal, the key frame slides sideways on the keybed, and it must fit the keybed perfectly. If the front rail of the key frame does not make firm contact throughout its area, it will knock when certain notes are played. To *bed the key frame,* or mate it with the keybed, screw the hammer action to the key frame without the keys, replace it in the piano, and screw the key blocks in place. Turn up all key frame glides in the balance rail so they do not hold the key frame up off the keybed. Tap along the front rail, listening for knocking against the keybed. Mark with chalk the beginning and end of any areas which knock. Remove the key blocks, insert a piece of 4/0 sandpaper face up between the key frame and key bed where there was *no* knock, and sand the bottom of the key frame lightly. Repeat this procedure at each place where there was no knock. Clean the sawdust out, replace the key blocks, and test again. Repeat the procedure until all knocks are eliminated. Never sand the keybed, and never insert shims to eliminate a knock.

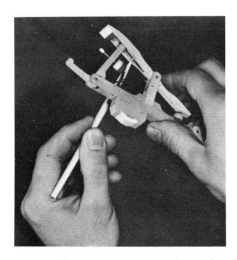
Illus. 5-44 Cleaning the repetition spring slot with a sharpened hammer shank.

Illus. 5-45 Sanding the key frame to remove high spots and eliminate knocks. The sandpaper is inserted with the abrasive side up.

73

Illus. 5-46 This Cable grand has front rail key frame glides built into the keybed, eliminating the need for sanding.

11. Regulate the *key frame glides*. All glides should already be turned up so they do not touch the keybed (in step #10). Insert a piece of newspaper under each glide and turn the glide down, clockwise, just far enough so the newspaper may be pulled out without tearing. If the glide is too high, the keys might bounce; if too low, or too tight against the keybed, the action will be thrown out of regulation and will be hard to shift sideways.

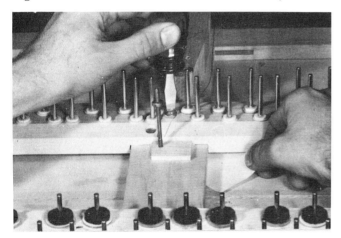

Illus. 5-47 Adjusting the key frame glides.

Illus. 5-48 Steinway key frame glides are adjusted with a tuning lever.

12. *Square and space the keys*; see #11, vertical regulating.

13. *Level the keys.* First, block the damper lift rail as high as it will go, to keep the damper levers away from the keys. With the action removed, place the key frame and keys in the piano. Screw down the keyblocks. Obtain a set of small lead clip-on weights from a piano supply house, and attach them to the rear ends of the keys or to the backchecks. Set each end white key to the proper height, according to the "Piano Action Handbook", or so the bottom of the key is about ⅛" (3 mm) below the top of the keyslip. Set middle E 1/32" (or 1 mm) higher than the end keys. Block each end key and middle E up to exactly the correct height with paper punchings, so they will support the weight of a straightedge. Lay a straightedge from one end key to middle E, and level the keys in between, leveling half of the keyboard at a time by adding or subtracting paper punchings under the balance rail cloth punchings. Middle E is higher than the end keys so the keyboard will have a slight crown. Because the middle keys are played more, they will gradually settle to the height of the end keys, resulting in a level keyboard. Repeat the procedure for the sharp keys.

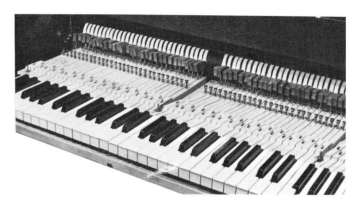

Illus. 5-49 Weighting the keys prior to leveling.

14. Regulate *key dip*. Using a ⅜" (10 mm) key dip block, regulate white key dip by adding or subtracting paper punchings under the front rail cloth punchings. Do not bend the paper punchings; if punchings are bent, the keys will get out of level when the punchings settle. Use tweezers if necessary. Set sharp key dip with a Jaras sharp leveler or ruler.

15. *Travel the hammers.* Remove the key frame from the piano and assemble the action to the key frame. With the action on the bench, check the stroke of each hammer to see that it travels

perfectly straight up and down. Lift each hammer with its neighbor, and see if it moves sideways as it goes up. Correct the hammer travel by inserting a thin paper shim under one side of the hammer shank flange to change the angle of the center pin.

16. *Space the hammers* to the strings. Replace the action in the piano. Lift each hammer, checking to see that it is centered on its strings. Align all hammers so when the soft pedal is depressed, hammers for three string unisons hit only two strings, and hammers for two string unisons hit only one string.

Illus. 5-50 While raising hammer by pressing up on jack with finger, look down into piano to check alignment of hammer with strings.

17. Regulate the *una corda pedal* so the action shifts just enough to align all treble hammers with two of their three strings. To adjust, loosen the lock nut and turn the capstan. When correct, tighten the lock nut. If an adjustable capstan is not present, regulate the pedal by shimming with buckskin between pedal rod and trap lever, or between appropriate links of the trap work.

If the piano has a hammer rail lift for the soft pedal, it is regulated later in procedure #33.

18. *Space the whippens* to the hammers. Place the action on the bench with hammers facing you. Tip or shim each flange as necessary to bring each jack and repetition lever cradle directly under its hammer knuckle.

19. Regulate the *jacks* to the knuckles. Adjust each jack regulating screw until the back edge of the jack is directly under the back edge of the wood core of the knuckle.

20. Regulate the *height of the repetition levers.* If the knuckles are not worn, adjust each repetition lever regulating screw so the top of the lever is .003"

Illus. 5-51 Regulating jack to knuckle core as described in #19.

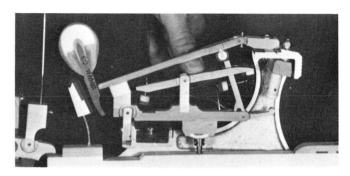

Illus. 5-52 Depressing repetition lever to check alignment of jack with knuckle.

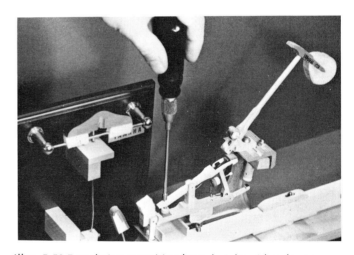

Illus. 5-53 Regulating repetition lever height with a drop screw regulating screwdriver. This tool has a narrow slot to accommodate the spade screw head.

(.075 mm) above the top of the jack. If the knuckle is grooved where the jack has worn it, the repetition lever must be lower than normal in relation to jack, to bring the jack up to the knuckle. Regulate the height of the repetition lever so the hammer knuckle is just barely in contact with the end of the jack. With the hammer resting on the repetition lever, move the jack slowly out from under the knuckle and let it slowly return. The jack should be able to slip all the way back under the knuckle.

75

Illus. 5-54 Measuring height of strings over keybed prior to regulating hammer height.

21. Regulate the *hammer height,* by adjusting the capstans. With the letoff rack adjusted to string height, adjust each end capstan in each section to bring the end hammers exactly 1⅞″ (22.5 mm) from the strings, (or other measurement, as given in the Piano Action Handbook). Then align the remaining hammers with the samples, using a straightedge. Replace the action in the piano to double check the hammer stroke, making any necessary corrections.

Illus. 5-55 Regulating a capstan screw to adjust hammer height.

Illus. 5-56 After regulating the height of the end hammers, the intermediate hammers are aligned with a straightedge.

Illus. 5-57 Alternate method of regulating hammer line, with letoff rack adjusted to correct hammer height.

22. Regulate the *height of the hammer rail,* if present, so there is ⅛″ (3 mm) space between it and the hammer shanks. *The hammers should not rest on the hammer rail.* Its only purpose is to help to cushion hammer rebound impact during loud stacatto playing.

23. Regulate *letoff.* With the action on the bench, set the letoff rack exactly 1/16″ (1.5 mm) *below* string height, and slide the action under it with the hammer striking point directly under the target. Turn each letoff screw or dowel up until the hammer blocks or jams against the target when the key is depressed. Depress each key, and turn the letoff screw down slowly until the hammer lets off. Repeat the procedure for each key, using the same finger pressure on every key to achieve uniform letoff. Replace the action in the piano, and recheck the letoff, making corrections as necessary.

Illus. 5-58 Regulating letoff.

24. Regulate depth of *hammer drop*. When each key is depressed slowly, the hammer should drop 1/16" (1.5 mm) after letting off. Adjust the target to string height (1/16" or 1.5 mm higher than the setting for letoff regulation). Depress each key slowly until the hammer lets off and drops, and set height of drop by turning drop screw. Measure hammer drop by inserting a 1/8" (3 mm) thick gauge between the target and hammer (1/16" letoff plus 1/16" drop = 1/8" total distance from strings). Replace the action in the piano to recheck drop regulation; correct as necessary.

Illus. 5-61 Measuring checking of hammers with 5/8" (16 mm) gauge.

Illus. 5-59 Regulating the drop screw.

26. Regulate *repetition spring tension*. Play each key so the hammer checks. When the key is released slowly, the hammer should rise slowly but positively. If the spring is too weak, the hammer will not rise; if too strong, the hammer will jump. Always clean the repetition lever spring slots prior to making this regulation.

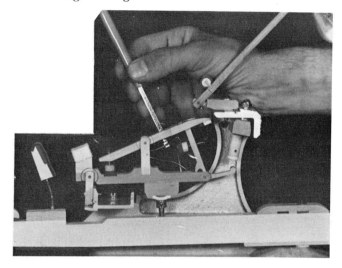

Illus. 5-62 Regulating a Steinway style repetition spring.

Illus. 5-60 Checking hammer drop with 1/8" (3 mm) gauge.

25. Regulate the *backchecks*. First, square them with the hammer heels. Then, with the action on the bench and the target set exactly at string height, play each key with a moderate blow. Each hammer should check exactly 5/8" (16 mm) from the strings (target). Measure with a 5/8" gauge, and bend the backcheck forward or backward to change checking distance from the strings. See details under #19, p. 69.

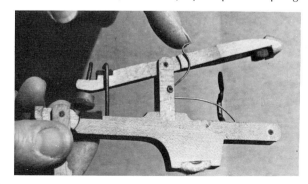

Illus. 5-63 Repetition springs have the distressing habit of becoming dislodged from their slots if care is not taken to relocate them after regulating.

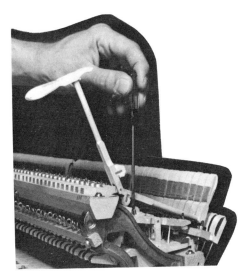

Illus. 5-64 Most grands have a screw adjustment for regulating the repetition springs.

Illus. 5-65 Regulating damper lever to lift rail, as described in #30. The tool is inserted between the strings.

27. Regulate height of *key strip rail*, if present. Loosen the lock nuts on top of the rail. Regulate the support nuts under the rail so the front end of each white key may be lifted barely ⅛″ (3 mm) with the rail in place. Tighten the lock nuts when regulation is correct.

28. Regulate the *dampers* to the keys. Each damper should begin to lift when the hammer is half way to the strings. To regulate, add or subtract paper shims from the back end of the key under the damper lever lift felt, or regulate the damper lever to the wire by loosening the damper wire screw. If the latter method is used, regulate one lever to the proper height. Make a jig which indicates that height, and regulate the rest of the levers to the jig.

29. Regulate the height of the *damper stop rail.* When the keys are depressed fully in each section, and the damper heads are lifted gently, there should be a little play between the white key dampers and the rail, but no play between the sharp dampers and the rail. If the stop rail is set too high, the dampers will bounce; if set too low, it will prevent the keys from going down all the way.

30. Regulate the *dampers to the lift rail.* If the rail has a capstan screw for each damper lever, regulate them so all dampers begin to lift at the same moment when the board is lifted. If the lift rail is not equipped with capstan screws, add or remove paper shims under the felt on the rail.

31. Regulate the *sustaining pedal.* Adjust the pedal rod by turning the capstan, or shimming, as described under #17, regulating the soft pedal. Adjust so there is ¹⁄₁₆″ (1.5 mm) between the

damper lift rail and damper levers, or so the pedal goes down about ¼″ (6.5 mm) at the front tip before engaging the dampers. If the piano has a damper pedal stop capstan, regulate it so the pedal stops immediately before the damper levers hit the damper stop rail.

If the piano has a bass sustaining pedal, regulate it in the same way as the regular sustaining pedal.

32. Regulate the *sostenuto mechanism and pedal,* if present. All sostenuto lever lips should form a straight line. Regulate their in-and-out adjustment by bending each damper wire in or out directly above the damper lever. Reseat dampers, if necessary. The sostenuto rod should be ¹⁄₁₆″ (1.5 mm) above the sostenuto lever lips when at rest. Adjust by repositioning or bending the support brackets. The sostenuto rod lip should overlap the lever lips by ¹⁄₁₆″ (1.5 mm) when the pedal is depressed.

33. If the soft pedal operates a *hammer rail lift,* regulate the linkage or trap work so the hammers move half way to the strings when the pedal is depressed fully. The keys may "wink" or move down a little. This is in contrast to the vertical piano, in which depressing the hammer rail pedal should not cause the keys to move.

34. Certain fine quality pianos have adjustable *hold-down screws* in the cheek blocks, which may be turned in or out to fine-regulate the striking point. The beginning technician should not tamper

with these unless he is clearly able to hear an improvement in tone quality when the cheek blocks are removed and the action is slid in or out. For further discussion of striking point, see p. 149.

Grand Regulating Checklist for Quick Reference

1. Tighten all plate and cabinet screws.
2. Remove action.
3. Tighten damper lever flange screws; repair damper action.
4. Clean piano.
5. Tighten all action screws.
6. Reshape hammers.
7. Clean action.
8. Remove action and keys from key frame.
9. Make necessary action repairs.
10. Bed key frame.
11. Regulate key frame glides.
12. Square and space keys.
13. Level keys.
14. Regulate key dip.
15. Travel hammers.
16. Space hammers to strings.
17. Regulate una corda pedal.
18. Space whippens to hammers.
19. Regulate jacks to knuckles.
20. Regulate repetition lever height.
21. Regulate hammer line.
22. Regulate hammer rail.
23. Regulate letoff.
24. Regulate hammer drop.
25. Regulate hammer checking.
26. Regulate repetition spring tension.
27. Regulate key strip rail.
28. Regulate dampers to keys.
29. Regulate damper stop rail.
30. Regulate dampers to damper lift rail.
31. Regulate sustaining pedal to lift rail.
32. Regulate sostenuto mechanism and pedal.
33. Regulate hammer lift rail, if present.
34. Regulate striking point, if adjustable.

Changing the Touch of a Grand Piano

The following adjustments may be made to stiffen a grand piano action. The pianist should practice on the instrument after each adjustment is made, prior to making the next one.

Regulate the action. Raise the sharps 1/16″ (1.5 mm). Reduce, but never eliminate, the lost motion between keys and dampers. The weight of the dampers added to the keys earlier in the stroke makes the touch heavier. If the whippens are equipped with auxiliary whippen springs, reduce the spring tension. These springs should be adjusted only if the action is completely regulated and all working parts are free to move properly. The springs must be bent very carefully for uniform regulation; this procedure is recommended only to the accomplished grand piano technician who is thoroughly familiar with grand regulating and hammer voicing.

Fine Action Regulating

Because of the many parts for each key in a grand action, and the effect of one adjustment on another, it is sometimes necessary to go back and correct a previous regulation after subsequent regulations are made. By adhering strictly to the above regulating sequence, the amount of re-regulating is minimized, but do not expect to fine regulate a grand piano by going through it "once over lightly". The uniform response necessary for fine playing (and the pianist's satisfaction with a piano) are in direct proportion to the amount of time taken to regulate the action properly.

SQUARE GRAND REGULATING

Tighten all screws, clean the piano and action, check for proper operation of all working parts, space and level the keys, space the hammers to the strings, etc., as in any other piano. Then regulate the action to the following specifications, referring to illustration 2-82. Set the key dip to 3/8″ (1 cm). Regulate the jacks (by adjusting the rocker capstans with a small offset or ratchet offset screwdriver or homemade tool) so there is no lost motion between jacks and hammer butts, and so each jack will slip under its butt without rubbing. Set hammer letoff to 3/16″ (5 mm) for the wound strings, and 1/8″ (3 mm) for the plain strings. The hammers should check as close to the strings as possible without having the hammer tail rub against the backcheck on the upstroke.

ACTION REGULATING PROBLEMS

If a hammer hits the string twice in rapid succession for each key stroke, it bounces or "blubbers". In a vertical piano, this is usually caused by inadequate key dip *in proportion to hammer stroke*. When a piano gets old and worn, the hammers become shorter, lost motion between the jack and hammer butt increases and the backchecks wear thinner, but the key dip does not increase proportionally. As a result, the key reaches the bottom of its stroke before the action finishes its cycle, and the backcheck is not able to do its job. To correct this situation, regulate the hammer stroke, lost motion, letoff and backchecks.

If grand hammers blubber during very soft playing, the repetition lever springs are probably too stiff. See p. 77 for regulating procedure. If grand hammers blubber during louder playing, the backchecks are not catching them properly and should be regulated.

If a hammer goes all the way to the strings and stays against them, damping out all tone, the hammer is *blocking*. Blocking hammers are usually caused by the jacks not letting off. Regulating the letoff corrects the problem.

If a hammer jumps just before letting off, the buckskin on the butt or grand knuckle has a depression or pocket where the jack pushes on it. When the jack is tripped by the letoff button, the jack has to ride out of the pocket over the resulting ridge in the buckskin, making precise letoff impossible. To correct this, replace the butt or knuckle buckskin, or build up the original buckskin by running several strands of yarn through the under-cloth. (See p. 117).

If a night club pianist repeatedly breaks strings or hammers, he is playing the piano too loudly. If he can not be persuaded to play softer, and if the piano is not used for subtle playing, set the hammer letoff at ¼" (or 7 mm) from the strings. This will prevent the hammers from hitting the strings with excessive force.

TONE REGULATING

Tone regulating is the fine art of adjusting the tone quality of a piano so that each note has the desired amount of brilliance or mellowness. It includes everything from changing the tone of a few notes which are more brilliant than their neighbors, to revoicing an entire piano. Although tone regulating is usually considered to be syn-onymous with hammer voicing (or changing the resilience of the hammer felt), it also encompasses anything which may be done to a piano that has an effect on tone quality, such as hammer reshaping (which changes the harmonic content of the tone), action regulating (which affects the amount of muscular power required to produce a tone of given loudness), tuning, replacing dead strings, adjusting string bearing, etc. For a complete tone regulating job, the piano must be brought into optimum condition. All mechanical problems such as sluggish or loose action parts, buzzing strings, loose bridge pins, etc., must be corrected. The hammers must be reshaped accurately so each hammer strikes all of its strings, the action regulated thoroughly, the ideal striking point established, and the piano carefully tuned. Only after these jobs are meticulously done is the piano ready for hammer voicing. Concert tone regulating may entail retuning or fine regulating of the piano during the voicing procedure.

Hammer Voicing

When fine quality hammers are made, the felt is glued around the wood molding under considerable pressure. This pressure puts tension around the outside of the hammer and compresses the felt inside. The tension and compression provide the resilience which is necessary for good tone quality. It also keeps the hammer striking point from going flat prematurely under heavy use. The tension in a good quality hammer may be demonstrated by cutting the striking point open with a sharp knife. The felt will spring apart as illustrated.

Illus. 5-66

New hammers, and old hammers which have been reshaped properly, are often too brilliant, and must be softened to make their tone more mellow. This is accomplished by careful needling of the felt, to break down the fibers and soften the cushion behind the striking point.

Hammers are voiced for loud playing, then medium, and finally for soft playing, in separate operations. In general, voicing for each loudness requires needling a different part of the hammer. Voicing a set of hammers for uniform tone quality at a loud playing level does not necessarily make them uniform at a softer level.

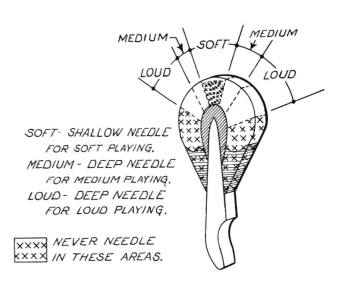

SOFT- SHALLOW NEEDLE FOR SOFT PLAYING.
MEDIUM - DEEP NEEDLE FOR MEDIUM PLAYING.
LOUD- DEEP NEEDLE FOR LOUD PLAYING.

NEVER NEEDLE IN THESE AREAS.

Illus. 5-69

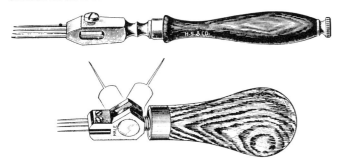

Illus. 5-67 Two types of voicing tool.

Tools Required

Hammer voicing tool with adjustable head
Supply of #6 sharp needles
Hammer support board—¼" thick, 4" x 10" (or 5 mm x 10 cm x 25 cm)

The small board is used to support the hammer being needled, as illustrated. Hold the hammer steady in one hand, and hold the voicing tool in the other, jabbing the hammer with short, firm strokes.

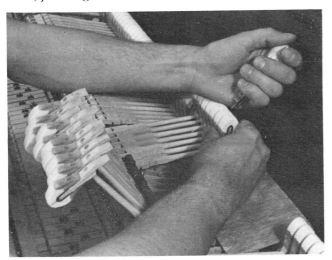

Illus. 5-68 Needling a hammer, illustrating use of the support board.

Procedure

To voice hammers at a loud playing level, insert one #6 sharp needle in the voicing tool. Play up and down the keys within an octave with heavy but uniform finger pressure. Listen for notes which are louder than others, and pull the action out of the piano. Deep needle the areas marked *loud* on illustration 5-69. Repeat the procedure until all the notes within the octave sound uniform, and continue throughout the piano. The tone quality will change gradually, of course, from the rich full bass tones to the brilliant, ringing high treble.

To voice for playing of medium loudness, deep needle the areas marked *medium* on illustration 5-69. Repeat the procedure used for loud voicing, but use lighter finger pressure to play the keys.

To voice for soft playing, insert three needles in the voicing tool so they protrude only ¹⁄₁₆ (1.5 mm) inch. Using very precise finger pressure, play up and down the notes of one octave as softly as is uniformly possible. Pick out any notes which are louder than their neighbors. Assuming that these notes are regulated perfectly, they should be shallow needled on the striking point, marked *soft* on illustration 5-69.

Notice that the shaded areas on illustration 5-69 are *never* needled. The area of felt which is glued to the wood molding must provide a firm foundation for the rest of the hammer and it must not be softened. Likewise, the crown is never softened by deep needling. To do so is to destroy the hammer.

Never over-needle! It is better to pull the action a dozen times, needling a little each time, than to soften a hammer too much. There is no way to regain tension and compression in a hammer which is broken down by excessive needling.

Making Hammers More Brilliant

Illus. 5-70 The hammer ironer.

New hammers and properly reshaped old hammers are rarely too soft, particularly after they have been played long enough to pack down the surface fuzz. If a customer complains that a piano is too soft, the action probably needs regulating; once this is done, the piano is usually loud enough.

In rare cases where piano hammers are too soft even when the action is regulated properly, strings are live and responsive, bearing is correct, etc., it is permissible to use a small amount of lacquer, thinned down with three parts of lacquer thinner, on the surface of the hammer. Never apply any solution to the crown, nor to the sides of the hammer. Apply just a little, and let the customer use the piano for a month before applying more. It is easy to destroy the tone quality of a set of hammers permanently by applying too much lacquer. Once this happens, new hammers will be necessary.

Another useful voicing tool is the hammer ironer, as illustrated. If a set of good quality hammers is voiced properly on a day with low relative humidity, and the air becomes extremely damp on the day of a concert, the dampness in the hammers will affect their tone. The ironer is used sparingly to drive the humidity temporarily out of the surface of the felt, restoring the tone to the way it was when the air was drier. This technique should be used on fine concert instruments only after the technician has practiced it on pianos of lesser quality, and is experienced in just the right amount of heat to apply. Excess heat damages the felt.

If the inner tension and compression of a set of hammers is gone due to old age or excessive needling, the felt may be packed temporarily back into shape by ironing from the heel toward the striking point. This reshaping lasts only until playing packs the felt back into its tired old shape.

Chapter Six
Repairing

Repairing usually involves maintenance, or fixing specific things which go wrong in a piano to keep it working properly. Rebuilding usually involves installing entire sets of new parts, or complete reconditioning of the old parts. Although there is some overlap between the two subjects, there is enough difference that repairing is covered in this chapter, and rebuilding in the next.

In some instances, more than one way to repair something is presented. Neither way is necessarily better than the other; the student technician should try both ways and decide which is the best for him. The student should not be afraid to invent new repair methods, providing that they are first tried on a piano with little value in case something goes wrong.

Before learning about piano repairing, the student should know a few woodworking basics, the proper use of tools, and the making of good glue joints. Anyone who is sincerely interested in piano servicing should be willing to obtain and use the correct tool for each job. Some tools are easily made in the home workshop; others should be purchased. The correct tools for each job are illustrated throughout this and the other chapters.

WOODWORKING BASICS

The most commonly abused tool is the screwdriver. Screws come in many sizes and shapes. The correct screwdriver must be used for each screw. The well-equipped piano technician should have five regular screwdrivers for cabinet screws, and a variety of specialized action regulating screwdrivers which are described in chapter five. Some pianos are assembled with Phillips screws of various sizes; the technician should have one medium and one large Phillips screwdriver. Using the wrong size screwdriver not only ruins the shape of the blade; it also leaves a trail of damaged screwheads wherever used. Disfigured screwheads are a reliable sign of a sloppy technician.

Use tools only for their designated purpose. Do not use a knife or chisel for a screwdriver or prying tool, nor a screwdriver for a chisel. Improper use eventually results in the tool breaking or the careless workman receiving an injury! Keep tools sharp and properly shaped. A sharp chisel is dangerous enough, but a dull chisel, knife or screwdriver is hazardous because it takes much more force on the handle to do its job. The more force, the more chance of slipping and injury.

Hands should always be kept behind the working end of a tool. Always aim a tool away from the body. Apply force to a tool with the strength of the arm, not the weight of the body. If a tool slips while you are leaning on it, you may fall into the sharp end of the tool or workpiece. Force should be aimed at an angle away from the work; this way, if you do slip, your hand will run into thin air instead of something sharp.

When doing any work which involves putting pressure on a part, such as cutting, scraping or drilling, secure the part in a vise. In a customer's home, use a small portable vise, or at least vise grip pliers. This allows you to apply more pressure to the part with the tool, without danger of slipping or running into your fingers. When holding a wooden part in a metal vise, insert thin wooden spacers between the vise jaws and the part, to protect the part from jaw imprints.

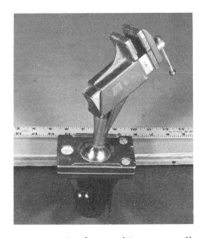

Illus. 6-1 A convenient vise for working on small action parts. It may be secured to any table with the built-in clamp, and may be turned on its ball and socket to any working angle.

Hold the part close to the area which will have pressure applied to it. This minimizes the chance of breakage. If a long slender wooden part is held by the opposite end, the working pressure is multiplied through leverage, and the part will break next to where it is clamped down. Whenever working on a part which is attached to another part, secure the part close to where pressure will be applied. Never hold it by the attached part.

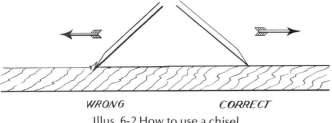

WRONG   CORRECT

Illus. 6-2 How to use a chisel.

When scraping glue or other materials from a strip of wood with a scraper or chisel, remember that wood grain usually runs at an angle to the surface being cleaned. In one direction, the chisel will scrape over the surface of the wood, and in the other direction it will dig into the wood and gouge it. Determine the grain direction in advance, and chisel only in the same direction as the grain runs to meet the surface. To remove old felts from backchecks, damper heads, and other small action parts, secure the part in a small vise, and scrape the felt off with short chisel strokes. It is sometimes possible to pull the felt from the wood with a pliers. If necessary, soften the glue by holding the part over steam. (See pp. 144-145).

No technician should be without a *pickup tool*, as illustrated, for reaching small screws which are dropped in hard-to-reach places.

Repairing Stripped Screw Holes

If a screw is tightened too much, or *overdrawn*, it will strip the threads in the wood and be impossible to tighten. The best way to repair stripped screw holes is to replace the wood. Drill a hole *perpendicular* to the screw hole large enough for a dowel to replace as much of the old hole as possible. A drill press produces the best results, or a hand drill will

work if held steadily. Knurl the dowel by rolling it under the edge of a file. Test the dowel for a snug but not tight dry fit. Coat the dowel with glue and drive it into the hole. When the glue is dry, cut the excess dowel off with a coping saw, and sand it flush.

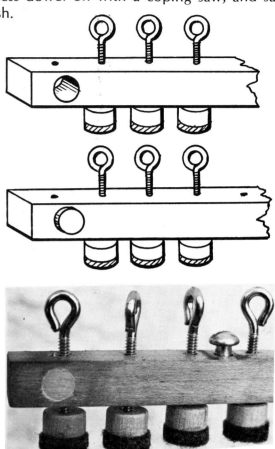

Illus. 6-3 A method of providing new wood for a stripped screw hole, using a dowel glued at right angles to the screw hole.

Steinway action rails are made of wood which is encased in metal tubing. The flange screws go through oversize holes in the tubing and are held tight by the wood core. If a flange screw hole is stripped, cut a piece of buckskin about 3/16″ wide by 1¼″ long (5 mm x 3 cm). Fold the buckskin in half, work glue into the hole with a pipe cleaner, and push the middle of the buckskin strip into the hole with a small screwdriver. Insert the screw without the flange, holding the ends of the buckskin in place, and trim the excess buckskin off with a sharp knife. After the glue sets but before it dries, remove the screw and carefully screw the flange in place. The buckskin lining should permit the screw to be tightened.

Inserting toothpicks or match sticks into stripped screw holes rarely helps, because the screw threads cut through the inserts, rendering them useless.

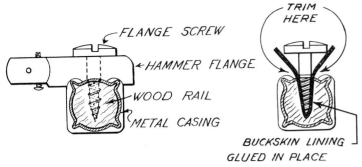

Illus. 6-4 Repairing a stripped Steinway action flange screw hole.

GLUE JOINTS

In a good glue joint, the wood surfaces just barely touch each other all across the surface of the joint, and the glue soaks into the pores in both pieces, forming a solid bond. A good joint does not have a sandwich of glue between the two pieces. (An exception is contact cement, which is not used for most wood joints). Glue sandwiches usually break apart somewhere in the layer of glue; good wood-to-wood bonds with the glue connecting the wood pores together tend to remain glued together.

Whenever a broken glue joint is repaired, remove as much of the old hard glue as possible. Secure the part in a vise, and scrape off the old glue with a chisel or knife, following the safety rules for such tools at all times. Leave the wood surface intact; removing original wood is worse than leaving old glue in place, unless the surface is filled with new wood or a suitable filler. After removing the old glue from both parts, hold them together to check the fit. Apply a thin layer of glue to both parts, rather than a thick layer to one part, press them together in proper alignment, and clamp. Check the alignment frequently while tightening the clamps. When the clamps are tight and alignment is perfect, remove any excess glue with a damp rag. When clamping close grained hardwood such as maple or birch, do not tighten the clamps so much that all of the glue is squeezed out of the joint. Do not remove the clamps until the glue is dry, or at least until it sets.

A broken or cracked piece of wood is usually easy to reglue, providing that the surface of the crack or break has not been damaged or warped. Nothing mates better than the two intact surfaces of a broken piece of wood. Open the crack as far as possible, and spread a thin coat of glue into the bad area with a toothpick or thin strip of wood, without disarranging any of the wood fibers. Align and clamp.

Several types of clamps are useful for piano repairing, including C clamps, spring clamps, pipe clamps, key clamps, rubber bands, thread and masking tape.

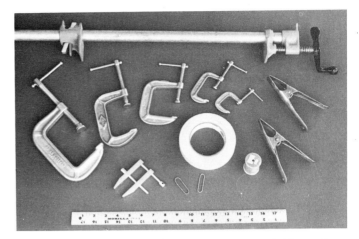

Illus. 6-5 An assortment of clamps which are useful for various types of piano repairs.

The proper type of glue is dictated by the nature of the joint, the amount of drying time, and the type of clamps available. Whenever two parts are screwed and glued together, they should first be assembled without glue to test for correct fit.

Types of Glue Used in Piano Making & Repair

TYPE:

Hot glue (hide glue)

Purpose:

Forms strong bond between porous materials found in a piano: wood, felt, leather. Not for metal.

Properties:

Good holding power. If necessary, old joint usually may be broken apart with a hammer and chisel or sharp putty knife. Easily sanded when dry. Old hot glue may be dissolved with solution of 30% acetic acid in water.

Instructions for use:

Although a certain amount of mystery surrounds the use of hot glue, anyone can obtain good results if these instructions are followed.

Hot glue is supplied in dry crystals, beads or chunks. Small crystals are recommended because they dissolve faster. Put just enough glue for the next day's work in an electric glue pot or glass jar, and add cool water, stirring constantly, until the water level is about ¼" (5 or 10 mm) above the level

85

Illus. 6-6 A thermostatically-controlled glue pot.

of the glue. No specific ratio between glue and water is given here because it is usually necessary to add a little water or let a little evaporate after the glue is heated. The purpose of adding enough water until there is about ¼″ over the top of the glue crystals is to insure that any bubbles which rise to the surface during the absorption period will be dissipated instead of remaining in the glue. Cover the container with a loose-fitting lid and leave it overnight. On the next day, plug in the glue pot, or put the jar in a pan of water on the stove, and slowly heat it to 140–145°F (60–63°C). Heating it any higher than 145°F (63°C) will reduce its strength. The most convenient glue cooker is the thermostatic electric glue pot, which automatically keeps the glue at the proper temperature. If glue is made on the stove, the heat should be raised gradually until the glue dissolves, and no higher.

Leave the container covered while heating. The glue is ready to use when it is completely melted, forming a smooth liquid the consistency of pancake syrup or slightly thicker, with no air bubbles.

If the glue is too thin, stir it every few minutes and wait until enough water evaporates to bring it to the desired thickness. If it is too thick, heat some water in a separate container and slowly add it, stirring the glue and checking it until it is thin enough. Never add cold water, which will gel the glue and make it lumpy. Keep the container covered at all times except when inserting the glue brush.

For most small repair jobs, a ½″ (or 1.5 cm) brush is used. Make a hole in the lid of the glue pot, and leave the brush in the hole when not in use, to keep the brush from drying and getting stiff. When using a bigger brush for large wood joints, devise another type of lid. When returning the brush to the glue pot after spreading glue, allow the glue to warm the bristles before using it again to keep the glue from gelling on the brush. A few seconds is usually adequate.

If a cheap metal glue brush is used, remove it from the glue overnight, to prevent formation of rust which discolors the glue. Clean the brush in warm water or discard it.

For the strongest joints, the wooden parts should be heated. If hot glue is spread on cold wood, it gels on the surface of the wood, instead of flowing into the pores. This causes a glue sandwich with reduced strength. An easy way to heat the parts is to suspend a bar containing one or more regular spotlights, not heat lamps, above the workbench on chains; the lights can be raised or lowered to provide the right amount of heat. Heat the parts just long enough to warm the surfaces to be glued; excessive heat applied to previously glued joints weakens them.

If hot glue is applied to a surface, and it gels before the joint can be assembled and clamped, the glue should be scraped off with a chisel, and the joint should be started over. The thicker the glue, the faster it gels. When gluing parts where clamping is impossible, such as gluing a jack to a whippen, use the above techniques, but hold the parts in place by hand until the glue begins to set. Then place the part in a position where no strain will be applied to the joint, and let it dry thoroughly before use.

Use clamps whenever possible, and leave them on the glue joint at least until the glue sets. Hot glue usually sets in a half hour to an hour in dry weather, and in several hours in humid weather. In a joint where great strength is necessary, allow the glue to dry overnight before applying any stress.

TYPE:

Liquid Hide Glue

Purpose:

Same as hot glue, where heat is not available.

Properties:

Same as hot glue, but takes longer to set and dry.

Instructions for Use:

Spread a thin coat on each part to be joined. Too much glue results in a sandwich and weakens the joint. Clamp when possible. Allow to dry overnight.

TYPE:

White glue (Elmer's)

Purpose:

Bonds wood and other porous and semi-porous materials. Corrodes some metals.

Properties:

Forms a strong bond. Water soluble before dry. After dry, turns to gummy mess when sanded, so it is not recommended for any joint which will have to be taken apart and reglued in the future. Causes white stain in finish if allowed to dry on bare wood. After dry, may be dissolved with ammonia.

Instructions for use:

Spread a thin coat on each surface to be joined. If allowed to set just slightly for about five minutes, the joint will not slip as much when clamps are tightened. Sets completely in a few hours. For maximum strength, allow to dry over night. If gluing a wood joint which will have varnish or other finish, remove every trace of white glue with damp rag before it sets, to prevent stains.

TYPE:

Aliphatic Resin Glue (Titebond)

Purpose:

Bonds wood and other porous and semi-porous materials.

Properties:

Similar to white glue, but more easily sanded. Sets faster and forms stronger bond.

Instructions for Use:

Same as white glue.

TYPE:

Burnt shellac.

Purpose:

For sticking felt to metal, such as the piano plate; for sticking non-porous materials together where strength of joint is not important; for sealing around hose connectors in player pianos.

Properties:

Very brittle when dry, adheres to almost anything, but does not form a strong bond. Easily sanded.

Instructions for use:

Pour a little orange shellac into a metal container in a well ventilated area. Light the surface of the shellac with a match and stand back. Shellac has an alcohol base, and burning some of the alcohol away causes it to thicken. After a minute or so, blow out the flame and let the shellac cool until it thickens. Repeat as necessary until when cool it is the consistency of warm cake frosting. Apply the shellac to the metal surface and then apply the felt. Allow it to dry overnight.

TYPE:

Contact cement

Purpose:

Sticks anything to anything else. Not recommended where hot glue, aliphatic resin glue or white glue will work, but recommended for gluing large surfaces such as veneer, where clamping is impractical. Good for gluing white keytops in place.

Properties:

Very sticky, can not be sanded easily. Thinned or dissolved with contact cement solvent.

Instructions for use:

Contact cement is different from other types of glue, because each surface to be joined is coated with a layer of cement which stays on the surface. The two surfaces are pressed together, and the instant the two layers of glue touch each other, they stick. Spread a thin layer on each surface. Allow it to dry according to instructions on the container. If the glue soaks in, apply another thin coat. One coat is usually sufficient on non-porous materials such as metal or rubber, while porous materials like wood or leather usually take two or three coats. When the surface is uniformly dry, touch a piece of kraft paper to the surface. If the glue is ready to be joined, the paper will not stick. Align both parts *perfectly* and press them together. If they are misaligned, they will stay that way, because once the two layers of glue touch each other they will not come apart. When gluing two large surfaces together, pound the entire surface with a soft rubber mallet until there is good contact throughout.

TYPE:

Hot glue gun

Purpose:

Sticks anything to anything else, where strength is not important. Good for sticking felt to metal in a piano, such as under string felt, hammer rail bumpers, etc.

Illus. 6-7 Hot glue gun, available from any hardware store. Handy for a few specific repairs where strength is not necessary.

Properties:

Glue is supplied in tough, rubbery sticks. Glue gun heat melts the glue into a sticky, gooey substance, which turns back into tough rubbery form as soon as it cools. Forms a glue sandwich, which is not strong enough for most wood joints.

Instructions for use:

Preheat the glue gun. Apply a thin layer of glue to metal or wood surface, smooth the glue with tip of gun, and immediately apply felt. If glue cools prematurely, clean the tip of the gun, and iron the felt with it. For long strips of felt, glue a short section at a time.

TYPE:

Epoxy

Purpose:

Sticks anything to anything else, fills cracks; forms strong bond.

Properties:

Comes in two tubes or jars; must be mixed prior to use. Very sticky before dry; very hard after dry. Unlike other glues, epoxy has body when dry, so may be used to fill small gouges in wood. May be sanded. Available in clear, amber and gray colors, and in quick and slow drying types.

Instructions for use:

Follow mixing instructions on container. When filling holes, gouges or cracks, apply glue and work into area to be filled with small tool. Use enough so it leaves a lump on the surface. When thoroughly dry, sand surface smooth. When gluing, apply thin layer to both parts, assemble and clamp immediately. Follow drying time on container. Because of its strength, epoxy should not be used for a joint which may have to be taken apart in the future. For conventional wood to wood joints, use hide, white or aliphatic resin glues.

TYPE:

Fiberglass polyester resin

Purpose:

To fill certain cracks and holes.

Properties:

This is more a filler than an adhesive. When mixed, it begins to set immediately, so it should be used quickly. Very hard when dry.

Instructions for use:

Fiberglass is used by some technicians to fill gaps between a grand pinblock and plate. See detailed discussion on p. 92 before using.

No matter what the job or type of glue, the proper amount is important. A good rule of thumb for making wood joints is: if a small amount of glue squeezes out of the joint when clamped, the right amount of glue was used. If no glue squeezes out, not enough was used, and if an abundance squeezes out, too much was used.

Glue joints should always be neat. A patch of dried glue on the surface of a part where there was none originally is a mark of a sloppy technician.

SOLVENTS AND CLEANERS

Several types of solvents are recommended in this book. They are poisonous and either flammable or explosive. Follow all warnings printed on the container. Adequate ventilation must be provided to prevent fire, illness or death.

EVALUATING THE CONDITION

Before any repair work is performed, the condition of the piano should be appraised thoroughly. Without this, much time and effort can be wasted. For example, it would come as a rude shock to spend hours fixing a piano action, only to find that the tuning pins are too loose to hold the strings in tune.

The aspiring piano technician would do well to obtain a well-battered old upright in need of almost everything, but having a solid plate and frame. Restoring it to new condition will give the technician valuable experience not only in repairing and rebuilding, but also in appraising the condition of other pianos.

THE FRAME AND PLATE

The first parts of the piano to evaluate for repairs are the frame and plate. If either of these is cracked or broken, it must be rebuilt prior to making other repairs in the instrument. Refer to chapter seven.

Broken Agraffe

If an agraffe breaks at the string holes, unscrew it with an agraffe remover, which fits in the combination tool handle. If broken at the threads, the stub should be center punched, drilled with a $7/64''$ drill, and then removed with an "EZ Out No. 2" reverse thread extractor. After removing the stub, renew the threads with a $7/32'' \times 36$ or $1/4'' \times 36$ thread tap, whichever size matches the original threads. Then screw in an appropriate new agraffe.

Illus. 6-8 An EZ out screw extractor.

Treble Strings Ring or Buzz

One cause for this condition is imperfect contact between strings and plate, caused by grooves worn by the steel strings into the cast iron plate where there are no agraffes. Ringing treble strings may sometimes be improved by sliding them sideways at the capo bar (in a grand) or upper plate bridge (in a vertical), just enough to move them out of their grooves in the plate. If necessary, the hammer should then be realigned with the strings in their new position. If the strings persist in slipping back into the old grooves, the strings and plate must be removed and the capo bar filed down. The least possible amount of metal should be removed from a grand plate, to prevent reducing string down-bearing on the bridge.

Illus. 6-9 Showing bottom of grand plate capo bar. Pointer shows grooves worn into cast iron by strings. These grooves are frequently responsible for troublesome noises.

THE PINBLOCK AND TUNING PINS

If possible, make a visual inspection of the pinblock. Although most of the pinblock is usually hidden from view, here are some places to look: In a grand, the bottom of the pinblock is visible when the fallboard is removed. Check it for cracks or separated laminations. In a ¾ plate upright, check the front of the pinblock for cracks. Tiny surface cracks in the veneer might not matter, but any large cracks indicate that the piano needs a new pinblock. In a full plate upright, check the back. This is a separate piece of wood, but if it is badly cracked, the pinblock probably is too. Remove the lid if possible. The top of the pinblock is sometimes hidden by another piece of wood or felt glued to it, but it is sometimes exposed. Check here for cracks, including the ends of cracks which run down into the block. If the block is completely hidden from view, the best way to check its condition is to tune the piano, marking loose pins with chalk. Another

excellent way to measure tuning pin tightness is with a tuner's torque wrench, fitted with a ratchet lever star tip. If it takes less than six pounds of force on the torque wrench to turn the pins counter-clockwise, they are probably too loose to hold the piano in tune for a reasonable length of time. If some of the pins are so loose that their strings go out of tune as soon as the tuning lever is removed, the pinblock is probably cracked. If so, there is no point in making any other repairs until the pinblock is repaired, because an untunable piano will never make music.

Illus. 6-10 Testing tightness of tuning pins with torque wrench.

If the pinblock is cracked, replace it with a new pinblock or fill the cracks with fiberglass polyester resin or epoxy. These are rebuilding jobs; before proceeding, refer to the rebuilding chapter.

All Tuning Pins Loose—
Block Not Cracked

If all of the tuning pins are just barely tight enough that the piano can be tuned, but not tight enough to hold it up to pitch for at least six months, the pinblock is probably not cracked but has merely loosened its hold on the pins. In this case, there are several repairs which might make the piano tunable without replacing the pinblock: restringing with larger tuning pins, applying a liquid called *tuning pin tightener* which swells the wood, or driving the original pins a little deeper into the pinblock.

The best way to cure loose tuning pins is to

restring the piano, using larger pins. If the pinblock is not cracked, this will add many years to the life of the piano without the expense of installing a new pinblock. Restringing is covered in the rebuilding chapter.

The use of liquid tuning pin tightener is controversial. Many technicians use it and achieve positive results, while many others avoid it, claiming that it does more harm than good, in the long run. In the experience of the author, when a pinblock is "doped" with pin tightener and the piano is restrung later with oversize pins, the new pins sometimes stick to the wood after a period of time, becoming jumpy and hard to tune. When deciding whether or not to use tuning pin tightener, the following guidelines are recommended: If a piano is in good overall condition and if its value is such that it is worth restringing, then restring it. If its value is on the borderline, and if restringing would cost more than the piano would be worth when the job is done, then pin tightener might profitably be used. Once pin tightener is used, however, it may be necessary to replace the pinblock if restringing is desired later.

One common type of tuning pin tightener contains glycerin (which swells the wood), resin (which adds friction), and alcohol (which acts as a vehicle to carry the solution into the pores of the wood and then evaporates). An easy way to apply it is with a "hypo-oiler" available from piano supply houses.

In a grand, remove the action and cover the keybed with enough newspapers, paper towels or rags to absorb spillage. Starting at either end of the pinblock, rest the needle on each tuning pin bushing or plate hole, and slowly squeeze the bottle, releasing it before any liquid runs onto the plate. Go from one end of the pinblock to the other. If the bushings project up from the plate, surface tension will keep the pin tightener from spreading all the way around the pins immediately. Rather than spilling liquid on the plate, apply just a little the first time. By the time it is applied to all the pins once, it will have spread around the first pins, allowing the next application to soak in immediately. Repeat the entire procedure until the piano does not soak up any more liquid, and leave it overnight. If the pins were extremely loose, repeat the procedure several days in a row. When all traces of liquid have dried remove the paper towels, replace the action, and tune the piano. If the block is not

cracked, the piano might stay in tune better than it did.

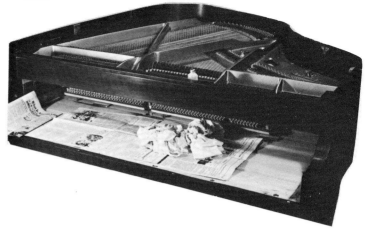

Illus. 6-11 Protecting the keybed from spillage prior to applying pin tightener.

When doping an upright pinblock, the piano must be laid on its back. (See p. 124.) Follow the same application procedure as in a grand. Do not tip the piano up again until *all traces* of liquid have dried; any pin tightener which runs down the front of the pinblock will end up on the strings, ruining their tone. Be very careful not to drip tightener on anything else in the piano, particularly action parts, which will swell and cease to function properly.

Illus. 6-12 Applying the pin tightener with a "hypo-oiler."

Driving the tuning pins a little deeper may be helpful in some pianos. Tuning pins are usually driven into a piano so there is at least 3/16" (5 mm) between the string coil and the surface of the plate. By driving the pins in so the coils almost touch the plate, there may be enough friction added between the bottom of the pin and new wood to make the piano tunable.

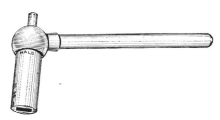

Illus. 6-13 A tuning pin setter, catalogue illustration and in use.

To drive pins, a large hammer, a tuning pin setter, and, for grands, a pinblock support jack, are needed. Use a hammer made specifically for driving steel objects; any other hammer may chip, sending fragments flying through the air.

Lay the upright on its back, place the pin setter on the pin, and drive it in with the hammer, leaving a small space between the wire coil and plate. The pin setter prevents the pin from turning when hit.

When driving pins in a grand, the pinblock *must* be supported with a pinblock support jack. Although an upright pinblock is supported by the upper frame beam, the grand pinblock is supported only by the plate, which will crack if subjected to heavy pounding. Remove the action, insert the jack, and move it along to keep it under the work area. This transfers the hammer blow into the keybed, which is strong enough to support it.

Illus. 6-14 Pinblock support jack.

Illus. 6-15 Support jack in use.

Several Loose Pins— the Rest are Tight

If a few pins are loose, but the rest are tight enough to hold the piano in tune, several repairs are possible. Tune the piano and mark the loose pins with chalk. To remove each loose pin, lower the string tension enough to pry the wire out of its hole, slip the coil up off the pin, and unscrew the pin the rest of the way. Measure the diameter with a micrometer or tuning pin gauge, and measure the length. Replace it with a pin one size larger in diameter, or one size longer if the pinblock hole is deep enough. If a larger pin is not available, a bushing may be used. Bronze tuning pin bushings are available from supply houses, or a bushing may be made by wrapping one layer of fine sandpaper around the bottom of the pin, with the grit facing outward, and driving the pin back in. Another repair method is to swab the inside of the tuning pin hole with fiberglass polyester resin (or "boat resin") with a razor cleaning brush. Dip the pin in the resin after replacing the string on it, and drive it in. Let it harden for a few days, and the pin should be tunable. Fiberglass resin may tend to lock the pin in place. If this occurs, work the pin back and forth a little with the tuning lever to soften the resin, and tune. The resin will reharden itself.

Illus. 6-16 A bronze tuning pin bushing, useful for tightening an occasional loose pin. Sandpaper may also be used (see text).

Jumping Tuning Pins

If oil soaks into the pinblock, the pins might *jump* instead of turning smoothly. Remove each jumping pin, swab the inside of the hole with naphtha and install a new pin. Use a new pin one size larger than the old if necessary. This repair will not be permanent if too much oil is present in the wood.

Removing a Broken Tuning Pin

If a tuning pin breaks at the string hole, remove it by screwing a reverse thread tuning pin extractor over the stump. As the extractor is turned counter-clockwise it will tighten itself on the pin, and then unscrew it from the pinblock. If a pin breaks flush with the plate in a grand piano, it may be driven out through the bottom with a machinist's pin punch of the appropriate size, providing that the tuning pin holes go all the way through the block. To extract a pin which is broken off flush in a vertical, drill a slightly larger hole next to the pin in the pinblock, removing the plate first if necessary. Work the stump into the adjacent hole and remove it. Plug both holes with hardwood dowels glued in place, and redrill the tuning pin hole.

Pinblock Loose in Grand Piano

If one end of a grand piano goes out of tune by the time the other end is tuned, and if the plate screws and tuning pins are tight, the pinblock is probably poorly fit to the plate flange, and is rocking on a high spot. When this condition exists, and if it is undesirable to restring or fit a new pinblock, the trouble may be corrected by filling the gaps with fiberglass polyester resin.

Fiberglass resin (also called "boat resin", and available from a well-stocked paint supply store) is as much a filler as an adhesive, and, as such, is valuable for filling various gaps such as the spaces between an ill-fitting pinblock and plate flange. Remove the action, lid and other loose parts, and turn the piano upside down on padded sawhorses. Build a dam out of putty or modelling clay on the plate flange to prevent spillage. Mix the resin according to instructions on the package; it is supplied in two parts. Pour it between the flange and pinblock. Let dry for a few days, remove the putty, invert the piano, and it should be ready to tune.

The use of fiberglass boat resin is relatively new, and remains in the trial stage at the time this is written. Rebuilders who have used it agree that it is worthwhile and does not prevent normal removal of the pinblock at a later time. It is not recommended, however, that the amateur use this procedure on a valuable piano until he is convinced by the results of his own experience that it is a valid repair technique.

THE SOUNDBOARD
Cracked Soundboard

Cracks in the soundboard are not inherently bad. This has been demonstrated in piano tuning schools by sawing slots in otherwise solid soundboards, which then had no apparent effect on the tone quality. Soundboard problems arise when the soundboard cracks and then comes unglued from the ribs.

Soundboard Unglued from Ribs

When this happens, one piece of wood can vibrate against another, causing an unpleasant buzzing sound. Make a visual inspection of the back of the soundboard to see if it is loose from the ribs anywhere. Then play each note loudly, from one end of the keyboard to the other. If a note vibrates or buzzes, have an assistant continue to play it vigorously. Press on the loose areas of the soundboard until the buzzing noise stops, and mark the spot. If it is at a place where both sides of the board are accessible, drill a ¼" hole through the board and rib, and clean as much of the dirt and old glue out from between the board and rib as possible. Insert liquid hide glue or Titebond into the crack with a small fingernail file, and immediately bolt it together. Remove excess glue. When dry, remove the bolt, and redrill the hole to clean out excess glue. Cut a piece of ¼" dowel rod to the correct length, and glue it into the hole.

If the buzzing area of the soundboard is behind the plate or strings, repair it from behind by inserting a #10 flat head wood screw through the rib into the soundboard. Drill and countersink the hole, using a depth gauge on the drill bit to keep from breaking through the front of the sound-board. (A rubber band or dab of red fingernail polish on the bit makes a simple depth gauge). Clean out the sawdust, insert glue, and screw together.

For complete illustrations of soundboard repairs, see pp. 128-132.

BRIDGES
Bridge Split at Bridge Pin Holes

A bridge often develops small cracks along the top where constant side-bearing pressure of the strings is exerted on the bridge pins. When the top of the bridge cracks, the pins are no longer held firmly in place, causing ringing and buzzing noises, false beats, and making the piano difficult or impossible to tune.

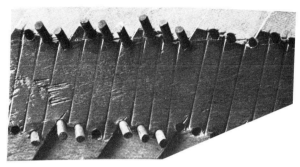

Illus. 6-17 A cracked treble bridge.

If the splits are so bad that they form one continuous crack, the bridge should be recapped or replaced, either of which is a rebuilding job. If the splits are small enough that they do not form one continuous crack, they may be filled with epoxy. If only a few repairs must be made, lower the tension on the appropriate strings just enough to slip them off their hitch pins, leaving them attached to their tuning pins. Lift the strings out of the way. Remove the loose bridge pins, mix some epoxy, and work it into each crack with a paper clip or piece of music wire, until the crack is completely full with no air bubbles in the epoxy. Reinsert each bridge pin as close to its original position as possible, and clean off *all* excess epoxy which squeezes out. Repeat the process for each crack until the pins are all inserted, and let dry. When thoroughly dry, put the strings back around their hitch pins and pull them up to pitch. If a number of strings have been loosened, the tension change will throw the whole piano out of tune, requiring several tunings to get it in tune again.

The above repair may be made if only a few pins are loose. If more than six or eight strings in the same section must be loosened at the same time, consult the rebuilding section. Lowering the tension of a whole section of strings should be done in a certain order to keep from creating a tension imbalance which might crack the plate.

STRINGS
Rusty at Bearing Points

Rusty strings are easily broken during pitch raising unless certain precautions are taken. When a string is rusty, there are usually tiny bonds of rust holding it to the other metal parts such as the pressure bar, upper plate bridge and guide pins. If an attempt is made to raise the tension of such a string, the added tension may be confined to the uppermost segment of the wire, and it may break, either at the tuning pin or at the upper plate bridge. To prevent this, let each rusty string *down* in pitch until a soft "tick" is heard, as the rust breaks loose. It will then be safer to raise the pitch to normal. If absolutely necessary, apply a drop of "Liquid Wrench" to the end of a toothpick and touch it to the rusty bearing point. *Do not* apply the solvent directly to the bearing point with the nozzle of the container; this always results in excess. *Never* apply so much that it runs down the string (in an upright) or down the tuning pin (in a grand) or gets on *any* part of the piano except the string bearing point. It is imperative to keep Liquid Wrench, in even the tiniest amounts, away from the tuning pins, action and other parts.

Broken Strings

If a two or three string unison has one broken string, the hammer for that note will wear unevenly. Such a hammer will have to be reshaped in order to play all three strings when the broken string is finally replaced. Also, the impact of the hammer will be absorbed by one side of the felt, putting a twisting strain on the hammer shank, butt, center pin and bushings, causing the hammer to get loose and wobbly prematurely. If a string breaks in the low bass where there is only one string per note, the hammer will travel too far, putting strain on the shank and butt. Therefore, broken strings should always be replaced promptly.

Fortunately for the piano technician, most string breakage occurs in the high treble and in the bass, where the strings are the most easily accessible; fortunately for the pianist, string breakage usually occurs near the tuning pin, so if the string flies through the air, it travels away from the pianist, toward the far end of the plate!

93

Tools Needed for String Repair

Tuning lever or T lever
Long nose pliers
Round nose pliers
Regular pliers
Wire cutters
String lifter and spacer
Stringing hook
Several screwdrivers
Music wire gauge or micrometer
Supply of music wire, sizes 12 through 20, including half sizes
For some repairs, a string looping machine or vise
Obtain a wire cutter which is specifically for steel wire. Most cheap wire cutters are made for copper or iron wire but not for hard steel music wire.

A micrometer is the best tool for measuring wire sizes, but in its absence a music wire gauge will suffice.

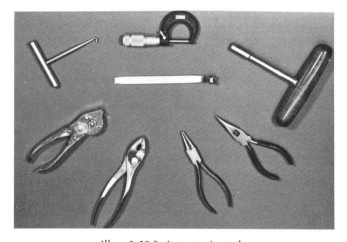

Illus. 6-18 String repair tools.

Handling Music Wire Coils

Music wire is very springy, and is hard to handle when coiled. To start a new coil, cut off the retaining loops and discard them. Remove the end of the wire with the metal flag, and unwind as much wire as needed from the *inside* of the coil. Do not let the wire push itself through the coil when the end is cut off, or it will become tangled. Leave the working end of the wire longer than the diameter of the coil. When finished with the coil, replace the flag, insert the working end through the hole in the coil holder, and bend enough over to keep it from slipping out. Always use the same end of the wire.

Illus. 6-19 *Left:* A one pound coil of music wire. *Right:* A reel and brake wire dispenser.

Another type of dispenser, which is more expensive but somewhat easier to use, is the *reel and brake*. To use it, bend the end of the brake almost straight to keep the wire from slipping through by itself. Loosen the nut just enough to allow the reel to turn when the brake is held with one hand and the wire is pulled through with the other. If the nut is loosened too much, or if the brake is not straightened enough, the whole affair will unwind like a huge clock spring until it becomes a tangled mess. Another handy dispenser is the canister type, as illustrated.

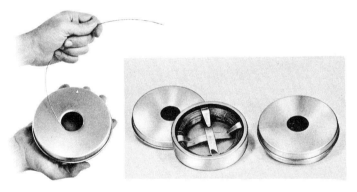

Illus. 6-20 Music wire canister.

Replacing Vs. Splicing

Replacing a broken string is easier than repairing it, but this is not always desirable. In old pianos, the bass strings lose their brilliant tone quality (because of corrosion and dirt in the windings), and become "dead" or "tubby" sounding. To replace a broken bass string with a new one in a piano with dead bass strings will make that note sound different from the rest of the bass notes. It is more desirable for all the notes to sound alike than for one note to sound different from its neighbors, even if it sounds *better* than the rest. For this reason, it is better to splice a new leader to a broken bass string, when possible, than to replace it with a new one, unless the original bass strings are still "live" enough to match the tone quality of a new string.

Old treble strings usually sound enough like new strings that if one breaks it should be replaced rather than spliced, since replacing is the easier procedure.

Splicing a String

Before attempting to splice a broken piano string, practice splicing scraps of music wire together. Begin with small wire, which is easier to handle, and work up to the larger sizes. Hold one piece of wire with a regular pliers, and form a loop in the end with a round nose pliers, as illustrated. Never kink or bend the wire at an angle, which will produce a weak spot. All bends should be rounded. Form a similar loop in the other piece. Face the loops in the proper direction, and assemble the knot, following the steps in the illustration.

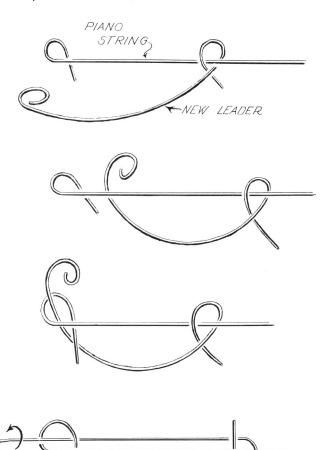

Illus. 6-21 Splicing a broken string in four steps, as described by Douglas Strong, PTG Journal, 11/72. The bottom drawing shows the position of the wires *after* rotating the new leader in the direction of the arrow, and before pulling on the leader to secure the knot.

Preparing to Install a New String

Since grand strings are exposed, there is no need to remove the action when making string repairs. In vertical pianos the action should be removed for access to the strings. One exception to this is when replacing a broken bass string in a spinet; it usually takes less time to replace the string with the action in place than it does to remove the spinet action with its drop lifters. When replacing a spinet string with the action in place, use extra caution to avoid damaging dampers with the loose string.

The following instructions apply equally to verticals and grands. The terms "up" and "down" however, refer to the vertical. When applied to a grand, "up" means "toward the keyboard" and "down" means "away from the keyboard".

Broken Treble String

Find the two tuning pins for the broken string. Remove the broken wire from the pins, and unscrew each pin counterclockwise three complete turns. Do not unscrew a pin with a wire stub still attached, or the wire may scratch the plate. If the wire breaks off at the pin, leaving a tight coil wound around it, pry the remaining coil out of the eye with a screwdriver and remove with a long nose pliers. When each pin is unscrewed three full turns, leave it with the eye facing downward, ready to accept the new string.

Measure the diameter of the old wire at a straight, clean spot with the wire gauge or micrometer. Measuring at a bend or rust spot will give an inaccurate reading.

Illus. 6-22 *Left:* Measuring the diameter of a broken string with a micrometer. *Right:* A music wire gauge. Do not confuse music wire sizes with any other standard.

PIANO WIRE SIZES

Size	Dia.	Feet per lb. (approx.)
12	.029	445
12½	.030	414
13	.031	384
13½	.032	366
14	.033	330
14½	.034	300
15	.035	295
15½	.036	290
16	.037	275
16½	.038	260
17	.039	248
17½	.040	234
18	.041	223
18½	.042	212
19	.043	200
19½	.044	190
20	.045	182
21	.047	165
22	.049	156
23	.051	140

Illus. 6-23 For the sizes listed in this table, double the gauge size and add 5 to determine the wire diameter in thousandths of an inch.

Pick out a new coil of wire of the proper diameter, estimate the length of the new string, including enough for the coils on the tuning pins, and cut off that much.

Insert one end of the new piece of wire up through the agraffe or pressure bar, and guide it through the eye of the tuning pin with the stringing hook. In a vertical, start with the right hand pin, and in a grand, the left hand pin, so the first new coil will not be in the way of the second.

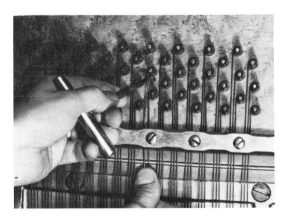

Illus. 6-24 Guiding the end of the string into the eye of the tuning pin with a stringing hook.

Illus. 6-25 Winding two and a half neat coils. The last half coil will be added when the string is pulled up to pitch and tuned.

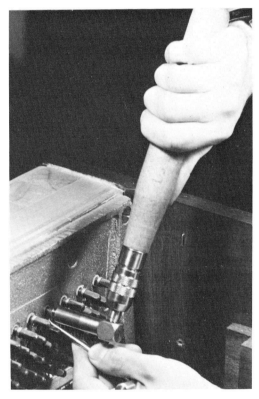

Illus. 6-26 Some technicians prefer to use a tuning lever instead of a T handle.

Slowly turn the tuning pin clockwise with the tuning lever or T handle, maintaining firm pressure on the string with the hook. Guide the wire as the pin is turned so it forms neat coils which do not cross each other, until there are about two and a half coils on the pin. Then feed the wire down across the appropriate bridge pins, pull it as tight as possible, and bend it around the hitch pin. Hold the remaining part of the wire next to its tuning pin, and cut it off about 3" (7.5 cm, or about the width of four fingers) above the pin. This is the right amount of wire for three coils around the pin. If your wire cutter is the type which is held parallel to the wire when cutting, mark the handle 3" (7.5 cm) from the blade, and use that for a guide.

Illus. 6-27 Securing the first half of the new string.

Illus. 6-28 Measuring the length of the second half.

Feed the wire up through the agraffe or pressure bar, guiding it into the eye of the pin with the string hook, and turn about two neat coils onto the pin. When the string is tight enough to stay in place, position it in the right place on the bridge. Snug the coil on the tuning pin with the string hook, string lifter or a screwdriver, and tighten the pin just enough to keep the coil in place. Then snug the coil on the other end of the wire, and tighten its pin just enough to hold the coil in place. Examine both tuning pins. Each should have almost three coils of wire, snug against each other. The end of the wire should be flush with the outside surface of the pin. Loose or uneven coils, coils of two or four turns, coils which cross each other, or wire that sticks out of the pin are all signs of sloppy work. If necessary, loosen the pin just enough to rearrange the coil, and tighten it again. Then, with a screwdriver and hammer, tap the wire where it goes around

Illus. 6-29 Using the string lifter to tighten a loose coil.

the hitch pin to seat it firmly on the plate. Squeeze the string together with pliers immediately above the hitch pin, to make both wires parallel. Check the spacing of the new strings with relation to their neighbors, and slide them sideways with a string spacer, if necessary. Tune.

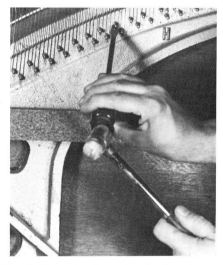

Illus. 6-30 Seating the string on the plate.

Illus. 6-31 Pinching the wires parallel as they leave the hitch pin hastens tuning stability.

The string lifter is a handy tool when there is room to use it. It should be used only for lifting, not for prying. Modern string lifters are made of plated cast iron, and will break if subjected to prying strain.

Attempt to make the coil right the first time. The more a tuning pin is turned back and forth, particularly in an old piano, the looser it becomes.

Do not bend, kink or twist music wire. This may cause *false beats,* or pulsations in the loudness of the tone, which make the string sound out of tune with itself, and make it impossible to tune.

Single Treble String Broken

Some treble strings are tied to their hitch pins like bass strings. The easiest way to make a hitch pin loop on the replacement string is with a commercially made string looping machine, as illustrated.

Illus. 6-32 A string looping machine.

Illus. 6-33 Winding the loop by hand.

In the absence of a looping machine, clamp a twelve-penny (8 cm) nail in a vise, with the head sticking up about ½" (13 mm). Bring about three inches (about 7.5 cm) of wire around the nail, and then about a half inch from the nail, wrap the wire around itself three times at a right angle. Wind the coils as tightly as possible. Snip the end off, leaving a stub about ⅛" (3 mm) long. Remove the nail from the vise, and slip the loop off the nail.

Treble String Missing

In some pianos, the wire sizes are printed or stamped on the pinblock or plate. If not, the size of a missing treble string must be deduced by measuring the surrounding strings.

If only one string is missing, gauge the remaining string for that note with a string gauge, without removing it from the piano. The replacement string should be the same diameter, because all strings for any unison should be the same size.

If several strings in a row are missing, gauge the strings on either side of the gap. If they are the same size, use that size wire. If not, gauge six or eight strings on each side of the gap and determine where the wire size should logically change.

If it is impossible to deduce the wire size by gauging the surrounding strings, such as when the surrounding strings have been replaced previously with various wrong sizes of wire, consult the formulas for wire diameter, length and tension on pp. 143-144.

Bass String Broken at Tuning Pin

When a bass string breaks at the *becket,* (the bend where the wire enters the eye of the tuning pin), enough of the original string is left to be tied to a new leader.

Remove the old wire from the tuning pin, and unscrew the pin three full turns, leaving the eye facing downward, ready to accept the repaired string.

Find a straight spot in the original string and measure the core wire. Cut a 14" (40 cm) piece of new wire of the same diameter, and lay it aside. Hold the original string in position in the piano, and locate the exact place where the splice will not interfere with the upper plate bridge or tuning pins. Add just enough to the measurement to allow for the knot, and cut off the rest of the old string. When the string is tuned, it will stretch a little, moving the knot closer to the tuning pin.

Tie the new leader to the old string, following the instructions on p. 95. Hitch the string to its hitch pin, position it on the bridge and upper plate bridge, hold it against the plate, and cut the new leader off 3" (7.5 cm) above the tuning pin. Wind it onto the tuning pin. After putting about two turns of wire on the pin, stop and unhitch the string from the hitch pin. Insert a small screwdriver or awl in the loop, and twist the string one full turn in the direction of the winding, to help insure that the winding will not come loose from the core. Grasp the twisted string just above the loop with pliers, remove the screwdriver, and hitch the sting over the hitch pin again. Check the position of the string on the bridge. Then snug the coil and pull the string almost up to pitch. Seat the loop on the plate at the hitch pin by tapping with a screwdriver and hammer, and tune the string.

Illus. 6-34 A spliced bass string.

Bass String Broken Near Hitch Pin

The string may be repaired if there is enough left to tie to a new leader. Tie a loop on one end of the leader first (see "Single Treble String Broken") and then splice it to the old string.

Bass String Broken Near Winding; Must be Replaced

The best replacement for a bass string is a custom-made duplicate from a piano supply company which specializes in making bass strings. If possible, send the original string as a sample, specifying two things: what number the *note* is in the scale, and how many strings there are for that note. For example, if the second B from the bottom is being sent in, state: "This string is for note 15 (B), and there are two strings per note."

Piano supply companies also make sets of "universal bass strings", which contain enough different sizes that one of them comes close to any original broken string. These are handy in situations where there is no time to wait for a replacement to be ordered through the mail, but an exact replacement is always better than a universal bass string which only approximates the original. Special instructions for installing universal bass strings are included in the catalogues of most piano supply companies.

Replacing a Missing Bass String

If the broken string is missing, measure the plate and adjacent strings to determine the following measurements of the missing string: diameter of core wire, length of winding, length of core wire from hitch pin to start of winding, name and number of *note* as it lies in the scale, and the number of strings per note. Send the measurements to a bass string maker, who will return a replacement string.

The piano manufacturer, if still in business, might be able to supply replacement bass strings, given the following information: the serial number of the piano, name and number of the note as it lies in the scale, and the number of strings per note.

Replacing Broken Strings in Baldwin Pianos Having "Acu-Just" Hitch Pins

Each string in this type of piano may be moved up or down its hitch pin in order to adjust the amount of down bearing on the bridge. To replace a broken string, follow the standard procedure, but adjust the string on its hitch pin just a little higher than the neighboring strings prior to adding tension. Pull the

Illus. 6-35 Tapping string down on Baldwin Acu-just hitch pin to increase bearing.

string up to pitch, and then tap it down gently with a screwdriver blade or special tool, as illustrated. Measure the down bearing on the bridge with a bearing gauge, and tap the string down a few thousandths at a time until the bearing is the same as for neighboring strings.

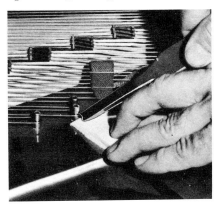

Illus. 6-36 If bearing is too great, lift string slightly by prying with coil lifting tool.

Illus. 6-37 Measuring downbearing in Baldwin with bearing gauge and feeler gauge. For details of bearing gauge, see p. 122.

Tuning Repaired or Replaced Strings

All new strings gradually stretch and go out of tune. Thus, when tuning a repaired or replaced string in a customer's piano which will not be tuned again for several months, follow these special instructions: If the string is a single-string unison in the low bass, tune it as sharp as possible without making it sound too objectionable. If it is one string of a two or three string unison, mute the new string with a rubber mute, and leave it muted until the next time the piano is tuned.

Treble String Dead; Tone Dies Away Too Quickly

This condition is usually caused by problems in the soundboard, but it is sometimes the strings themselves which have gone dead. If a string loses its resilience where it bends around the bridge pins or other bearing points, it will not vibrate properly. The tone sometimes may be improved by changing the position of the wire in relation to its bearing points. Loosen one tuning pin about half a turn, tighten the other to take up the slack and slide the wire around the hitch pin, and tune. New portions of the wire will be in contact with the bearing points, and the tone might be improved.

If a string loses its resilience throughout its entire length, it will have to be replaced. If this condition is present, it is usually generalized throughout the entire treble so that restringing is necessary.

False Beats in Treble Strings

"Beats" are pulsations in the loudness of the tone when two strings are out of tune with each other. "False beats" are pulsations in the loudness of one single string, which can not be eliminated by tuning. Most false beats in treble strings are caused by improper contact between the string and one of its bearing points, due to grooves in the plate bridge, loose pins in the soundboard bridge, or absence of downbearing.

In many old pianos having a cast iron upper plate bridge (or capo bar, in a grand), the string tension forms grooves or troughs in the metal, causing improper contact. If the grooves are shallow enough, the strings may be moved sideways just enough to get them out of the grooves onto a new surface of iron, where they will make good contact. If the grooves are so deep that the strings slip back into them, the surface of the plate bridge or capo bar will have to be ground smooth. This is a rebuilding job.

If the downbearing is inadequate, the string may ride up the bridge pin away from the top of the bridge, causing false beats. Sometimes this situation may be corrected temporarily by tapping the string gently down to the bridge with a screwdriver and hammer, being careful not to nick the wire. It may be corrected permanently by restringing the piano, moving the plate closer to the soundboard to restore proper downbearing.

Illus. 6-38 Tapping a string down to the bridge sometimes eliminates false beats temporarily.

If there are false beats in a piano with adequate downbearing and a good plate bridge or capo bar, the bridge pins are probably loose. If the bridge appears to be solid, loosen each string one at a time, remove the bridge pins, insert a little epoxy in the holes, and drive the pins back in. When dry, replace the strings and tune. Do not allow any epoxy to get on the strings. If the bridge is cracked or split, refer to pp. 93 and 133.

Other causes for false beats include twists, bends, kinks, rust spots on the wire, or raising the string too far above pitch during tuning. If the bridge pins are tight and the strings make firm contact with the soundboard and plate bridges, try replacing the offending string(s), being careful not to twist or bend the wire nor to raise it more than ¼ step above the correct pitch.

Ringing or jangling noises in treble strings have the same causes and repairs as false beats.

Bass Strings "Dead"; Tone is "Tubby"

Poor tone in dirty or corroded bass strings may sometimes be improved by the following method. Pick a string somewhere near the middle of the bass section, where any improvement will be the most obvious. Loosen the tuning pin just enough to slip the string off of its hitch pin. If it was previously twisted, note the number of turns that it untwists itself. Put a 6" (15 cm) loop in the string and run it up and down from one end to the other, to flex the wire and loosen the dirt, as illustrated. Remove the loop, twist the string as many turns as it untwisted when it was removed, plus a half twist more, replace it, add tension, seat the loop on the plate, and tune. If there is a noticeable improvement in the tone quality, repeat the process for each string in the

bass, one at a time. Remove only one string at a time, to keep the plate stress even.

Illus. 6-39 Loosening dirt and corrosion in a bass string sometimes improves its tone. The tuning pin is loosened just enough to remove the string from its hitch pin, leaving it attached to the tuning pin.

Dead bass tone may also be caused by the bridge being broken from its shelf, or by a poor repair job done previously on such a break. If this is the case, refer to bridge rebuilding.

Bass Strings Rattle or Buzz

A rattling or vibrating noise in the bass is usually caused by a loose or split bass bridge, or an unglued soundboard rib.

A metallic buzzing in a bass string is usually caused by a loose winding. To correct, loosen the tuning pin, remove the wire at the hitch pin, add a twist to the wire in the direction of the winding, in addition to any twists that it may already have, replace and tune. If the winding still buzzes, gently crimp the end of the winding with a rotating motion of a long nose pliers. Be careful. Too much pressure with the pliers will make it worse. If the string still buzzes, apply a small drop of white glue to the offending part of the winding with a toothpick. If that does not help, or if it noticeably deadens the tone, replace the string.

Strings Look Unsightly

Refer to "Cleaning a Piano" at the end of this chapter.

THE KEYFRAME

The only usual keyframe problems are deterioration of the cloth, and rusting of the key pins. Replacing the cloths and polishing the pins are discussed on p. 144.

THE KEYS

Piano keys are almost always embossed at the factory with numbers, from #1 in the bass to #88 in the treble. These numbers are necessary because no two keys in a piano are exactly alike. Unscrambling a set of mixed up keys can be a very time-consuming, if not impossible job. Unfortunately, even when the numbers appear to be legible, as soon as the keys are removed from the piano, all of the 6's, 8's, 9's and 0's look the same. For this reason, any time more than one key is removed from a piano at once, number or index the keys as illustrated.

Illus. 6-40 Drawing several diagonal lines on the keys prior to removing them helps to get them back in the right order.

Key Stays Down

Push down on the back end of the key, near the capstan. If both ends of the key go down at once, the key is broken. See "Repairing a broken key" on pp. 104-105.

If the back end of the key will not go down, a foreign object like a crayon has probably fallen under it.

If the back end of the key goes down and the front comes up, determine whether the key or action is sticking. Hold the key down in the back with one hand, raise the whippen with the other hand, and release the whippen. If the whippen drops to its rest position properly, the key is stuck. If the whippen stays up, the trouble is in the action.

If the front of a white key binds on the keyslip, remove the keyslip and insert shims made of paper or business card stock in the appropriate places so the shims will hold the keyslip away from the front ends of the keys when it is screwed down.

Illus. 6-41 Showing location of cardboard shims between key frame and keyslip to prevent latter from binding on keys.

If the key binds on an adjacent key, either the balance rail pin is bent, or the key is warped. See if the front of the key is square with the adjacent keys, and the capstan is centered under the whippen or sticker. If the front and back are both leaning in the same direction, the balance rail pin is bent. Square the key by tapping the top of the pin lightly with the palm of the hand on a screwdriver, being careful not to slip onto the key itself. If the front of the key leans to one side and the back leans to the other, the key is warped. Bend the balance rail pin sideways until the front and back of the key are both centered as well as possible, and then sand the back of the key on the binding side.

If the key sticks but does not bind on the keyslip or an adjacent key, one or both bushings are binding on their pins. If the pins are rusty, clean with silver polish, and spray with silicone to retard future rusting. If the key still sticks, gently squeeze, or "ease" one or both bushings with a "key easing pliers", as illustrated. Ease the bushing just enough for free movement of the keys without excess side play.

Illus. 6-42 Key easing pliers. Note that the construction permits the jaws to remain parallel.

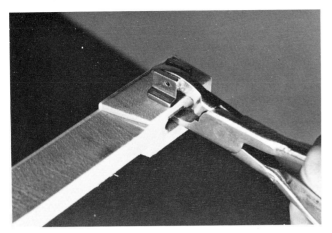

Illus. 6-43 "Easing" a key by squeezing the wood on either side of the bushing. Care must be taken to keep from enlarging the hole so much that the key wobbles or knocks.

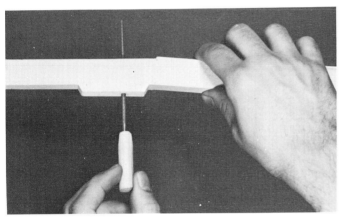

Illus. 6-44 If the unbushed hole in the bottom of the key binds on the balance rail pin, ease it with a 4" Nicholson bastard file. *IMPORTANT:* Grind the teeth off two sides of the file, and insert it with the flat sides facing the ends of the key, to keep from enlarging the hole from front to back.

Key Does Not Go Down

Determine whether the problem is in the key or the action. Try to lift the whippen by hand. If it will not go up, the problem is in the action. If it will go up, and the key will not go down, either the key is binding or a foreign object has fallen under the front end.

Many old player pianos have a *key lock*, consisting of a rail mounted under the front of the keys. By moving a small lever under the keybed, the rail moves up and prevents the keys from moving. Once in a while, a customer accidentally locks the keys on his old player piano, and, being ignorant of

the operation of the key lock, will call the technician because all of the keys are jammed.

Key is Sluggish

If a piano key plays the action properly, but is slow in coming back up, test the key and whippen separately to isolate the trouble. If the key is sluggish, ease the tight bushing, or sand any spots which bind on adjacent keys.

A sluggish spinet key sometimes is caused by the drop wire or lifter dowel binding against the hole in the back end of the key. To correct, bend the wire.

In spinet pianos having "dog leg" keys (see illustration), the weight of the action is supported by one side of the center bushing when the key is depressed. When the bushing becomes worn, it develops an indentation on the side receiving the weight, and this indentation prevents the key from returning properly when released. To correct, replace the worn bushings.

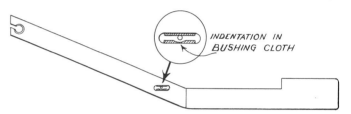

Illus. 6-45 An indented balance rail bushing in a "dogleg" key makes operation of the key sluggish. To correct, replace the worn bushing.

Most keys are weighted with lead slugs for proper balance. If the keys are sluggish, do not assume that more lead should be added. When the piano was new, the keys worked properly, and lead weights do not change their position in the keys by themselves! Correct the sluggishness by one of the above methods, and not by attempting to change the balance of the keys.

Keys Rattle From Side to Side

The purpose of the cloth bushings in piano keys is to allow the keys to work properly without being noisy. If the bushings are worn, compressed or missing, the keys will rattle.

If there is only a slight amount of excess side play, the front bushing may be tightened somewhat by swedging it with a *bushing tightener* as illustrated.

Illus. 6-46 A key bushing tightener.

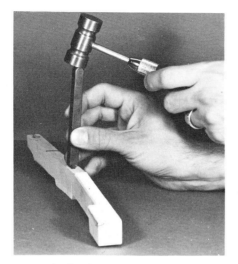

Illus. 6-47 Using the bushing tightener sparingly to eliminate side play in a key.

If a bushing is badly worn, or missing, obtain a piece of bushing cloth of the proper thickness. Clean as much of the old cloth and glue out as possible without disrupting the wood fibers, and glue the new bushing in place with hide glue and a spring or plug bushing clamp, as illustrated on p. 145.

If a key has end play because the center rail hole is elongated, the wood should be "sized". Needle the wood with a single needle in a hammer voicing tool, and apply a drop of water. Keep the water away from the bushing. While the water is drying, clean the balance or front rail pin with silver polish and spray with silicone. When the water evaporates from the surface of the wood, apply a drop of Titebond glue, which will penetrate into the newly-opened wood fibers. Wipe off excess glue and put the key on the pin. The wood will swell to the size of the pin, and when the glue is dry, the key should fit properly.

Never turn a front rail pin to take up side play in the bushing. If the pin is turned, the corner will wear the bushing away even faster, aggravating the condition.

Repairing a Broken Key

Breaks usually occur near the middle of a key,

where the wood is the thinnest. Separate the broken parts, coat the broken surface with Titebond and reassemble. It is sometimes helpful to use the adjacent keys for a splint, to hold the broken key in proper alignment while the glue is drying. Let the glue dry thoroughly before using the key. If a joint looks like it will be weaker than the original key was, glue a piece of veneer on the side of the key, clamping it firmly until the glue dries. When dry, sand the veneer down so the key will fit between the adjacent keys.

Illus. 6-48 A typical broken key.

Illus. 6-49 Coat the mating surfaces with glue, *align carefully*, and clamp.

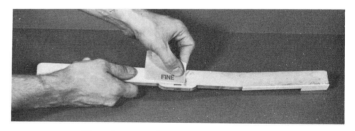

Illus. 6-50 Sanding away excess glue.

Illus. 6-51 Showing veneer patch cut to size, ready for gluing.

Illus. 6-52 Gluing and clamping the patch.

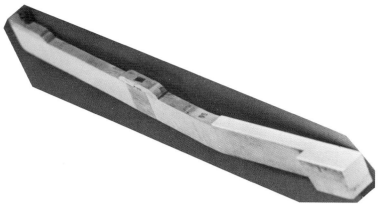

Illus. 6-53 The completed patch, after sanding.

White Key Covering Materials

Four types of keytops have been used commonly for white keys: ivory, celluloid, pyralin, and molded plastic. Ivory is the covering on most old upright and grand keys. Celluloid was used on cheaper pianos made until the 1940's; it is sometimes a little more yellow or gray than ivory, and usually has a fine "grain" of thin lines running through it. Pyralin is a thin plastic which comes in blanks, and must be trimmed to the size of the key after it is glued on. Molded plastic keytops are thicker and have pre-rounded edges. Almost all pianos made since the late 1960's have molded plastic or pyralin keytops. Since ivory and celluloid tops are difficult to obtain, the technician should save an assortment of old keytops of various materials, colors and thicknesses from junk pianos, for replacement purposes.

Replacing a Missing or Broken Ivory

Remove the remaining original keytop. Old ivory may be removed by heating it for a minute with an iron set on medium, and then slipping a 1" wide putty knife under it. Some old plastic keys may be removed with methylene chloride, a highly volatile solvent which softens the glue. Never apply heat to plastic or celluloid keytops. Ivory can be identified by its grain pattern, which with careful examination

will be seen to resemble a wood-grain. Plastic and celluloid sometimes have a simulated grain, which will be much more uniform than that of genuine ivory.

After removing the keytop, remove the old glue by sanding. To keep from rounding the edges of the key, tape a piece of sandpaper down to a flat surface and rub the key over it until clean and flat.

Illus. 6-55 Sanding the key as described above.

Pick a replacement keytop which matches the adjacent keys, and glue in place, using contact cement for molded plastic, pyralin glue for pyralin, and ivory cement or an ivory wafer (a glue-impregnated piece of cloth, available from supply houses) for ivory. Clamp as illustrated, except when using contact cement. To use the ivory wafer, heat the clamp in boiling water, wet the wafer in room-temperature water, apply it to the key, position the ivory on top of it, and apply the hot clamp. After the glue is dry, trim the edges of the new keytop with a fine file if necessary. Remove excess glue, and buff the key with tripoli buffing compound (available from hardware stores) on a felt buffing wheel to bring its surface to the same gloss as the adjacent keys.

To recover an entire keyboard, see pp. 145-148.

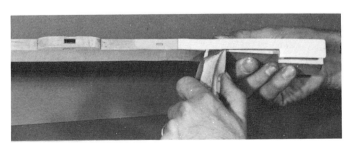

Illus. 6-54 Cutting the old keytop loose with a sharp knife.

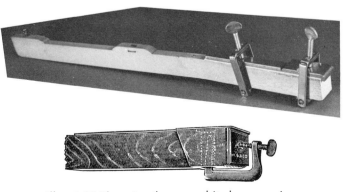

Illus. 6-56 Clamping the new white key covering.

Black Keytop Missing

Black keytops are usually made of hardwood or plastic. Obtain a new one of the correct type from a piano supply company. Sand the old key smooth to remove old glue, and glue the new sharp in place. For an ebony or hardwood sharp, use Titebond; for a plastic one, use contact cement or plastic glue. Clamp, and remove excess glue. Do not allow glue to run down into the front bushing.

A new wood sharp may be made by cutting and sanding a piece of close grained hardwood to the correct shape. Glue it in place, and apply several coats of black lacquer.

Discolored Keys

Ivory keys may be lightened in color somewhat by scraping the surface with an ivory scraper and then buffing to restore the surface finish. Little can be done to enhance keys with ink or crayon stains or cigarette burns, except to replace them. Worn sharps may be sprayed with several coats of black lacquer. To hold the keys upright while spraying, make a spraying rack out of an old key frame, or finishing nails and a piece of ¾" plywood, as illustrated.

Illus. 6-57 A homemade sharp key spraying rack.

ACTION REPAIRS
Note Does Not Play

Is the action for the "dead note" regulated right? Improper regulation can cause various problems, even if nothing is broken. For example, if the bridle wire is bent, holding the whippen up too high, the jack will not reset itself under the butt, and the hammer will not work. Other problems caused by improper regulation are covered in chapter five.

Broken Jack or Spring

In a vertical action, a note will fail to work if the jack flange comes unglued from its whippen. Remove the action, unhook the bridle tape from the wire, and unscrew the whippen with an *action flange screwdriver,* as illustrated. The narrow round shank of the screwdriver will allow the screw to be loosened without damaging the damper lever or spoon. Remove the whippen, pull the jack loose, remove as much old glue as possible, and reglue. When dry, replace the jack spring under the jack and replace the whippen in the action.

Illus. 6-58 *Left:* removing a whippen screw with the action flange screwdriver; *Right:* the jack flange is unglued from this whippen.

If the whippen is rounded, the jack will rock from side to side. In this case, as soon as the jack is reglued, but before the glue dries, replace the whippen in the action and rock the jack sideways until it is directly under the hammer butt. Allow the glue to dry, and reposition the jack spring.

A broken jack spring can also cause a note to fail. Without its spring, the jack will not reset itself under the hammer butt. In a vertical, remove the whippen, and clean the old glue and broken spring out of the hole in the whippen with a jack spring hole reamer. Glue a new spring in the whippen with

106

hide glue, insert under the jack and replace in piano. Jack springs come in two sizes: long for uprights, and short for spinets. Grand jack springs are made of heavier wire than upright jack springs, and seldom need replacement. If one does break, however, remove the silk cord holding the spring, with a center pin punch. Replace the spring, gluing a new cord in place. In addition to an assortment of action springs, the technician should have a supply of brass spring wire for making odd replacement springs for old pianos.

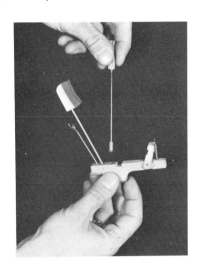

Illus. 6-59 The jack spring hole reamer for cleaning out old glue.

Broken Hammer Shanks

Hammer shanks usually break at the middle, as illustrated. To repair, remove the butt (or flange, in a grand) from the action with a flange screwdriver. In an upright, do not apply excess pressure to the jack. Apply glue, align the parts, and press together. Remove excess glue, and wrap the joint with heavy thread. The thread may be removed and the shank sanded clean after the glue is dry.

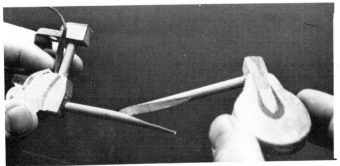

Illus. 6-60 A typical broken hammer shank.

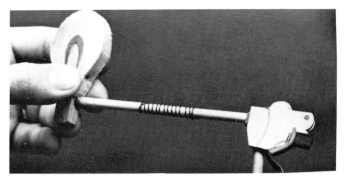

Illus. 6-61 Wrapping the glue joint with thread.

Broken shanks may also be repaired with *shank repair sleeves*, which come in two styles. The short sleeve is continuous, while the longer one is slit so it may be drawn tight around the broken shank. With either type, glue should be applied to the broken wood joint before assembly. The use of repair sleeves is not recommended in fine quality pianos because the added weight of the sleeve changes the touch of the repaired note.

Illus. 6-62 Cutaway view of one style of hammer shank repair sleeve.

To replace an irrepairable grand shank, remove the old stump from the hammer head with a *grand shank press*, as illustrated. Because the grand shank goes completely through the hammer, the press merely pushes it back out. Select a new shank which is identical to the original, to insure that the knuckle will be the correct distance from the center pin, or axis of rotation. If an exact replacement is unavailable, obtain a universal replacement shank which may be adjusted to the correct position, as illustrated.

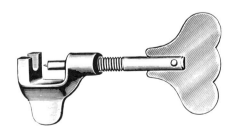

Illus. 6-63 The grand hammer shank press.

Illus. 6-64 An adjustable replacement grand hammer shank.

To replace a broken vertical shank, remove the old stump from the hammer and butt with an *upright hammer extractor.* Because the vertical shank does not go completely through the hammer head, the vertical shank extractor is used with a clamp on the shank, as illustrated. Prior to using this tool, chip the old glue away from around the shank to weaken the joint.

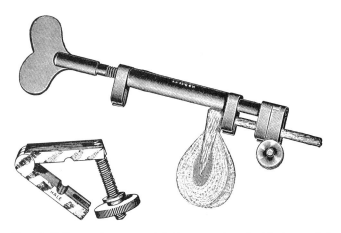

Illus. 6-65 Removing an upright hammer head with the upright hammer extractor and clamp.

If the shank breaks off at the surface of the butt, indent the exact center with an awl, and bore the remaining shank out with a *hammer head and butt borer,* as illustrated. Adjust the drill guide carefully before boring.

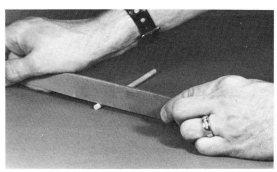

Illus. 6-67 *Top:* the hammer shank knurler; *Bottom:* knurling with the edge of a large file.

Illus. 6-66 The hammer head and butt borer.

Illus. 6-68 The hammer shank reducing tool, for use in any situation where it is necessary to remove old glue from a shank or reduce its diameter.

Cut a new shank to the correct length, and knurl each end with a shank knurler or by rolling it under the edge of a large file. Screw the butt to the action, and test the shank and hammer head for proper fit. Then glue the shank to the butt, and the hammer to the shank, aligning the hammer with its neighbors.

Hammer Missing

If a hammer is missing, inspect the inside of the piano thoroughly; missing hammers can usually be found lying somewhere in the bottom of the piano. If not, replace with a similar hammer from a junk action, usually available from any piano technician who has replaced the hammers in several pianos and has kept the old ones.

Broken Whippen

A whippen occasionally breaks where the sticker is pinned to it. This is repaired with a *Peniston whippen repair pin,* as illustrated. In an emergency, a piece of veneer glued to the side of the whippen will do the trick, providing that the new hole for the center pin is drilled in exactly the right spot after the glue is dry.

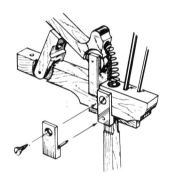

Illus. 6-69 The Peniston whippen repair pin.

Broken Spinet Lifter Elbows

A number of spinets were built in the 1940's and 50's with plastic lifter elbows connecting the drop sticker wires to the whippens. The plastic in most of these elbows eventually degenerates into a crumbly, sticky mess. Two types of replacements are available: "Vagias" snap-in plastic elbows, and wood elbows. Snap-in elbows are very convenient to use, because they may be slipped into place on the whippens without removing the action from the piano. They presumably are made of higher quality plastic than the originals, so they should last longer. Pick all remains of the old plastic elbows from the whippens and lifter wires, screw the lifter wires into the new elbows, snap the elbows in place in the whippens, insert the lifter wires into the keys, and regulate lost motion.

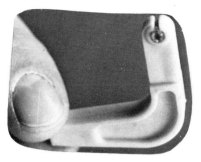

Illus. 6-70 The easy to install Vagias replacement elbow.

To install a set of wood elbows, remove the action, number and remove the whippens. Punch out the old center pins with a center pin punch or extractor, as illustrated. Screw the wires into the new elbows, pin them to the whippens with new center pins the same size, clip the ends of the pins off with a side cutter, and reassemble the whippens to the action. Replace the action in the piano, insert the lifter wires in the keys, and regulate lost motion.

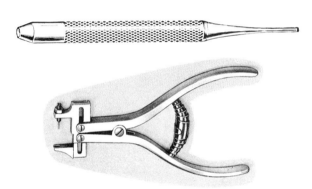

Illus. 6-71 Two types of tools for removing center pins.

Sluggish Action

To find the offending sluggish part, test each action component separately. For example, in a grand, first lift the hammer to see if it drops promptly when released. Then swing the hammer up out of the way, hold the key down in back, and lift the whippen to see if it is free. Then hold the whippen up and check the key. This same process of elimination is useful for locating any action problem quickly.

If a part does not move freely on its flange, the cloth center pin bushing is binding either on the side of the moveable part, or on the center pin. If a bushing is sticking out of the side of the hole and binding on the moveable part, remove the center pin with one of the tools illustrated, and trim the bushing with a sharp hobby knife or single edge razor blade. Measure the diameter of the center pin, and replace with a new one. Never put an old center pin back in the hole; the blunt end will damage the bushing as it is pushed through.

CENTER PINS

Size	Diameter	Size	Diameter
18	.046	22	.054
18½	.047	22½	.055
19	.048	23	.056
19½	.049	23½	.0575
20	.050	24	.059
20½	.051	24½	.061
21	.052	25	.063
21½	.053		

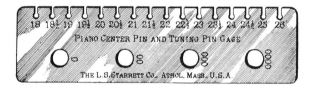

Illus. 6-72 A handy center pin holder.

Illus. 6-73 A combination center pin and tuning pin gauge.

If the bushing binds on the center pin, apply a mixture of eight parts naphtha to one part mineral oil. This should shrink the bushing to its proper size, and add a little lubrication. If it does not help, ream the bushing, as described under "repairing a flange". Keep the solution away from all plastic parts, including keytops, and use only in a well ventilated area. In the past, some technicians have recommended a mixture of alcohol and water for shrinking bushings, but this mixture is not as desirable because it takes longer to dry and may cause corrosion.

Other causes and remedies for sluggishness include corroded capstans (clean with silver polish or by buffing), rusty or broken vertical hammer springs (clean, or repair as illustrated), or lack of lubricating graphite on dowel capstans, jack tips, hammer butts and knuckles, etc. (rub in a paste of powdered graphite and a little denatured wood alcohol).

Illus. 6-74 Installing a hammer butt repair spring.

Clicks in Action

See that all cloth and felt is present on the butt, jack and catcher. Replace missing felt or cloth with material of the proper thickness and texture. Hot glue is the best glue for felt or cloth, but in an emergency a hot glue gun is handy.

Tighten all action screws. Loose whippen, hammer and sticker screws are common sources of clicking. Do not overlook the screws which hold the letoff rail in place. If this rail is loose, the clicks it produces are particularly hard to locate.

Check the bridle and back check wires, which sometimes click against each other. Bend sideways to correct.

Unglued hammer heads and catcher shanks are common offenders. If either part wobbles, it will click. Reglue.

If the bridle tape tips are hard and the holes are enlarged, they will click against the bridle wires. Replace the bridle straps or apply a drop of PVC-E glue to each tip at the hole. This glue remains somewhat rubbery after dry, and will silence the clicking.

In a grand, clicking or thumping noises may occur if the key frame does not make firm contact throughout with the keybed. See "bedding the key-frame" on p. 73.

Wobbly Parts—Repinning a Flange

If hammers, whippens or jacks wobble when their screws are tight and nothing is unglued, the center pins are loose. Remove the loose part from the action, and remove the center pin with a pin punch, extractor or pliers. Insert a new pin of the same size in a pin vise and try its fit in the unbushed wooden hole. It should take moderate pressure to fit the new pin in place; if loose, select a bigger pin. Be careful; if the pin is too big, the part will crack.

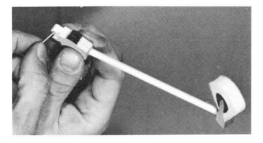

Illus. 6-75 Testing the fit of a new center pin in a hammer butt.

When a pin is found which fits tightly in the wooden part, remove it and try its fit in each side of the bushed flange. Test each bushing separately, because they sometimes wear unevenly. If the pin is loose in either bushing, the flange will have to be rebushed.

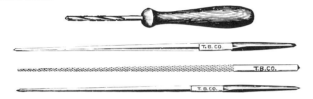

Illus. 6-76 Flange repinning tools, top to bottom: Bushing drill, cornered reamer, rat tail file and burnisher.

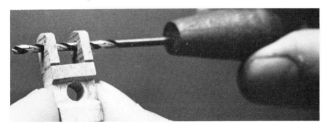

Illus. 6-77 Drilling the old cloth bushings out of the flange with a 7/64″ drill.

Remove the old bushings with a hand-held flange bushing drill. Obtain a piece of flange bushing cloth, which is supplied in strips, cut to a width equal to the circumference of the bushing hole. Cut a point on the end of the bushing strip and insert it into the flange. Pull it through both sides of the flange, as illustrated. Apply a little hide glue to the cloth, next to each hole in the flange, and pull the cloth a little more, to drag the glue into the hole. Cut the end of the strip away, leaving a little excess cloth on both sides of the flange, and insert a center pin the size of the original pin, which will press the bushing in place until the glue dries. When dry, remove the pin, and trim away the excess cloth and glue with a new razor blade or very sharp knife.

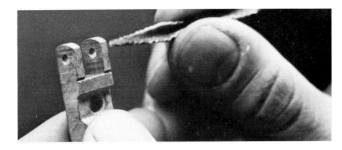

Illus. 6-78 Flange bushing cloth and a flange ready for rebushing.

Illus. 6-79 Pulling the cloth through the flange with long nose pliers.

Illus. 6-80 A new center pin in place while glue is drying.

Illus. 6-81 Trimming the bushing with a single edge razor blade.

Take the center pin which fits properly in the wooden part, and test its fit in each new bushing. It should fit snugly but loose enough to rotate in the bushing. If it is too tight, ream each bushing with a flange bushing reamer, and polish the cloth with a burnisher. Remove the least possible cloth, and try the fit; keep doing this a little at a time until it is just right. It is better to ream it several times in tiny amounts than to ream too much and have to rebush the flange a second time! Since the reamer and burnisher are tapered, each side of the flange must be treated separately in order to achieve uniform results.

Illus. 6-82 Enlarging the bushing slightly with a reamer.

When the center pin fits properly in the wooden hole as well as in both bushings, pin the parts together and clip the pointed end off of the pin with a side cutter, as close to the wood as possible. Never nick the working area of a center pin by grasping it with a pliers, or it will wear out the cloth.

Illus. 6-83 Clipping the pin with a side cutter.

It takes practice to learn how a pin feels when it fits correctly in the wood and the bushing. When the fit is just right, the part will work freely, but will not wobble. A good test is to see if the flange drops under the weight of a flange screw inserted in the hole. A jack should fall from its own weight when the spring is removed and the whippen is tipped up or down.

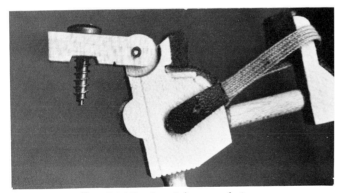

Illus. 6-84 Testing tightness of pin.

When a pin is loose in the bushings, always rebush, and ream the new bushings to the size of the pin which fits properly in the wooden part. Do not accommodate old worn out bushings with an oversize pin. This requires enlarging the hole in the wooden part, something which is very difficult to do uniformly and which can never be made smaller again.

A simple bushing reamer may be made by roughening the surface of a center pin with a light file and inserting the pin in a pin vise. Use a pin a half-size smaller than the one which will be used in the flange.

Teflon Bushings

In search for a center pin bushing material which is not affected by humidity changes (as cloth is), the Steinway Company has pioneered the use of solid teflon center pin bushings. Although they do not change their dimensions with humidity changes, they are not completely trouble free, and their servicing requires a technique and tools which are different from those used on conventional bushings.

Illus. 6-85 Steinway teflon flange bushings and inserter.

One problem with teflon bushings is that although they do not change size with humidity changes, the wood surrounding them does. Holes in wooden parts change dimension across the grain, shrinking when they dry and expanding when they gain moisture. Piano technicians sometimes attempt to service these bushings using conventional techniques, which makes matters worse, resulting in clicking and rattling noises.

Teflon bushings should be reamed with a parallel sided reamer rather than a tapered reamer. The technician should obtain a set starting at .049" and going up to .053", graduated in .0005" steps.

A loose center pin is usually looser in one side of the flange than the other. Remove the original center pin, and find a new one which has the proper fit in the looser of the two bushings. To test the fit, insert the pin in the looser bushing, hold the pin in one hand, and allow the flange to hang by that bushing. When the pin is rotated slowly, the flange should rise almost to the horizontal position, and then drop under its own weight almost vertically. When a pin is found which fits properly in the looser of the two bushings, the tighter bushing is then reamed to fit the pin. Start with the reamer the size of the pin, and test the fit of the pin again. Ream the bushing with increasingly larger reamers, one size at a time, until the pin fits perfectly.

If a bushing comes loose during the pin fitting process, replace it with another bushing, or size the wood surrounding the hole with water and then glue, as in sizing a loose key. Press the bushing back into place after the hole is sized. Seat it, and ream for proper fit.

Brass Flanges Broken

A broken brass flange rail is repaired with one of several types of *brass flange rail repair clips,* as illustrated. Type A is used when the rail breaks at the groove, and type B is used when the rail breaks at the screw hole. Determine whether the flange rail is of the regular or Kimball type. The regular type has a threaded hole in the butt plate, with the screw going in through an unthreaded hole in the rail. The Kimball type has a threaded hole in the rail, with the screw going in through the butt plate. Do not interchange Kimball and regular butt plates or repair clips. A *butt plate inserter* is handy for holding the plate while tightening the screw.

Illus. 6-88 A butt plate inserter.

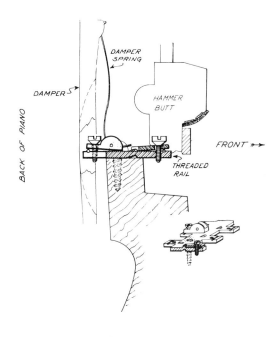

Illus. 6-89 Another type of brass rail is the *Kimball double flange rail,* on which both hammers and dampers are mounted.

Billing flanges are manufactured intermittently. If a new replacement is not available, a broken Billings flange must be replaced with one from a junk piano, or, in an emergency, with a flange taken from one of the infrequently played notes at the extreme end of the action.

Illus. 6-90 A Billings brass flange.

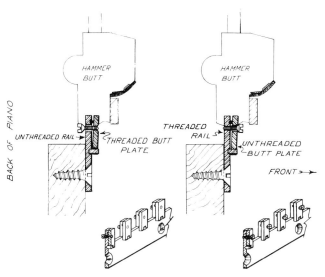

Illus. 6-86 Regular (left) and Kimball (right) brass flange rails, showing opposite mounting of flange screw and butt plate.

Type A   Type B   Type KA   Type KB

Type A is used when the tongue is broken at the groove. One half of the old groove is used and the broken part replaced by the repair clip.

Type B is necessary when the tongue has broken at the screw hole.

Type KA is special for Kimball pianos.

Type KB is special for Kimball pianos when the tongue has broken at the screw hole.

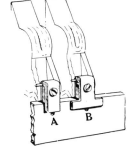

Illus. 6-87 Repair clips.

Reshaping Worn Hammers

Illustration 6-91 shows the shape of new and worn hammers. To restore a flat hammer to its original shape, draw a line on each side and across the face with a sharp pencil, to locate the striking

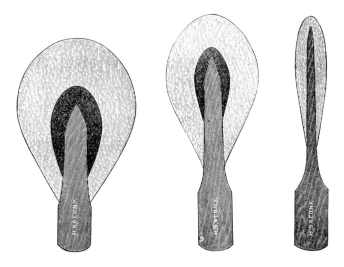

point, as illustrated. Then file the hammer in the direction shown until the grooves are gone and the shape is correct. Support the hammer firmly with one hand during filing to prevent damage to the center pin or bushings, Use a flat stick with medium garnet sandpaper glued to it, or a commercially available sanding stick with replaceable sandpaper.

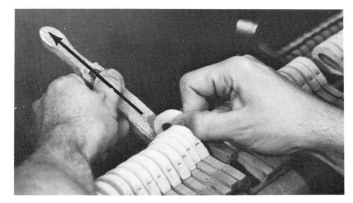

Illus. 6-91 New and worn hammers.

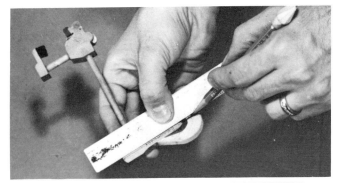

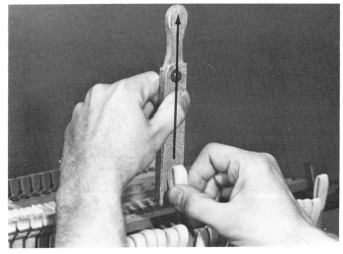

Illus. 6-93 Always file hammers toward the striking point, as indicated by the arrows.

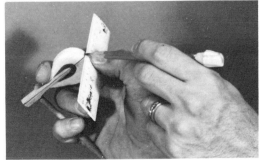

Illus. 6-92 Locating the striking point.

114

Sand carefully to keep from rounding the surface sideways. Never file extreme treble hammers if doing so will expose the wood, or will weaken the felt so the strings will cut through it to the wood rapidly. Flat treble hammer felt is better than wood striking the strings.

It is important to file the hammers accurately, maintaining the striking points in their correct positions, in order to preserve tone quality. If hammers are reshaped carelessly, with one striking point out of line with the next, the tone quality will vary from one note to the next. An equal amount of felt should be removed from the top and bottom of each hammer, so the crown will have symmetrical support. If more felt is removed from the top than the bottom, playing will gradually beat the felt into a different shape, distorting the crown and striking point. For further discussion about the importance of the correct striking point, see p. 149.

Illus. 6-94 Careless reshaping is worse than none at all.

To check the accuracy of filing, each hammer should be inspected from several angles, of observation. The overall shape should be symmetrical and rounded as in illustration 6-91. The top and bottom of each hammer should be perpendicular to the sides. Looking down on each hammer, the striking point should be parallel to the strings. Feel the crown of each hammer with one finger, to make sure the striking point is where it should be, directly in line with the wood molding. As a final test, after all hammers are shaped, install the action in the piano, and test the hammers for all multiple string unisons by holding each hammer against its strings with one hand, and plucking each string separately with the other. Each hammer should dampen all strings equally. If one string rings, the hammer is not hitting all of its strings equally, and should be corrected.

Another tool for hammer reshaping is the hand-held motorized tool fitted with a drum sanding attachment and guide, available from piano supply houses. Using a motorized sander is quicker than sanding by hand, but it increases the risk of nicking the felt or filing the hammers crooked. Its use should be confined to pianos in which tone quality is relatively unimportant; fine concert pianos should always have the hammers reshaped by hand.

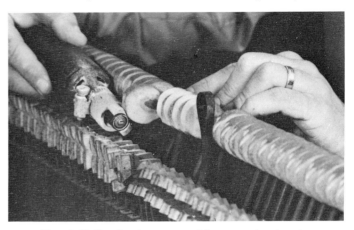
Illus. 6-95 Shaping hammers with a motorized tool.

If treble hammers are worn to the wood, they should be replaced with a new partial set. In an emergency, they may be capped temporarily by filing the grooves down and gluing buckskin or dense felt in place. If the technician is away from home servicing old pianos in a rural area and finds himself in need of hammer capping material, felt bunion or corn pads from a local drug store may provide a temporary remedy in the extreme treble.

Damper Does Not Damp

In order for dampers to work properly, the levers must work freely, the springs must be good (in a vertical), the wires must be free in their guide rail holes (in a grand), and the felt must meet the strings squarely. If a vertical damper spring is broken, replace it with a damper repair spring, as illustrated.

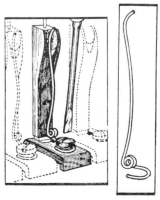
Illus. 6-96 Damper repair spring for vertical piano.

If a grand damper stays up when the key is released, check the action to see that it is not too far back in the piano, with the keys binding on the damper levers. If that is not the problem, remove the action and determine whether the damper wire is binding in its bushed guide rail hole or whether the lever is sluggish. To correct a binding damper wire, remove the damper by unscrewing the wire from the lifter, polish the wire with silver polish, and ream the guide rail bushing slightly with a center pin bushing reamer or file, if necessary. If the lifter lever is sluggish, treat it with center pin lubricant (see p. 110.) If this does not help, remove the lever from the piano and ream the flange bushing. It sometimes is possible to remove the offending lever simply by removing its damper, but it may be necessary to remove all of the dampers and the entire damper lever rail to gain access to the flange screw. Number the dampers as they are removed, and replace them in order.

If a damper works freely, and is regulated properly, but fails to damp, it is not seating on the strings. Allow the damper to seat itself, and pluck each string. Double check the contact visually, and bend the damper on its wire until the felt lies squarely on the strings.

If a string twangs when the damper makes contact, the felt is probably hard or crusty. To soften it, needle it with a hammer voicing tool, or file it *gently* with fine sandpaper, being careful not to pull the felt out of shape. If the damper still does not seat properly, replace the felt with new damper felt.

Damper in Vertical Does Not Lift

If a damper in a vertical piano fails to lift when the key is depressed, the spoon is either bent or broken. If bent, regulate. If broken, remove the whippen from the action, punch the old spoon stump back out the same way it came in, insert a new spoon, and regulate.

Squeaks

If a pedal squeaks, operate the action mechanism (damper lift rod, grand shifting lever, hammer rail, etc.) to determine whether the squeak is in the action or the pedal. If a metal part squeaks against another metal part, such as a pedal squeaking on its metal pivot screw, lubricate with a drop of oil. If two

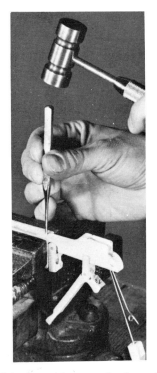

Illus. 6-97 Punching out broken damper spoon. Spoons are normally serrated instead of being threaded as shown in the picture.

wooden parts, as in wooden pedal trapwork, squeak against each other, lubricate with graphite.

Corroded damper springs in vertical pianos are a common source of squeaks. If the same squeak is heard when the sustaining pedal is depressed and when individual notes are played, the damper springs are probably the culprits. Remove the action and polish any offending springs with silver polish. The dummy damper has a stronger spring, and is a common troublemaker. Rub all squeaky damper spring felts with the end of a hammer shank sharpened in a pencil sharpener and dipped in the powdered graphite and alcohol mixture. Pure

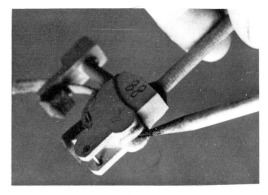

Illus. 6-98 Polishing a squeaky hammer spring slot with a sharpened hammer shank and graphite.

graphite applied in this way is better than rubbing with a pencil or graphite stick, which leaves a clay residue, and may become sticky.

Jacks sometimes squeak when they slide out from under their hammer butts (in verticals) or knuckles (in grands). If graphite applied to the buckskin does not cure the squeak, the buckskin should be cleaned. Fill a hypo-oiler (see illustration on p. 90) with a solution of eight parts naphtha to one part mineral oil, and insert it into the cloth under the buckskin. Apply enough to flush the old dirt and graphite out of the pores of the buckskin. Apply new graphite, and the squeaks should be eliminated.

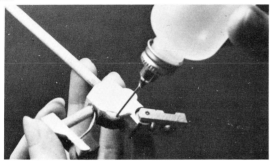

Illus. 6-99 Flushing the dirt out of the buckskin with naphtha-mineral oil solution. Following this treatment, new graphite should be rubbed into the buckskin.

Hammers Jump During Letoff

If the buckskin on the butt or knuckle is indented where the jack pushes on it, the hammer will jump when the jack rubs across the high spot. If the buckskin is packed down but still has enough thickness to be usable, its shape may be restored temporarily by sewing yarn between the buckskin and under-cloth, as illustrated.

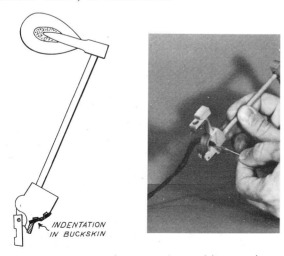

INDENTATION IN BUCKSKIN

Illus. 6-100 Eliminating indentation by padding underneath buckskin with yarn, drawn by a 2" fine steel yarn needle.

If hammer butt, knuckle, or catcher buckskin is worn out, it must be replaced. At the same time this book is being written, buckskin is in short supply, and a dark brown woven cloth is being sold as a substitute. If this material is used, it should be sprayed with aerosol silicone to reduce friction.

Regulating Screws Will Not Turn

When a regulating screw rail absorbs enough humidity over a long period of time to rust the regulating screws, the screws become bonded to the wood, and they will break off if any attempt is made to turn them. Badly rusted regulating screws should always be replaced. Take the regulating rail out of the action, and heat the end of each screw with a soldering iron or pencil flame propane torch, without scorching the wood. When the regulating screw is hot, remove the heat, and twist the screw back and forth with pliers, which should loosen it in the wood and enable it to be removed. If both ends break off, punch the stump out with a pin punch, plug and redrill the hole, and insert a new regulating screw.

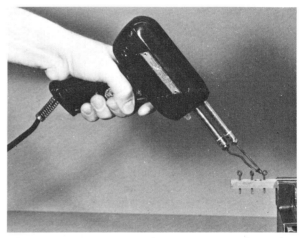

Illus. 6-101 Heating a rusty regulating screw in order to free it. Do not scorch the wood.

Bridle Tapes Broken

If a few bridle tapes are broken, the rest of them are probably ready to break, so the whole set should be replaced. The best replacement tapes are new ones glued to the catcher shanks like the original. This preserves the original leverage of the tape as it tugs on the butt. Cork-tipped and clip-on tapes are available, but these should be avoided when possible because the position where they attach (near the end of the catcher shank) affords different leverage than that of the original. Cork tapes come with small, medium or large corks, to fit various size catcher holes. The cork is pushed into the hole with an inserter, as illustrated, and glued if necessary. Care must be taken with old brittle catchers, or they will break off. If the catchers have no holes, clip-on tapes may be used.

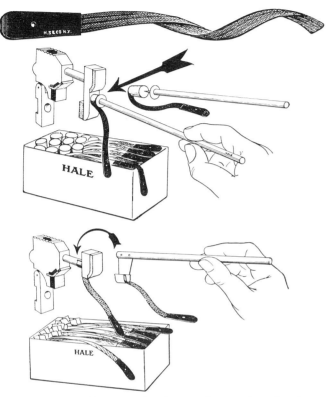

Illus. 6-102 *Top to bottom:* glued-in, cork-tipped, and spring-clip bridle tapes.

RATTLES

The most obvious sources of rattles are loose cabinet parts, or a cracked soundboard vibrating against a rib. Less obvious rattles include such things as a caster vibrating against the floor, a foreign object laying on a grand soundboard, a grand bass string buzzing against a damper wire, the nuts loose on vertical action bolts, or sympathetic vibration of another object in the room. A diligent search will locate the rattle.

PEDAL REPAIRS

A large variety of new pedals are available from piano supply companies, to replace broken pedals. If a new pedal does not match the old ones, install a whole new set. If both pieces of the old pedal are present, it might be possible to have them welded,

polished and replated, if replacement pedals are not available.

To repair a loose grand lyre, remove it, plug and redrill the screw holes, and install new screws if the original ones are worn. Longer screws may be used, providing that they do not go all the way through the keybed into the key frame.

To repair loose pedal mounting blocks in a vertical, number and remove them. Plug and redrill the screwholes. Clean the blocks and piano bottom. Reglue and screw the blocks in their original positions. Never mix pedal mounting blocks, even if they look alike.

If the bottom of a vertical piano is cracked and provides inadequate support for the pedals, remove the pedal action, tilt the piano on its back see p. 124), and unscrew the bottom. Glue and clamp the bottom as illustrated. If it is warped when

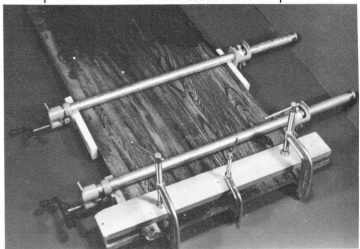

Illus. 6-103 Gluing and clamping a cracked upright bottom.

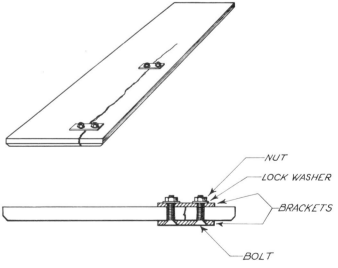

Illus. 6-104 Reinforcing a cracked upright bottom with reinforcing brackets or plates.

118

the crack is reglued, dampen it, and place it under weights to straighten it. If the bottom is high enough above the floor, when installed in the piano, to allow room for reinforcing brackets, install several as illustrated. Insert flat head bolts through the bottom in places where they will not interfere with the pedals, add another bracket on the top side, and tighten with lockwashers and nuts.

THE EFFECTS OF CLIMATE ON A PIANO

The best possible climate for a piano is a very dry climate, providing that the piano is shipped there when new, and remains dry all year long. The next best climate is one which is somewhat humid all year long. Any climate which changes from humid in the summer to dry in the winter (such as any place where a building is dried out by a furnace in the winter and allowed to become humid in the summer) causes the wood and felt in a piano to expand and contract. Expansion and contraction from seasonal humidity variations are a major cause of many piano problems, such as loose glue joints, checked varnish, loose tuning pins, a cracked soundboard, etc. The worst thing which can be done to a piano is to leave it in a very humid climate for a number of years and then move it to an extremely dry climate, where it will fall apart.

Protecting a Piano from Climate Changes

Never place a piano over a hot air register or next to a radiator. Never place a piano in front of a

Illus. 6-105 This location has three counts against it: the radiator, the window and the outside wall.

window. When possible, place a piano against an inside wall, which will minimize the effect of condensation when the outside and inside temperatures are different. Avoid placing a piano in a concrete block building or on a concrete floor, either of which is usually very damp.

For the best protection, the climate surrounding the piano should be controlled. If a building or room humidification/dehumidification system is impractical, the piano may be protected by installing a Dampp Chaser® or a similar climate control system, available from any piano supply company. The Dampp Chaser piano dehumidifier, humidifier, and humidistat control as illustrated, may be used individually or in combination, depending on the climate requirements. In climates having moderate seasonal change of relative humidity (10–20% change), the dehumidifier and control provide adequate protection. In climates having more extreme changes, the entire system is recommended. If the humidifier is used, it must be refilled with water faithfully. It is better not to use a humidifier than to forget to fill it part of the time.

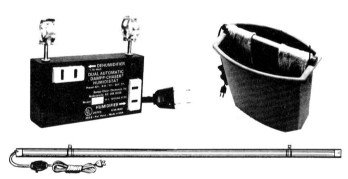

Illus. 6-106 A typical moisture control system. As this book is written, two prominent brands are the Dampp Chaser and Moisture Master.

MOTH PREVENTION

Moths like to lay their eggs in piano action felts. When the eggs hatch, the larvae eat the felt, leaving the piano with holes in the hammers and other parts. To prevent moth damage, use moth spray, available from piano supply companies, or put a few ounces of paradichlorobenzene in a muslin bag and hang it in the piano. Do not use any mothballs or other moth preventative containing DDT, because the fumes contain acid which rusts metal parts.

CLEANING A PIANO

Over a period of years, the inside of a piano collects an amazing amount of dust and dirt on the soundboard, among the tuning pins, and in other places where it is hard to get out. A thorough cleaning not only enhances the looks of a piano, but also keeps the old dirt from acting as an abrasive on moving parts.

Remove the action, all removeable cabinet parts, and in a vertical, the keys.

Clean the tuning pins. A wire brush may be used to remove thick rust, providing that care is taken not to scratch the plate. Polish the pins with a "Travis Tuning Pin and Coil Cleaner" in a hand or electric drill. Apply a small amount of cleaning compound (supplied in the kit) to the tip of each tuning pin, insert a rubber bushing in the holder, center the hole in the bushing over the tip of the tuning pin, and work it in and out.

Vacuum the inside of the piano as thoroughly as possible. In a vertical, use a narrow crevice tool to vacuum the keybed without vacuuming away the keyboard punchings. If an air compressor is available and if the piano may be moved outside, alternately blow the piano out with compressed air and then vacuum it, until all loose dirt is gone.

The exposed areas of plain strings may be cleaned by rubbing lightly with fine steel wool, providing that care is taken not to snag particles of steel wool around bridge pins or other parts of the piano. The accessible surfaces of the wound strings may be cleaned by brushing them lightly with a fine, flexible rotary brass brush in a variable speed electric drill. Do not apply much pressure to the ends of the string windings, which might make the windings loose. Do not expect this treatment to help the sound of dead bass strings, because it will only clean the exposed surfaces of the strings, leav-

Illus. 6-107 The Travis tuning pin and coil cleaning kit.

Illus. 6-109 Cleaning the bridge with a toothbrush or razor cleaning brush.

Illus. 6-108 Vacuuming loose dirt from the keybed.

Illus. 6-110 Scrubbing away residual dirt with a rag. Do not rub so hard as to remove gilding.

ing enough dirt and corrosion to deaden the tone.

Clean the bridges and tuning pin areas. Scrub the dirt loose with an electric razor cleaning brush dampened in a household liquid detergent-ammonia solution (such as "Sea Mist", "409", or other commonly available products which may be used on varnished surfaces), diluted 50% with water. Do not spill any liquid on any part of the piano. After scrubbing each area, clean up the remaining film of dirt with a rag wrapped around the end of a bluntly sharpened hammer shank or other small tool.

Paint the tuning pins with "tuning pin bluing" from a piano supply house, to inhibit future rust.

Clean the soundboard. Obtain a "soundboard steel", or flexible piece of spring steel with a hole punched in one end. Dampen a rag in a solution of two tablespoons vinegar to a gallon of warm water. With one end of the rag attached to the soundboard steel and the other end tied to a piece of string, work the rag back and forth on the soundboard under the strings, as illustrated. A thorough job of cleaning a soundboard and plate takes several hours.

Clean the action by scrubbing with a small toothbrush, and blowing the loose dirt away with a hand blower, the pressure end of a vacuum cleaner, or an air compressor.

Clean the keys. For the wooden parts, use a rag dampened in the water-vinegar solution. For the white keytops, use a rag dampened in warm water or a weak solution of Ivory soap. If necessary, polish the white keys on a clean buffing wheel.

Assemble the piano.

Clean the cabinet thoroughly with a rag dampened in the water-vinegar solution. Polish with furniture paste wax, which buffs up to a hard, glossy finish. *Never* use conventional aerosol furniture polish on a piano. This type of polish contains alcohol, which damages lacquer and varnish.

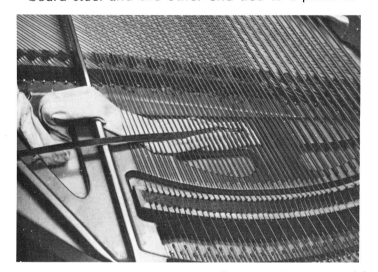

Illus. 6-111 Showing use of the soundboard steel and rag.

Chapter Seven
Rebuilding

Rebuilding involves the complete overhauling or replacement of major parts of a piano. Because rebuilding usually requires a relatively large expenditure of time and money, several factors should be weighed carefully before "taking the plunge". How good will the instrument be when the job is done? Will its market value be more or less than the total rebuilding cost? If a partial rebuilding job is contemplated, does the condition of the rest of the instrument justify it? Does the customer put more emphasis on sentimental value or market value? One customer may want his family heirloom restored to new condition regardless of expense, even if it costs more than the instrument will be worth; another may be interested only in keeping the piano for a few years until he can trade it in for a better one, in which case a complete rebuilding job may be impractical.

It is usually worthwhile to replace a grand pinblock if necessary. The upright pinblock is built into the cabinet, making it harder to remove, and good quality upright pianos may usually be obtained for less than the price of a complete rebuilding job. Therefore, it is not usually practical to replace an upright pinblock. If there is evidence that an upright pinblock is cracked, so that restringing with oversize pins will not keep the piano in tune, rebuilding is usually not advisable. Exceptions are in the case of an electric player piano of the coin operated or reproducing variety, which is worth enough to make this large job practical.

Whatever the circumstances, the technician should always explain the potential musical and market value of the instrument to the customer, along with an honest estimate of the rebuilding cost, before any decisions are made.

It is strongly recommended that the new piano technician completely rebuild a half dozen old uprights or junk grands before attempting to restring or repair the soundboard or install a set of new hammers in a fine quality grand.

PREPARATION

A complete rebuilding job involves removing the strings and plate from the piano. The height of the plate over the soundboard is very critical, because it determines the amount of downbearing of the strings on the bridges, and hence, the tone quality. Before taking a piano apart, the tightness of the tuning pins, the height of the plate, the amount of downbearing, and the piano technician's opinion of the tone quality should all be noted.

Before measuring down bearing, tune the piano, and note whether or not the tone is appropriate for that type and size of piano. If downbearing is inadequate, the tone is usually weak but long-sustained, providing that the strings are still good. If downbearing is excessive (a rare condition in an old piano) the tone is usually loud and short-sustained. When evaluating tone quality, take the condition of the strings and hammers into consideration.

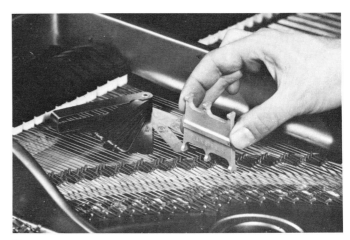

Illus. 7-1 *Top:* A bearing gauge; *Bottom:* showing use of the bearing gauge with a feeler gauge in a piano with conventional hitch pins.

To measure downbearing, obtain or make a bearing gauge of the type supplied by the Baldwin piano company, as illustrated. Place the center foot of the gauge exactly half way between the two rows of bridge pins for the string to be measured, and align the outside feet over the same string. If bearing is present, the gauge will rock on the middle foot. To measure bearing, rock the gauge toward the hitch pin, and measure the gap between the other foot and the speaking portion of the string, with a feeler gauge. Start with a thin gauge, and add thickness until the bearing gauge no longer rocks. Note the amount of bearing at the points indicated on illustration 7-2. In a Baldwin with Acu-just hitch pins, bearing is measured by rocking the gauge toward the speaking length and measuring the gap under the other foot. Before restringing a Baldwin of this type, write to the factory for specific restringing instructions for that particular instrument.

After noting the overall tone quality and making a list of downbearing measurements, take the piano apart.

DISASSEMBLY OF THE VERTICAL

Remove the front panels, upper pillars, lid, music shelf, fallboard, key strip, key slip, cheek blocks, action, keys and key frame.

Lay the piano on its back. If a piano tilter is available, one man can perform this job, as illustrated. If not, three men should be on hand. Before tipping the piano, place a large block of wood on the floor where the pinblock will rest, to allow space for the fingers. Two men stand behind the piano to tip it back, and a third remains in front to keep the bottom of the piano from kicking forward. Remove the front legs (if a spinet) or pillars (if an upright). This should expose all of the keybed screws.

There are usually three large screws on each side of the keybed going up into the cabinet arms; some pianos also have one or two screws attaching the keybed to the plate. When all screws are removed, lift the keybed straight up and out of the piano.

Illus. 7-4 Screwdrivers indicate locations of screws holding the front leg assembly. In the piano illustrated, the half pilaster flush with the cabinet also has two screws reached from inside the cabinet.

Illus. 7-5 *Left:* Arrows show two of the three screws which are usually found in each end of the keybed; *Right:* Removing the keybed.

Remove the bottom. It is attached with screws around its perimeter, going up into the piano back, sides and toe board. In some pianos, the bottom may be removed with all pedals and trapwork still attached; in others, some or all of the pedal mechanisms will have to be removed before removing the bottom. The piano should now look like illustration 7-6; it is now ready for string removal.

Illus. 7-3 Showing use of the one-man folding piano tilter.

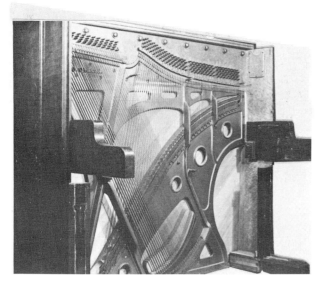

Illus. 7-6 The upright ready for string removal.

DISASSEMBLY OF THE GRAND

With the legs and pedal lyre removed, place the body of the piano on sturdy sawhorses. Remove the key slip, cheek blocks, fallboard, action, music rack, music rack guide rails, lid and lid prop.

Remove the dampers. Make a damper storage rack out of any convenient piece of wood by drilling a row of 75 holes spaced about ¾" (or 2 cm) apart, and mark "bass" at one end. Unscrew the damper wires from the damper levers; pull the dampers out of the piano one at a time, number them, and place them in order in the storage rack. Secure them to the rack with masking tape.

The piano is now ready for string removal.

Lowering the String Tension

Removing the strings from a piano is not a job to be taken lightly. Each string has an average tension of 160 pounds (72.5 kg), adding up to a total of 18 tons (16,300 kg) in a medium size piano! When dealing with tensions of this magnitude, as the technician does any time he rebuilds a piano, the stress must be kept uniform to keep from cracking the plate or damaging the soundboard! This is so important that it bears repeating: any time the technician changes the string tension in a piano (such as when removing the strings), *the stress must be kept uniform*. If the tension is changed suddenly on part of a piano, there is always a risk of cracking the plate or damaging the soundboard. Keeping the importance of stress in mind, always follow the correct sequence when lowering string tension.

Make one cardboard jig to record the height of the tuning pins, and another for the pressure bar. Set these aside for reference during restringing. Using a regular tuning lever (or a T handle, if the

Illus. 7-7 Cardboard height jigs for tuning pins and pressure bar.

Illus. 7-8 String tension may be lowered with a tuning lever, T lever or ratchet wrench equipped with a tuning pin socket, as illustrated.

pins are very loose), let the tension down on the left hand string of the lowest three-string unison. Turn the tuning pin counterclockwise one full turn, just enough to remove all tension from the string, without disrupting the tuning pin coil. Proceed all the way up the scale, lowering each left hand string. Then go to the bass section. Lower the left hand string of each two-string unison, and then lower *every other* single string unison. Going back to the treble, lower the middle string of each three-string unison, then the rest of the bass strings, and finally the right hand string of each treble unison. Following this sequence will take longer than going directly from one end of the keyboard to the other, but will reduce the possibility of damage.

Illus. 7-9 All of the strings in this piano are loose; notice that the pressure bar has been removed.

Removing the Wound Strings

Remove the wound strings first. Turn each tuning pin counterclockwise just far enough to pry the becket (the bend in the wire where it enters the eye of the tuning pin) out of the pin with a screwdriver, and slip the wire coil off of the pin. The best tool for turning tuning pins during this operation is a ratchet socket wrench with socket wrench tuning lever tip. In the absence of this tool, use a regular tuning lever.

Hang the strings by their hitch pin loops in order on a piece of copper electrical wire with a large knot tied in one end, indicating the position of any missing strings in the sequence with balance rail punchings. If the strings are still like new, and if the coil ends are still in good enough condition to wind onto new tuning pins, lay them aside for restringing. If they are dead sounding or dirty, or if the piano is of fine quality, they should be replaced. Attach a tag with the following information: name and address; brand name, style or size, and serial number of piano; how many strings are one per note, how many are two per note, how many are three per note, and how many (if any) lie on the treble bridge. Package them in a sturdy box, and send them to a string maker for duplication.

Removing the Treble Strings

When restringing, treble strings should always be replaced. Any savings gained by not having to purchase new wire are more than offset by the additional time it takes to preserve and re-use original treble strings.

Before removing the treble strings from a vertical piano, the pressure bar must be removed. Record the positions of any screws of different lengths on a chart for future reference. If any of the pressure bar screws are rusted to the bar, apply a sparing amount of Liquid Wrench or WD-40 solvent, being careful not to get the solution on any wooden part of the piano. Tap the pressure bar around the screw with a punch and mallet to loosen the rust. If a pressure bar screw is rusted to the pinblock, heat the screw head with a large soldering iron, being careful not to scorch the wood.

Starting with the lowest non-wrapped string, turn the tuning pin counterclockwise until the string may be pried out of the pin. Repeat the procedure for the other end of the string at the next tuning pin. Remove the string from the piano and measure its diameter (at a straight place in the wire) with a micrometer or music wire gauge. Proceed, in order, to the last note in the treble. List the number of strings of each size as you go, noting the position of any single treble strings which are tied to individual hitch pins. Keep a record of the stringing pattern if any strings go around two hitch pins, or skip a pin, as illustrated. If any treble strings are missing, leave blanks in the list in the appropriate places. Discard the old strings.

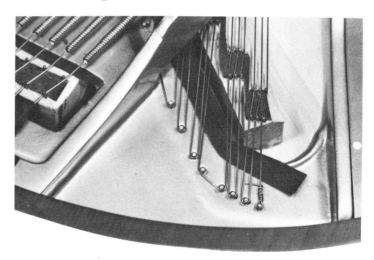

Illus. 7-10 Always sketch odd stringing patterns, such as this one in a Cable grand, to remember how to restring properly.

If the piano has a duplex scale, and if the aliquots do not have guide pins which fit into holes in the plate, mark the position of each aliquot with a tiny scratch on the plate. If the plate will be regilded, cut pieces of masking tape the size and shape of the aliquots, and stick them to the plate exactly where the aliquots were. After the plate is sprayed, remove the tapes, and the masked areas will show exactly where to replace the aliquots.

Removing the Tuning Pins

Check each tuning pin, and clip off any excess wire still attached to it which might scratch the plate when the pin is unscrewed.

The quickest way to remove tuning pins is with a half-inch variable speed reversible electric drill, with a special tuning lever tip made for insertion in a drill chuck. A smaller electric drill is not recommended; it will wear out rapidly if subjected to the torque involved.

Avoid any sideways pressure on the tuning pins, which will enlarge the holes in the pinblock. Lift the drill with the pin as the pin unscrews, to prevent the weight of the drill from pushing downward on the pin.

Illus. 7-11 Removing tuning pins with a half-inch reversible variable speed drill, after the strings are removed.

Illus. 7-12

If a large variable speed, reversible electric drill is not available, use a hand brace with a drill-chuck tuning lever tip.

Note the length of the tuning pins and measure their diameter with micrometer or tuning pin gauge. If any of the pins were previously replaced with oversize pins, note their size and position on the plate or a pattern. (If the pins are in good condition, save them; although they will be replaced with larger pins, they might be useful for restringing another piano in the future.)

Removing the Plate

Before removing the plate, sketch its shape on a piece of cardboard about 16" (about 40 cm) square. Then, as each plate screw is removed, screw it into the cardboard in a position corresponding to its actual location in the plate, for future reference.

Illus. 7-13 Storing the screws in a piece of cardboard.

Unscrew the plate over the pinblock first. Then remove the nose bolt nuts, and the screws around the rim (in a grand) or sides and bottom of the cabinet (in a vertical). With the help of several strong friends (or a block and tackle attached securely to one of the main I-beams of the building), lift the plate straight out of the piano. In a vertical, it is usually necessary to lift the plate enough to clear the bridges, and then slip it out the top of the cabinet. Do not drag it along the bridges! Although a plate weighs as much as several hundred pounds, treat it carefully. Dropping a plate even a few inches may cause it to crack.

CABINET AND FRAME

Inspect the body of the piano for loose or unglued joints. Because of the construction of the grand piano, it is uncommon for the rim or frame members to come loose. It is not uncommon, however, to find the lower or upper back beam loose in old vertical pianos. To repair loose frame parts in an old vertical, clean out as much glue as possible from the old joint, fill the crack with white glue, Titebond or epoxy, and pull together as tightly as possible with large C clamps, pipe or bar clamps. Remove excess glue. Whenever possible, insert large screws to help prevent the joint from separating again in the future.

Occasionally, the pinblock in a ¾ plate upright is partially separated and pulled forward from the back beam. If the pinblock is still good enough to hold the piano in tune, and if the piano is worth repairing, take it apart, remove the lag screws which originally held the pinblock to the back, and drill the holes all the way through. Remove as much sawdust as possible. Replace each lag screw with a large bolt and washer, countersinking the hole in the back deep enough to accept a washer and nut so they will not stick out. If the piano originally had only three lag screws, add an extra bolt between each of the original holes, for a total of five bolts. Insert the bolts, pour glue into the crack, and draw the nuts as tight as possible without cracking anything. Remove excess glue.

THE SOUNDBOARD

The soundboard should be rebuilt if it is cracked or loose from the ribs. Prior to rebuilding, it should be dried out as thoroughly as possible to help prevent it from cracking again after it is rebuilt. If possible, the drying period should be spread over a period of several months or longer, during which time the humidity should be lowered gradually. This will allow the wood to shrink gradually, spreading the strain over a larger area than if it dries suddenly. Gradual drying will reduce the number and size of the cracks. If a piano is moved from a humid climate to a very dry one, however, after it dries over a long period of time the soundboard should be heated to drive out all remaining excess moisture to prevent it from cracking again after it is repaired. Place two heat lamps about four feet from the board for 24 hours a day for a week. If the surrounding air is humid, keep the board warm during rebuilding.

When removing the damper guide rails from a grand soundboard, mark their positions carefully for precise reassembly.

Illus. 7-14 Showing soundboard broken loose from ribs.

Inspect the back of the board along each rib to find places where it is loose. They usually occur along each crack in the board. Wherever the board is loose from a rib, drill a ¼" hole about ⅝" (16 mm) from the crack, all the way through the board and rib. To keep the wood from splintering, drill from the front and have an assistant hold a block of soft wood against the back of the rib. When the bit comes through the rib and goes into the block, the block will keep the wood fibers of the rib from splitting. When all necessary holes are drilled, remove the sawdust. Obtain a number of bolts small enough to slip through the holes and long enough to go through the soundboard and rib and extend about ½" (about 15 mm). For each bolt, obtain one nut and two fender washers. (A fender washer is about 2" (5 cm) in diameter with a small hole).

Illus. 7-15 Mark location of ribs with small strips of paper, and drill through soundboard and rib from the front.

Illus. 7-16 An assistant should hold a block of wood behind rib during drilling to prevent splintering of wood when drill breaks through.

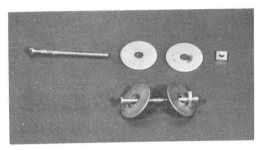

Illus. 7-17 Simple soundboard clamp made of bolt, nut and two fender washers.

Wherever the board is loose, work a moderate amount of Titebond glue between it and the rib with a fingernail file or other thin metal strip. Insert the bolt with one washer on each side of the board, and tighten the nut to clamp the glue joint together. Remove excess glue. When dry, remove all bolts. Make a plug for each hole from a piece of

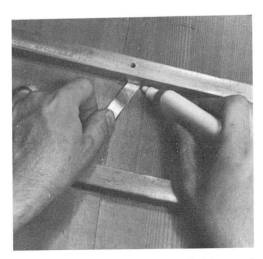

Illus. 7-18 Working glue into space with thin metal strip.

¼" dowel rod a little longer than the combined thickness of the soundboard and rib. Knurl with a shank knurler or by rolling it under the edge of a large file. Coat the plug with a thin layer of glue, swab the inside of the hole with glue, and pound the plug into the hole from the front until the back end is flush with the back of the rib. Leave the excess plug sticking up from the surface of the soundboard.

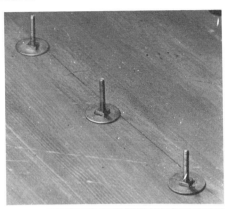

Illus. 7-19 Rear and front views of bolts in place.

Illus. 7-20 An alternate method; temporarily insert screw through soundboard into rib to draw the two together.

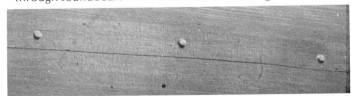

Illus. 7-21 Bolts or screws removed and dowels glued in holes.

If the soundboard is loose around the edges, drill a screw hole at each loose spot, work glue into the joint, and screw it together. Countersinking the screw and hiding it with a dowel plug is not recommended because a future technician may wish to remove the soundboard and will not realize that the screw is there.

Under the middle of the soundboard, insert wedges between the ribs and back beams, to force excess crown into the board.

The next step is to fill the cracks with wedge shaped spruce *soundboard shims*. With a V-shaped soundboard shimming chisel or roller, open each crack as uniformly as possible so the width of the crack is the same from one end to the other. The purpose of the chisel or roller is not to cut wood fibers away but rather to separate the fibers into a relatively straight V-shaped slot. Cut a shim to the length of the crack with a coping saw, and test its fit. Do not press it too firmly into the crack, or part of it may become lodged in the crack and break off. Open the crack until the shim fits as perfectly as possible, without any gaps. If necessary, cut the shim into several sections, to compensate for variations in depth of the crack. Do not open a crack any wider or deeper than necessary; the larger the crack, the harder it is to fit the shim. Warm the shim and soundboard, coat the shim with hot glue and pound it into the crack. Repeat for each crack in the soundboard. The shims will not all go into the wood the same amount, due to variations in the original cracks and the amount they were opened.

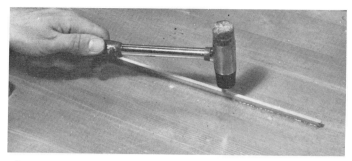

Illus. 7-24 Tapping shim into crack after coating shim with glue.

Illus. 7-25 Shim and dowels ready for trimming after glue dries.

When all cracks are shimmed and dry, remove the wedges from between the back of the soundboard and beams. The board will settle a little, losing some of its crown, and compressing the shims tightly. Plane the shims and the protruding ends of the dowel plugs with a block plane. (Before planing, double check to be sure that there are no screws coming through from the back, which may have been installed by a previous technician).

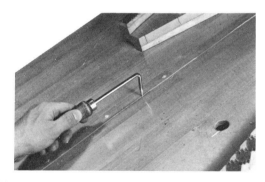

Illus. 7-22 Spreading the crack with a shimming chisel.

Illus. 7-23 Showing a triangular-shaped shim ready to be fitted.

Illus. 7-26 Trimming shim and dowels with block plane.

130

Illus. 7-27 Sanding shims with straight-line reciprocating sander.

Illus. 7-28 A completed repair.

If the soundboard is cracked under the bridge, shim from the back, and add two screws through the back of the soundboard into the bridge, with soundboard buttons. At this time, make all necessary bridge repairs.

Repairing Large Cracks and Damaged Areas

If an old crack is too wide to be repaired with a shim, the damaged portion of the board will have to be cut away and replaced with a new strip of spruce. This operation requires a router and a table saw with tilting blade. Obtain a piece of old soundboard with the same grain configuration as the surrounding area of the board. Lightly tack a wooden straightedge parallel to the crack and at the proper distance from it so a router may be used to cut the old wood away, using the straightedge as a guide. Insert a tapered bit in the router, set its depth to cut through the soundboard but not into the ribs, and carefully cut a slot in the board along the crack. Repeat the operation for the other side of the crack, making certain that the two cuts are parallel. Insert

a veneer cutting blade in a table saw, and set it to the same angle as the side of the router bit. Cut a strip of spruce of the same width as the slot in the soundboard, and glue in place.

Filling Soundboard Cracks With Epoxy

An easier but more noticeable way to fill soundboard cracks, providing they are not too wide, is with a mixture of spruce sawdust and epoxy. Reglue and dowel all loose spots in the board, but do not sand the old varnish off yet. Lay the board flat, and apply masking tape along the bottom of each crack. Make a batch of spruce sawdust by sanding an old piece of spruce. Mix a small amount of amber or clear epoxy, *not* the quick drying variety, and mix in as much sawdust as possible. Before the mixture hardens, pour and work it into the cracks. When dry, remove the masking tape, and sand the soundboard. The excess epoxy will sand off with the old varnish.

Refinishing the Soundboard

Remove the old finish by scraping carefully with a broad (1" or wider) chisel or scraper. Do not allow the corner of the tool to dig in and scratch the wood. Scratches will be magnified, not concealed, by the new finish. After scraping, sand the board with increasingly finer sandpaper, either by hand or with a straight line reciprocating sander. Always sand with the grain, and do not use an orbital sander, which will scratch the wood across the grain. Use 7/0 garnet paper for final sanding.

After all varnish is removed from the surface of the wood, there will still be traces of old shellac in the pores. If the board is varnished in this condition, the shellac residue will show up as unattractive dark stripes. To reduce striping, bleach the soundboard carefully with a two part wood bleach (such as "Dexall" or "Blanchit") available from a paint supply store. Use rubber gloves, and apply the bleach with a cellulose sponge. Do not bleach a soundboard in direct sunlight; the sun will add to the bleaching action, leaving dark areas where there were shadows. Allow the board to dry. If desired, apply a weak coat of yellow aniline stain, not oil stain, to enrich the color of the finished board. When dry, rub the board with 4/0 steel wool until smooth. The smoothness of the final finish depends upon the smoothness of the bare wood.

Vacuum away all sawdust. Lightly go over the board with a "tack rag," or a rag slightly dampened with varnish, which will pick up the remaining powder.

Experts agree that varnish is the best finish for soundboards because it remains more flexible after it dries than shellac or lacquer, and does not restrict the vibration of the soundboard as much as the other types of finish do.

When dry, install the damper guide rails (in a grand), aligning them carefully with the marks made when they were removed.

The Soundboard Decal

If the soundboard originally had a decal, it may be replaced or preserved. Hundreds of different decals are available from piano supply houses. Piano decals are not water decals; they are applied with varnish. After the first coat of new varnish applied to the soundboard is completely dry, clean the area where the decal will be with a rag dampened in benzine. Fold one corner of the decal back about ¼" (or 5 mm), and peel the heavy paper backing away from the decal at the corner only. With a camel's hair artist brush, apply tacky varnish to the lettering and gold work of the decal, not the spaces in between. Allow it to dry for about five minutes or until tacky. Position over the soundboard and apply. The decal must be applied in the right place the first time; sliding it around on the wood more than a fraction of an inch will ruin it. Carefully peel the heavy paper backing off of the decal, starting at the corner previously separated. With a piece of clean dowel rod, roll the air bubbles out of the decal from the center to the top and bottom, until perfectly smooth. Do not allow any varnish to get on the surface of the decal! Leave it for a few days, until the varnish is *completely dry.* Then soak the decal with water, and peel the thin backing away. When dry, give the soundboard two more coats of varnish.

Applying a new decal is a delicate operation. The first time this job is attempted, the technician should order two or three decals in case the first one is spoiled.

If it is desired to preserve the original decal, mask over the decal and a one inch border with a piece of wax paper taped down with masking tape. Sand, bleach and stain the rest of the soundboard, leaving the decal area intact. When the rest of the board is ready to be varnished, remove the masking, and clean the decal area gently with a damp rag, being careful not to damage the decal. Then varnish the entire board, decal and all.

Illus. 7-29 Andrew Nicholas shows a new spruce soundboard ready for installation in a 9' concert grand Mason & Hamlin piano at the Aeolian-American factory.

THE BRIDGES

For ease of tuning and equalization of string tension, the top of each bridge should have as little friction as possible. Regraphite the top of both bridges by rubbing with the alcohol-graphite paste described on p. 116.

Loose Bass Bridge or Apron

If any part of the bass bridge assembly is cracked or loose, it must be removed from the soundboard. Remove the screws from the back of the soundboard. If necessary, drill a hole through the back beam to gain access to the screw. The entire bridge assembly will sometimes fall off. If not, apply acetic acid or vinegar to loosen the glue. Be very careful not to crack or split the soundboard.

Inspect each part for warpage. If the riser, apron and bridge are all flat, sand them just enough to remove the old glue, and reglue with hot glue or Titebond. If any part is warped, it must be sanded flat. Unfortunately, too much sanding will reduce the height of the bridge and consequently the string downbearing. If any part must be sanded so much that all downbearing is lost, make a new riser or apron out of hard maple. If the bridge is split or cracked where the bridge pins enter it, repair it (see p. 93) or send it to a piano supply company for duplication. Reglue and screw the bridge assembly to the soundboard.

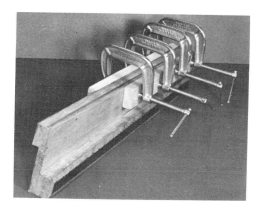

Illus. 7-30 Repairing a loose bass bridge apron.

Split Treble Bridge Cap

Repair with epoxy; or, if badly split, replace the cap. Having a treble bridge or cap duplicated is expensive, so prior to replacing the cap, weigh the cost against the potential value of the instrument.

Remove the screws going into the bridge from the back of the soundboard. Separate the bad section of the cap from the good section, by cutting through the cap with a fine-tooth back saw held at a right angle to the length of the bridge and at a 45° angle from the vertical. Remove the cap from the rest of the bridge carefully. Use a chisel or sharpened putty knife, dilute acetic acid or heat lamp as necessary, to remove it in one piece, and send the old cap to a piano supply house for duplication. Plug the old bridge pin holes in the main body of the bridge with shoe pegs, little wooden pegs which are available from well-equipped shoe repair shops. Glue them in place and sand off flush. Fit the replacement cap carefully to the old bridge, drill and countersink several screw holes, glue and screw in place. Drill the bridge pin holes into the body of the bridge, using the holes in the new cap for guides. Hold the drill steady to keep from enlarging the holes; the bridge pins *must* fit tightly to prevent false beats. Install new bridge pins of proper size, and file the ends flat with a medium file or portable belt sander.

Cracked Single Piece Treble Bridge

If a single piece treble bridge (without a cap) is split so badly that it can not be repaired with epoxy, the entire bridge must be removed from the soundboard and sent to a piano supply company for duplication. This is a very difficult job which should be attempted only by someone who has adequate experience and skill to chisel the old bridge off without damaging the soundboard. (In some cases, however, when a bridge is badly cracked, the old glue is so loose that the bridge almost falls off the soundboard). Mark the original position of the bridge carefully. An offset soundboard bridge chisel is handy, as the blade rests flatly on the soundboard with the handle in the air. If any slivers of soundboard wood come off with the bridge, cut them off of the bridge with a sharp knife, and reglue them to the soundboard with hot glue.

Make every attempt to repair the old bridge with epoxy before attempting to remove it. If a soundboard is damaged beyond repair by an unsuccessful attempt to remove a bridge, the entire soundboard must be replaced; making and installing soundboards is beyond the scope of this book.

Rusty Bridge Pins

Heat each pin with a soldering iron, without scorching the wood. Grasp the end of the pin firmly with a pliers, twist back and forth until loose, and pull out. Pound new pins of the correct diameter in place, and file the ends flat with a file or portable belt sander.

Broken Bridge Pin

If a bridge pin breaks off and the stump can not be extracted, drill a small hole next to the broken pin so the stump may be worked sideways and removed. Plug the extra hole with wood or epoxy, and insert the new pin in the original position.

THE PINBLOCK
Should the Pinblock be Replaced?

The old block may probably be re-used, if no cracks, splits or loose laminations are visible, providing that larger tuning pins can be used. Removing the old tuning pins always enlarges the holes a little, requiring the new pins to be larger. If the old pins were the largest available size, or if the block is cracked or split, it must be replaced.

Fitting a Grand Pinblock

In order for a piano to stay in tune for a reasonable length of time, the pinblock must fit snugly with the plate so the two act like one piece in the piano. Fitting a new pinblock to a plate is a time-consuming but important procedure. For the rebuilt piano to have a long life of tuning stability, always fit a new block carefully.

Remove the original block. In most grands, it may be unscrewed and lifted out of the rim once the plate is removed. In many Steinways and some Victorian grands, however, the pinblock is mortised and glued into the rim, and dowelled around its perimeter into the cabinet. Removing such a pinblock requires careful sawing and chiselling, and should not be attempted until the technician is experienced in fitting regular pinblocks. When ordering a new block, there are two alternatives. The old block may be sent to a piano supply company, or in some cases, to the manufacturer, who will return a "rough cut" replacement block. Or, if the technician has access to a table saw, band saw and planer, an uncut pin block blank may be purchased and may be rough cut in the shop.

Lay the plate upside down on two sawhorses. If it had tuning pin bushings, punch them out with a bushing punch or with a hammer and dowel rod of appropriate diameter.

Rub the plate flange with blue chalk. Lay the pinblock blank in place and tap it toward the plate with a mallet until all high spots on the block are colored with chalk. Remove the block. Cut down all high spots carefully, removing just a little wood at a time with a hammer and chisel, spoke shave or wood rasp. Replace the block on the plate in its exact previous position. Repeat the entire procedure, adding chalk to the plate when necessary, until the entire surface area of the pinblock is covered with chalk when removed from the plate,

Illus. 7-32 Applying blue chalk to plate flange.

Illus. 7-33 After clamping block at its narrowest point to the flange, the technician prepares to tap the leading edge of the block toward the flange in order for the chalk to indicate the high spots.

Illus. 7-31 The photographs in this sequence are of Andrew Boisvert fitting a pinblock to a new Knabe piano in the East Rochester (N.Y.) factory of the Aeolian-American Corporation. In this picture we see a pinblock as would be supplied to a technician by a piano supply house.

134

showing that it makes solid contact throughout. It is important that the edge of the block make good contact with the plate flange, because this area bears much of the string tension.

Illus. 7-34 *Left:* Inspecting edge of pinblock for high spots revealed by chalk; *Center:* Coarse removal using a hammer and chisel; *Right:* The technician uses a spoke shave for more delicate work as the shaping progresses.

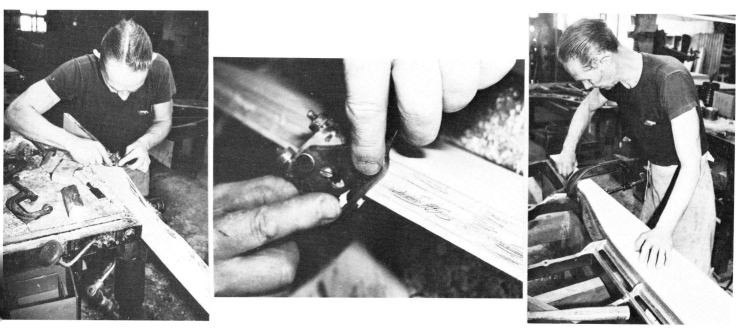

Illus. 7-35 *Left and center:* Further use of the spoke shave; *Right:* After removing, shaping and replacing the pinblock numerous times as shown in this sequence of pictures, the technician makes final inspection for close fit.

Illus. 7-36 Coating the pinblock with shellac prior to final fastening to plate.

Illus. 7-37 Clamping pinblock to plate prior to drilling plate screw holes.

Illus. 7-38 Drilling the plate screw holes.

Clamp the pinblock tightly to the plate with several large C clamps, and mark and drill the holes for the screws which attach the block to the plate. Insert and tighten the screws.

Illus. 7-39 Fastening the pinblock to the plate.

Lay the plate and pinblock in the piano. If necessary, cut the ends of the new block to leave a small gap between each end and the rim of the piano, to allow for proper fit in case of future expansion caused by an increase in humidity. If the ends of the old block were screwed into the rim, locate and drill the holes in the new block very carefully. Remove all sawdust, and screw the pinblock and plate into the piano.

Drilling the Tuning Pin Holes

The tuning pins must all lean uniformly toward the keyboard at a 7° angle. There are two ways of drilling the holes to achieve this angle: using a hand-held electric drill, or a drill press. Prior to drilling, clamp a flat board to the bottom of the section being drilled, to keep the drill bit from splitting the wood when it breaks through the bottom.

To drill a new block with a hand electric drill, attach a round leveling "bubble" to the handle, for guidance. This should be adjusted accurately so the bubble is centered when the drill is held exactly at a 7° angle. Center punch the tuning pin hole centers, using the plate holes as guides. Obtain a .271″ brad point tuning pin drill (for 2/0 tuning pins) from a piano supply house. The brad point will keep the drill from wandering sideways. With the drill turning at a low speed, feed it into the wood slowly to prevent overheating. Use the bubble as a guide to keep the drill at a 7° angle. Overheating will expand the bit, making some of the holes larger than others; it will also char the wood, making the inside of the hole shiny. Shiny tuning pin holes cause the pins to squeak or jump during tuning.

Illus. 7-40 Brad point pinblock drill.

To drill a pinblock with a drill press, leave the plate and pinblock screwed to the piano as when drilling with a hand drill. Mount a table model drill press on a wooden base which rests at a 7° angle. Lay a new double-width pinblock blank or other *flat* piece of wood across the piano, and slide the drill press on this board from one tuning pin hole to the next.

Illus. 7-41 Drilling the tuning pin holes with a drill press inclined at a 7° angle.

Drilling an Open Face Pinblock

If the piano has an open face pinblock (in which the plate does not cover the tuning pin area of the block), a template for locating the proper positions of the tuning pin holes must be made. After rough-cutting and fitting the new block, with the plate screwholes drilled, remove the block from the piano. If the old block is in bad enough condition, it may be possible to chisel the top lamination off. Lay the top lamination of the old block on the new one, and use it to locate and center punch the tuning pin holes. If it is not possible to use the old lamination for a pattern, it will be necessary to make a paper pattern. Cut a piece of brown package wrapping paper to the exact shape of the top of the old pinblock, and tape it down around the edges. Rub over each hole with the side of a sharp pencil, as in making a coin rubbing. The holes will show up as light spots with black outlines on the rubbing. Remove the pattern and tape it to the top of the new block. Center punch the position of each hole through the pattern, remove the pattern, and drill the block as described above.

Illus. 7-42 Making a paper pattern of an open face pinblock. This pattern is then taped over the new block and the holes are center punched through the pattern.

Replacing a Vertical Pinblock

To replace a vertical pinblock, major cabinet work must be performed. Break the pinblock loose from the back beam and soundboard. If it is necessary to split or damage anything, split the old pinblock rather than any other parts which must be reused. Clean all splinters and glue from the back so the new block will make good contact. Obtain a new rough cut block of the proper thickness, cut it to the exact length of the old block, and fit it in place. Fitting a vertical block is more difficult than a grand, because it should fit snugly to the back beam, the top of the soundboard, the plate flange and back face of the plate, all at once. When the plate is the correct height over the soundboard for proper string downbearing, it must fit flatly on the pinblock without rocking. Because of the difficulty of this job, it should not be attempted until the technician gains extensive experience in cabinet making and grand pinblock replacement.

When the block is shaped properly, glue it to the back. Screw the plate into the piano. Locate and drill the plate screwholes in the pinblock; screw the plate to the pinblock. Mark and drill the tuning pin holes.

Fitting a Pinblock with Fiberglass Resin

Although the best way to insure good contact between the plate flange and pinblock is by careful fitting of the block, some rebuilders advocate the use of fiberglass resin to fill any gaps which might be present after the piano is ready to string. See p. 92.

THE PLATE

If the plate was installed for the fitting of a new pinblock, remove it. Make all necessary repairs. Replace broken agraffes. If the capo bar of a grand plate, or the upper plate bridge of a vertical plate is grooved, file it just enough to remove the grooves. Remember that removing metal from a grand capo bar *reduces* down bearing, while removing metal from a vertical plate bridge *increases* it. Maintain the original shape; do not make it too flat or pointed.

Cleaning and Gilding

Remove the old felt. If the tuning pin bushings have not already been removed, punch them out with a mallet and dowel rod. Scrub both sides of the plate with a scrub brush and detergent; rinse well.

Obtain one or two large aerosol cans of metallic gold spray lacquer (depending on the size of the plate), and one can of clear spray lacquer, preferably of the same brand. "Bright gold" or "Metallic gold" matches most old plates; "Antique gold" usually is a richer orange color similar to many Japanese piano plates. Check the label to see that the material is actually *lacquer*. Many aerosol cans which are labelled "spray finish," "spray enamel," or even "spray lacquer" actually contain acrylic, which does not build up to a glossy finish like lacquer does. Spray the top side of the plate with several thin coats of gold, followed by several coats of clear. When dry, paint the raised lettering with gloss black enamel and a small artist brush.

Illus. 7-43 As this book is written, there is a distinct possibility that aerosol propellants may be banned, in which case conventional spraying equipment will have to be used. In the absence of a spray booth, this work should be done out-of-doors.

Repairing a Cracked Plate

If the crack is in a place where a steel brace may be fitted and bolted to hold the parts in position, a successful repair might be made. When deciding on the position of the brace, the technician should consult someone with some mechanical engineering ability who can analyze the best placement of the brace to support the stress.

Although it is possible to weld cast iron, it is doubtful that a welded plate will withstand the enormous tension exerted by the strings when they are pulled up to pitch. If the crack is in a place where bracing is impossible, having the plate welded will probably be a waste of time. For every welder who "could fix that crack so it will *never* come apart again" there is a piano technician who has seen one that did.

If the plate can not be repaired, it might be possible to obtain a replacement from an identical piano, or from the factory, if the model is still in production.

Installing the Plate

The plate must be installed at exactly the correct height for proper string down bearing.

Put the plate in the piano. It should lie flat on all supports without rocking. Screw it down with one screw at each corner, using the correct screw for each hole.

Check the bearing. Make a test "string" by tying a hitch pin loop in the end of a piece of fishline. Loop the "string" over the hitch pin, thread it over the bridge, agraffe, capo bar or plate bridge, pull it tight, and tie or tape the end down. A bearing gauge will give a fairly close idea of what the final bearing will be, providing that the "string" is not deflected by pressing on it with the outside foot of the gauge. Check the bearing at each of several test points.

There should be slightly more bearing now than after the piano is fully strung and raised to pitch, when the string tension will force the board down a little.

If the bearing is inadequate, the height of the dowels in a grand, or shims in a vertical, must be reduced by sanding or planing. Remove only a little wood at a time until bearing is correct, with the plate resting simultaneously on all supports. If necessary, screw the nose bolt in so the plate just touches it without rocking.

When the bearing is correct with the plate resting evenly on all supports, screw it down.

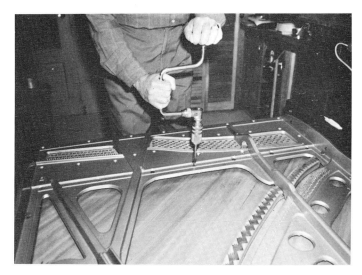

Illus. 7-45 Screwing the plate down with a hand brace and screwdriver bit.

RESTRINGING
Tools Needed

Restringing tools include the usual string repairing tools (see p. 94) plus a tuning pin crank, tuning pin punch, coil winder, bushing punch, tuning pin height gauge, small sledge hammer (not a ball peen, claw or other hammer which might chip), pair of leather gloves, pinblock support jack (for grands) and, in some cases, a pinblock reamer.

Illus. 7-46 Restringing tools. The leather gloves are recommended for people who have a tendency toward heavy perspiration, which causes rust.

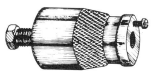

Illus. 7-47 The coil winder, used with the tuning pin crank for winding neat coils of wire on the tuning pin prior to driving the pin into the pinblock.

NOTE	PIANO SIZE				
	5'10" Brand A	another 5'10" Brand A	5'7½" Brand A	5'8" Brand B	5'2" Brand C
C8	.022	.051	.023	.032	.055
C6	.025	.015	.015	.030	.040
E 4	.018	.005	.015	.015	.015
Bass end of treble bridge	.015	.002	.010	.043	xxx
Treble end of bass bridge	.020	.030	.023	.024	.020
A1	.020	.051	.032	.026	.026

Illus. 7-44 String downbearing in various new grand pianos, measured in thousandths of an inch with feeler gauge and bearing gauge, as illustrated on p. 122.

Determining the Correct Size of the New Tuning Pins

If the piano still has its old pinblock, the size of the new pins is determined by the tightness of the original pins. If the old pins were uniformly tight, use new pins one size larger. If the old pins were uniform but barely tight enough to hold the piano in tune, use new pins two sizes larger. If the old pins were quite loose, and the holes in the block are deep enough, use pins two sizes larger and ⅛" longer.

Size	Dia.
1/0 x 2" 1/0 x 2½"	.276
2/0 x 2¼" 2/0 x 2⅜" 2/0 x 2½"	.282
3/0 x 2¼" 3/0 x 2⅜" 3/0 x 2½"	.286
4/0 x 2¼" 4/0 x 2⅜" 4/0 x 2½"	.291
5/0 x 2¼" 5/0 x 2⅜ 5/0 x 2½"	.296
6/0 x 2¼" 6/0 x 2⅜" 6/0 x 2½"	.301

Illus. 7-48 Tuning pin sizes.

The Use of the Reamer

Pinblock reamers for use in an electric drill are available in various sizes, one for each diameter of tuning pin. The use of the reamer is controversial, with some technicians claiming that it is neither necessary nor desirable. In the opinion of the author, the tuning pins will be of more uniform tightness if a reamer is used. However, careless reaming is worse than none at all. If the loosest old pins were fairly tight, use a reamer and pins one size larger; if the old pins were very loose, use a reamer and pins two sizes larger.

Illus. 7-49 A pinblock reamer.

Restringing Procedure

Replace the hitch pin punchings and understring felt, if originally present. Glue the latter to the plate with burnt shellac or the smallest possible amount of glue from a hot glue gun. Place the aliquots, if present, in their correct positions.

Wear leather gloves while stringing, not only to protect the hands, but also to protect the strings and tuning pins from perspiration and skin oils.

If the decision has been made to ream the holes, ream only one or two at a time to keep the reamer from overheating and charring the holes. Keep the reamer handy during stringing, and ream a few holes in advance of the new pins before pounding them in.

If the plate had wooden tuning pin bushings, measure the thickness of the plate at the tuning pin area, and obtain a set of bushings of the same *thickness*. All sizes of bushings have the same diameter. After each hole is reamed, pound the bushing all the way in with a dowel rod or plate bushing punch and hammer until it stops on the pinblock. If no reaming is performed, insert all bushings at once. Bushings are larger in diameter than most plate tuning pin holes, but they compress as they go in, if driven squarely.

Illus. 7-50 Driving tuning pin bushings in place, as done at the factory. These are available in various lengths, to suit various plate thicknesses.

When pounding plate bushings or tuning pins into a grand, a pinblock support jack *must be used*. This is placed between the keybed and pinblock to prevent the pinblock or plate from cracking. In an upright, the pinblock is supported by the back beam, so no support jack is necessary.

Before starting, attach a piece of masking tape to each hitch pin where the wire size changes. These serve as reminders to change to the next larger size during stringing.

In all pianos, the treble section of strings is installed first (as opposed to the overstrung bass section). Most right handed technicians prefer to hold the hammer in the right hand, in which case it is more convenient to go from right to left, starting in the extreme treble in a grand and the low tenor in a vertical. (Because the vertical piano is strung while laying on its back, the high notes are on the left.) Most "lefties" prefer to string from left to right, holding the hammer in the left hand.

Decide where to start, and determine the wire diameter by referring to the chart made during unstringing. Unwind enough wire from the coil for the entire string plus a little excess. Insert a new tuning pin in the coil winder, and insert the end of the wire into the pin so the wire is flush with the surface of the pin. If the wire sticks out the job will look sloppy; if it doesn't go all the way through the pin, it may slip out of the hole later. Adjust the height of the tuning pin in the coil winder so the string lines up with the guide screw. With the tuning pin crank, turn the pin clockwise 2½ times to turn as many neat coils on the pin. Remove it from the winder, and apply a little powdered chalk to prevent corrosion from perspiration. Pound the pin into the pinblock with a hammer and tuning pin punch, using the cardboard

pin height gauge made prior to unstringing the piano (See p. 125). In most pianos, each pin has about ³/₁₆" (5 mm) space between the bottom coil and the plate after the string is brought up to pitch. The punch will keep the hammer from battering the top of the pin.

Tuning pins should be *driven*, rather than *turned* all the way in, because the driving process roughens the wood and increases the friction. Turning the pins smooths the wood, decreasing the ultimate tightness.

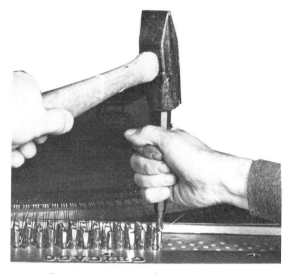

Illus. 7-52 Driving in the tuning pin.

Thread the string through the agraffe (if present) and across the bridge. Pull it tight and bend it around the hitch pin. Thread the remaining portion across the bridge and lay it next to its tuning pin hole. Measure 3" (75 mm) beyond the hole, and cut the string from the coil. Thread the string through the agraffe (if present) and wind 2½ coils onto another tuning pin, with the winder and crank. Pound the pin in, using the height gauge for a guide.

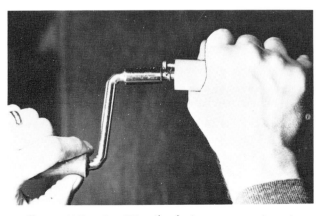

Illus. 7-51 Turning 2½ coils of wire onto a tuning pin.

Illus. 7-53 Adding tension to the string after both pins are in place.

When both pins are in place, snug each coil with the coil lifter, and turn each pin clockwise to add *just enough* string tension to hold the coil in position, with a tuning pin tip in a ratchet socket wrench or a regular tuning lever. Squeeze the becket with pliers, as illustrated.

Illus. 7-54 Tightening the becket, or bend in the wire where it enters the pin.

Repeat the procedure for all treble strings. Observe and follow any odd stringing arrangements indicated on the stringing pattern, such as single treble strings tied to their hitch pins, strings which skip a hitch pin, and strings which go around two hitch pins.

String the bass in the same direction that the treble was strung. Hitch each string on its hitch pin, thread it over the bridge and plate spacer pin, and cut the new end off 3" (75 mm) beyond the pin hole. Wind a tuning pin on the end of the wire, twist the string one full turn in the direction of the winding to inhibit the winding from coming loose in the future, and pound the pin in. Add just enough tension to hold the coil in place, but do not pull the string up to pitch yet. Install new stringing braid wherever it was used originally, by threading it over and under alternate strings, and secure each end by doubling it back over itself.

Installing the Pressure Bar in a Vertical

If the back of the pressure bar is grooved, file it smooth, maintaining the original curve. If the front is pitted or corroded, clean it with fine steel wool and spray it with a few coats of metallic silver or aluminum aerosol spray lacquer followed with a few coats of clear, or have it replated.

Start all of the pressure bar screws in the same holes from which they were removed. Turn them all down snug, with the bar resting on the loose strings. Then, tighten the bar to its original height using the cardboard height gauge. The bar should deflect the strings downward from the upper plate bridge about 4°. Go back and forth from one screw to the other, tightening each a little at a time, to keep the bar level and to distribute the pressure evenly across all screws. If the pressure bar is too high, the strings will slip sideways; if it is too low, the strings will be bent too much, making the piano hard to tune.

Chipping the Piano

The newly strung piano does not yet have an action, and the strings are not necessarily aligned with the hammers (unless the piano has agraffes throughout the treble,) so the initial tunings are done by plucking the strings with a small chip of wood (hence the term "chipping").

Unless the technician has a good sense of perfect or relative pitch, (the ability to remember what each note sounds like without using a pitch reference), he should use a pitch pipe, another piano, or an electronic tuning aid as a reference when chipping.

Raising the pitch of a newly strung piano is done slowly so the added tension is distributed evenly all across the plate. The down bearing pressure of the strings on the soundboard should also be applied in the proper sequence, to keep the soundboard from developing dead spots. Begin chipping at the bottom of the high treble section, going up to note 88, followed by the lowest unwrapped strings up to the bottom of the high treble, and then note 1 up to

Illus. 7-55 Aligning the strings to the hammers. For purposes of illustration, the piano action has been removed.

the highest bass note. During the first chipping, raise the strings to about an octave below their correct pitch. At this point, install the action, and align the treble strings with the hammers, using a string spacer. Force the spacer down over the strings, and tap it sideways with a small hammer until the strings are aligned with the hammers. Remove the action. Squeeze each string at the hitch pin with pliers, to make both sections of the wire parallel. Then tap each string where it goes around the hitch pin to seat it on the plate. Repeat the chipping procedure until the piano is no more than a half step below pitch. Replace the action (including the dampers, in a grand), make any final string spacing adjustments which may be necessary, and tune the piano. It usually takes two or three chippings, followed by two or three tunings, before a piano will still be in tune by the time the tuning is completed. New strings will continue to stretch for several months of hard use, or for up to several years if not played much. The more often a piano is tuned during this initial stretching period, the sooner it will stay in tune for longer periods of time.

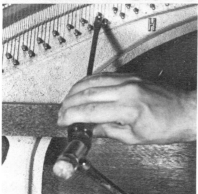

Illus. 7-56 Pinching the strings parallel (top) and tapping the loop to seat it on the plate (bottom) hasten tuning stability.

Restringing a Baldwin with Acu-just Hitch Pins

For a description of these hitch pins, refer to p. 13. The technician should send the model and serial number of the piano to the Baldwin Piano and Organ Company, requesting specific restringing instructions.

DETERMINING THE SIZE OF A MISSING TREBLE STRING

In some pianos, the wire sizes are stamped on the pinblock, plate or bridge. In others, they are not, but the correct size of a missing treble string sometimes may be determined by an educated guess, based on the sizes of the adjacent strings, and points in the scale where the next smaller and larger sizes begin. All three strings of any unison should be the same size, so if only one string is missing, replace it with the same size wire as the remaining strings of that unison.

Using the Music Wire Formulas

For the mathematically inclined, there are formulas which may be used for computing string tension and the diameter of a missing string. Large numbers are used in these formulas, so a good slide rule or electronic calculator will save time.

Any piano string has the following four properties:

F = Frequency, in cycles per second.
L = Length of the vibrating portion of the string, from the bridge pin to the agraffe, capo bar, or plate bridge, in inches.
W = Grain Weight per inch of music wire.
T = Tension, in pounds.

To find the diameter (weight) of a missing string, its *tension* must be known. To find the correct tension, the tension of the neighboring strings must be determined.

The tension of a string is found by inserting its length, weight and frequency in the tension formula. Measure the length to the nearest hundredth of an inch. Measure the diameter with a micrometer or music wire gauge, and convert into grain weight, using the numbers listed. Look up the frequency on p. 41. Insert the three numbers in this formula, and solve:

$$T = \frac{F^2 L^2 W}{675,356}$$

The answer is the string tension. Find the tension of at least three notes on each side of the missing string to deduce its correct tension.

Measure the length of the vibrating portion of the missing string, and look up its frequency on page 41. Insert the length and frequency, and the average tension of the neighboring strings in the weight formula:

$$W = \frac{675,356\ T}{F^2 L^2}$$

The answer is the grain weight of the missing string. Find its size below.

GRAIN WEIGHT OF MUSIC WIRE

Wire Gauge Size	Weight in Grains per Inch
12½	1.4211
13	1.5125
13½	1.5860
14	1.7143
14½	1.8168
15	1.9351
15½	2.0198
16	2.17565
16½	2.2710
17	2.3809
17½	2.4783
18	2.6075
19	2.7963
20	3.1645
21	3.4259
22	3.78025

Taken from the January 1914 issue of The American Piano and Pipe Organ News

Illus. 7-57 Grain weights of music wire.

For the mathematically inclined technician who is interested in tonal theory and scale design, the music wire formulas are invaluable when evaluating the potential of an old piano in need of restringing, and for improving the quality of a piano which was poorly designed in the first place.

Anyone who has the occasion to measure string tension, or who is interested in the theory of piano scale design, should obtain a copy of "Tension Calculations Made Easy," a copyrighted article by Ladislas Rysy which appeared in the December 1966 "Piano Technicians Journal." It contains complete charts of the logarithms of various string lengths, frequencies and diameters, making possible the computation of string tension by means of simple

addition. Reprints of the eight page article are available for a nominal fee from the home office of the Piano Technician's Guild.

THE KEY FRAME

Remove the old punchings. Clean the wooden parts with fine steel wool if necessary. Clean the key guide pins with silver polish, and spray with silicone. Remove the glides from a grand key frame and polish if necessary.

If the back rail cloth is compressed or worn, replace it. To order new cloth of the correct thickness, measure the old cloth at an unworn spot, such as the end where no keys rest on it.

Replace all cloth punchings with new ones of the original thickness, and place a .01" paper punching under each one. Later, during regulation, set the key height by adding or removing shims under the balance rail, measuring the height of the highest keys. Follow the usual leveling procedure.

THE KEYS
Rebushing Keys

If the old bushings are worn, allowing side play and rattle, the keys should be rebushed. An electric bushing remover is a handy tool for this job. Wet each bushing lightly, and insert the heated tip of the tool. The heat will turn the water into steam, loosening the glue and the bushings. In the absence of an electric bushing remover, a whistling teakettle makes an excellent steam generator. Adjust the heat under it so a minimum amount of steam comes out, and hold the bushing directly over the opening

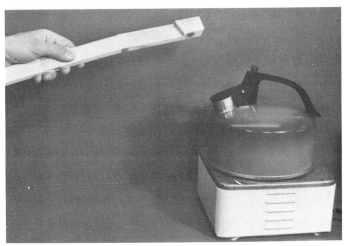

Illus. 7-58 A simple steam generator. Adjust the heat so a small amount of steam comes out.

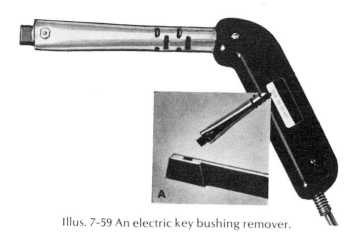

Illus. 7-59 An electric key bushing remover.

Replacing White Key Tops

Since complete sets of ivories are difficult to obtain, keys are recovered with one of two types of key tops: molded plastic tops, and pyralin blanks. Molded key tops are glued in place by hand; for mass production, pyralin blanks are installed with special key covering machines.

Removing the Old White Tops

To remove old ivories, heat with an iron on medium setting for about a minute; then cut them loose with a sharpened 1″ putty knife. It is helpful to insert a damp towel between the iron and the ivory, to keep from drying out the original glue and baking the ivories on even tighter.

To remove old celluloid key tops, brush methelyne chloride around the edges. When the glue softens, pry the plastic up, and brush more solvent into the joint, until the whole piece comes off. Methylene chloride is available from plastic supply companies. Use it with caution, as it is toxic and highly flammable.

Never use heat on celluloid or plastic keys.

for a few seconds. This will loosen the glue enough so the bushing may be removed with a sharp knife. Do not remove any wood. Hold the bushing over the steam for as short a time as possible, to keep the wood from getting soggy.

Obtain a roll of new bushing cloth the same thickness as the old, and a set of key bushing clamps. Cut the cloth into pieces of the proper length, and glue in place with hot glue, clamping as illustrated.

Preparing the Wood Surface

If a wood chip or splinter comes off with an old key top, chisel it from the top, and glue it back to the key. Then sand the key lightly on a belt sander to remove the old glue, being extremely careful not to round the surface or make it crooked. If no belt sander is available, tape a large piece of medium sandpaper to one end of a flat tabletop, and sand as illustrated on p. 105.

As little wood as possible should be sanded from the keys. If the wood is pitted, molded keytops with contact cement should be used. The plastic glue used with pyralin tends to soften and sink the pyralin into any irregularities in the wood surface, resulting in rippled keys.

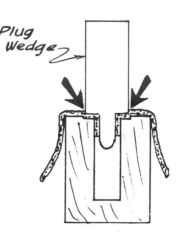

Plug Wedge

Illus. 7-60 *Above:* Spring key bushing clamps. *Right:* Wood plug wedge. The bushing cloth is trimmed where indicated by the arrows.

Installing Molded Key Tops

Remove the action and the black keys from the keyframe, and insert the white keys, after preparing them as described above. Square and space the keys if necessary. (See p. 64.) Clamp a straightedge to the key slip, using wooden shims to bring it up to the level of the key tops. The key tops should overhang 3/32″ (2.5 mm) from the front of the keys; align the straightedge so there is exactly 3/32″ (2.5 mm) space between it and the fronts of the bare key tops. If necessary, weight the keys in front so they will rest in the "down" position. Molded key tops are made in seven different shapes, and each one has the key name molded into the bottom side.

Apply a thin layer of contact cement to the top of the wooden key and the bottom of the appropriate key top, and allow the cement to get tacky, so a piece of writing paper will not stick if lightly touched to it. Align the key top with the key, and press it firmly in place. Be neat! Do not spill glue on the side of the key or keytop. Be sure the keytop is perfectly aligned with the key prior to pressing it in place, because once the contact cement takes hold, no adjustment is possible.

When all the white keys are done, remove the straightedge, and insert the black keys one at a time. File the notches in the white keys as necessary with a medium file.

Installing Pyralin Key Tops

Pyralin key tops are glued on with "pyralin cement" which dissolves the plastic into the pores of the wood, and should be clamped for best results. They are made slightly oversize, and must be trimmed after the glue dries. Although it is possible to use pyralin key tops without any special equipment, it is faster to use molded plastic tops when doing the job by hand. For mass production, however, a set of Oslund key covering machines, for pyralin tops, is recommended.

Prepare each blank key top with the key surfacer. (This is also a handy tool for recovering with molded key tops.) It produces a perfectly flat surface more accurately than when using a belt

sander or when sanding by hand. A flat, smooth key surface is absolutely necessary when using pyralin keytops, because the plastic will sink into pockmarks if the wood is pitted.

Illus. 7-62 Surfacing the key.

Illus. 7-63 Keys before and after surfacing.

Apply a thin coat of pyralin glue to the blank and the key, allow it to soak into the wood a little, and put the key top in place. Insert the key in the key clamp. The multiple key clamp has room for several keys, and by the time the last key is clamped in place, the first one may be removed. In this way, an entire keyboard may be glued without waiting.

Illus. 7-61 Key surfacing machine.

Illus. 7-64 Commercially made multiple key clamp.

146

Illus. 7-65 An inexpensive home-made key clamp, using pedal trap springs.

When the glue has dried overnight, trim the key tops with the key trimmer. (Like the key surfacer, this machine does the job neater and faster than doing it by hand.) Finish the job by rounding the corners and edges neatly with a fine file.

Illus. 7-66 Key trimming machine.

Illus. 7-67 Detail of key trimmer with guide table removed, showing blades.

Illus. 7-68 Trimming the front.

Illus. 7-69 Trimming notch for black key.

Illus. 7-70 Trimming side of key.

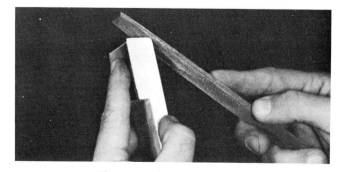

Illus. 7-71 Filing corners.

147

Illus. 7-72 A finished white key.

The Black Keys

If the original sharp keys are smooth, but the black color is worn, they may be painted. Make a jig as illustrated on p. 106, mask the bare wood behind the sharps, and spray with high quality black lacquer.

If the sharps are pitted, chipped or badly worn, they should be replaced. Remove the old sharps carefully with a chisel. Reglue any wood splinters which split from the keys, sand the keys flat, and glue new ebony or plastic sharps in place. Ebony sharps should be glued with Titebond, and clamped. Plastic sharps may be glued with model airplane cement or contact cement. Clean off all excess glue which squeezes out around the edges, and touch up any bare spots on the black wooden part of each key with black stain or an indelible black Magic Marker.

Finishing Touches on the Keys

Repair any capstans which are too loose by plugging and redrilling the holes. Polish the tops of the capstans with silver polish.

Ease the keys if necessary. If they have been rebushed, the bottom center holes will probably be tight, having swollen from the steam. If so, ease them *sideways* but do not enlarge them from front to back.

At this time, inspect the nameboard felt. If it is dirty or worn, replace it with a new piece, using hot glue. It should protrude from the front of the nameboard so it almost touches the back edges of the sharp keys. Self adhesive nameboard felt is available, but is not recommended because it falls off when the weather turns dry, and because the white adhesive shows on the exposed surface behind the sharps.

ACTION REBUILDING

If an action needs extensive repairs, a decision must be made whether to rebuild the old parts or to install new ones. Rebuilding the old parts usually takes longer, but the cost of materials is less. If an action has obsolete parts, it is necessary, of course, to rebuild them. On the other hand, if new parts are available, and if time is at a premium, the technician will have fewer problems if all defective parts are replaced with new ones.

Rebuilding a whole action of old parts is nothing more than an extensive repair job. If a number of parts of the same type are worn out, all parts of that type should be repaired. For example, if half of the jacks in a vertical action are unglued, the rest should be broken loose and the whole set reglued, to avoid having the problem recur.

Rebuilding the Vertical Action with New Parts

Disassemble the action. Number the damper levers and stickers, which will be re-used. The two hammers at each end of each section should also be numbered as they lie in the scale, because these will be used for samples.

To order new hammers, send the first and last hammer from each section to a piano supply house for duplication. Be sure each is numbered as it lies in the scale, and include a chart showing how many hammers are in each section. Specify whether the hammers will be used on the original or new shanks, so the duplicator will know what size to bore them. State if *reinforced* felt is desired (for more long-lived resilience at a slightly higher cost) and the weight of the new hammers. Hammers are made in 12, 14 and 16 lb. weights for small, medium and large pianos, respectively. The weight refers to the weight of a sheet of felt from which several sets of hammers are made, and has nothing to do with quality. For the best tone quality, select new hammers whose weight relates to the size of the piano.

At the same time the new hammers are ordered, send for new butts, whippens, damper flanges (if necessary), damper heads and felts, hammer shanks, and miscellaneous action felts, springs, regulating screws, etc.

Prepare the action frame. Disassemble, clean, replate or paint the action brackets if necessary. Plug and redrill any overdrawn screw holes. Rebush the hammer rail swing holes and damper lift rod hangers if necessary. Polish the damper lift rod. Replace the hammer rail cloth. Replace the regulating screw punchings. If the regulating screws are rusty or hard to turn, replace them and their buttons. Replace the hammer butt springs, and refelt the spring rail, but do not screw it in place yet.

Preparing to Install New Hammers

Screw the new hammer butts to the action rail.

Unwrap the new hammers and number them on the bottom, starting with #1 in the bass, to avoid confusion if they get mixed up. A new set of hammers has several spares; lay aside those at the upper end of the bass section and the last few in the treble.

Prepare each new hammer by placing a pencil dot at the exact center of the striking point. Then prick a tiny hole in each hammer molding with a sharp awl, inserting the awl from the bottom. This hole will let air escape when gluing the hammer to the shank.

Roll each new shank on a flat surface and discard any which are badly warped.

Insert a new shank in each butt, knurling the bottom end with a shank knurler to allow space for the glue. Shank and butt diameters vary; match the shanks to the butts so each shank fits snugly but not too tightly.

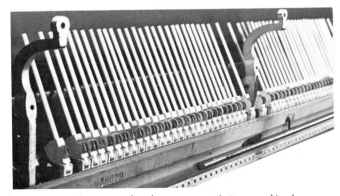

Illus. 7-73 New hammer shanks temporarily inserted in the new butts.

Travel the shanks. First, space the butt flanges so the shank tops are equally spaced at their rest positions against the hammer rail. Then swing each shank forward to see if it veers to one side. An easy way to spot sideways travel is to swing each two adjacent shanks forward simultaneously, and see if the distance between them changes. Insert paper under the appropriate side of each flange until every shank travels in a straight line, perpendicular to the hammer rail. To avoid problems with hammer alignment later, it is important to travel the shanks accurately.

Importance of the Correct Striking Point

One of the most important areas of piano design is the point at which each hammer hits the strings. A vibrating string subdivides itself into many different fractions which vibrate simultaneously to produce partials. Any point at which the vibrating string divides itself is called a *node*. The exact middle of a string is a node for the two vibrating halves; each point which divides a string into thirds is a node for the three vibrating portions, and so on. If a string is struck at one of its nodes, the striking action of the hammer will cancel out the partial which is associated with that node. Thus, if a hammer strikes a string at one sixth of the string length, the resulting tone will have a weak sixth partial. It so happens that the seventh partial and certain other higher partials are quite flat of their corresponding pitches in the musical scale, so the striking point in most pianos is set at somewhere around one seventh of the string length. (The actual measurement deviates somewhat from this theoretically ideal point, particularly in the high treble, because of other factors such as string stiffness which alter the partial series of the string.) In any piano, the tone will be loudest and clearest when the hammers hit the correct striking point, particularly in the high treble. The importance of correct striking point may be demonstrated in a grand piano by loosening the action and sliding it in and out while playing and listening to the tone quality. One point will be found at which the tone is the best; in a piano which has not been altered since it left the factory, this ideal point will correspond with the place where the action is held down by the cheek blocks.

It is very important to maintain the correct striking point when new hammers are fitted. If the old hammers were not the original ones, and were glued on carelessly, experiment with new sample hammers to find the ideal striking point.

Vertical Hammer Installation

Prior to installing the new hammers, certain old hammers must be reinstalled as *temporary guides*.

149

The temporary guides are the second hammer and the second-to-the-last hammer in each section. Their striking points serve as an example for aligning the *new guide hammers* (the first and last in each section). After the new guide hammers are glued in place, the temporary guides are removed, and the new ones become the standard for aligning all of the intermediate hammers.

Mark the exact center of the striking point on each temporary guide hammer, and screw them to the action.

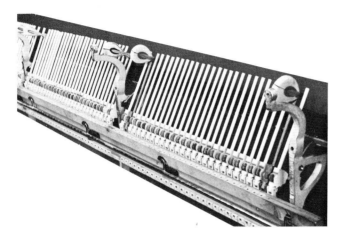

Illus. 7-74 Old guide hammers installed amidst the new butts.

Cut the new shank for hammer #1 in the bass to the proper length. When the hammer head, shank and butt are assembled, and the hammer is aligned with its neighbor (the temporary guide), there should be a little space between the bottom of the shank and the bottom of the butt hole. This space insures that each hammer may be aligned vertically, and gives room for a little excess glue which is pushed into the butt by the shank. The new shank will not necessarily be the same length as the original one because new butts and hammer heads are rarely drilled at the original angle or to the original depth. When a good dry fit is achieved, glue the shank to the head by dipping the end of the shank in hot glue, Titebond, or white glue, inserting it in the hammer head, and twirling the hammer around the shank a few times to distribute the glue. If it is possible to see the grain pattern in the end of the shank, turn it until the grain is parallel with the hammer head. This will help prevent the shanks from breaking. Do not remove the bead of glue from around the shank, as it adds to the strength of the joint.

Dip the other end of the shank into the glue, and insert it in the butt. Before the glue sets, hold an 18"

aluminum or steel straightedge in line with the striking points of *both temporary guide* hammers in the bass section, and move the new #1 hammer up or down until all three hammers form a perfectly straight line.

Repeat the procedure for the last hammer in the bass, making certain that the striking points of all four hammers (the two temporary guides and the two new guides) are perfectly aligned. The new heels need not be aligned with the old ones, but the striking points must be.

Illus. 7-75 New end (guide) hammers glued in place.

After installing all of the new guide hammers, remove the old temporary guides and replace them with new butts and shanks. Then cut all of the shanks to the correct length.

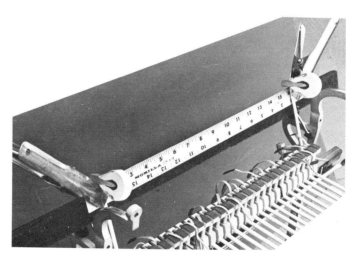

Illus. 7-76 The bass section ready for new hammers.

The action is now ready to have the rest of the hammers installed. Beginning in the bass section, clamp a straightedge to the guide hammer shanks with the top edge of the straightedge touching the bottoms of the two guide hammer tails, as illustrated. This will serve as a guide for aligning the intermediate hammer tails. Push each new bass hammer down on its shank until it touches the straightedge. Check the striking point (indicated by the pencil dot) with another straightedge. In most cases, when the tails form a perfectly straight line, the striking points are irregular. To remedy this, ream each hammer hole with an appropriate drill bit or large round file so the striking point wobbles up and down *just barely enough* to be aligned properly when the tail rests on its straightedge.

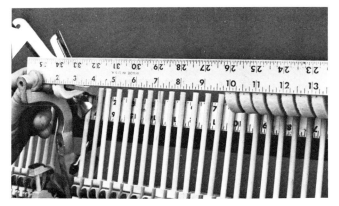

Illus. 7-77 Checking alignment of the new hammers as they are being glued in place.

When each bass hammer has a good dry fit, glue it in place. Push it into the butt until the tail touches the straightedge. Then, before the glue sets, check the striking point with the other straightedge and align the hammer so it forms a perfectly straight line with all other hammers already glued in place. After gluing each hammer, stand back and check it from a different angle, to be sure it is aligned in all planes. When the bass section is done, repeat the operation for the other sections.

Summary

1. Preparation: Install the new butts, number and prick the new hammers, mark their striking points, insert and travel the new shanks.
2. Install the temporary guide hammers.
3. Install the new guide hammers and remove the temporary ones.
4. Install all intermediate hammers, one section at a time.

Because the bass hammers are mounted on an angle, one tail might rub against the next hammer. If so, sand or file the tails where they rub.

If the last few hammers in the low tenor section

Illus. 7-78 Filing the sides of the bass hammer tails if they rub on adjacent hammers.

were originally mounted on a curve, install the rest of the treble hammers which are on a straight line first. Then replace those on the curve, using the old hammers as guides.

To complete the job, shape the new hammers by filing off the outer layer of felt. This is necessary because new hammers are slightly concave across the striking point from one side to the other, and do not always hit all three strings equally. See p. 114 for hammer shaping instructions.

Installing the Dampers

After the hammers have dried, unscrew them from the action and set them aside. After removing the old damper felt and glue from the damper blocks, screw the damper levers in place and put the action in the piano. Coat each new damper felt with hot glue and slip it in place between its block and strings. The damper lever spring will press the lever, and thus the block, against the felt, clamping the glue joint until it dries.

Illus. 7-79 Installing new damper felts.

If the entire damper heads or levers are replaced, screw them in place and bend each one until it damps properly. Then regulate all dampers to lift at the same time when the sustaining pedal is depressed.

Final Assembly

Remove the action from the piano. On the bench, install the spring rail and screw the hammers in place. Lay the old stickers in order, and divide the set of new whippens into those with spoons pointing to the left, to the right, and those without spoons. Pin the appropriate whippens to the old stickers, and attach them to the action. Secure the bridle tapes to the bridle wires, and the new action is ready for regulating.

Installing New Vertical Piano Hammers on Old Shanks

If the original shanks and butts are still in excellent condition, break off the old hammer heads with side cutters, being very careful not to damage the shanks. Leave the second hammer from each end of each section in place to serve as a temporary guide, and proceed as when installing new hammers.

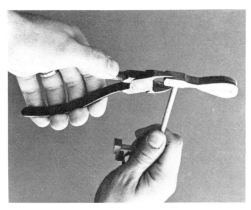

Illus. 7-80 Splitting the old hammer from shank, being careful to preserve the shank.

GRAND ACTION REBUILDING

Number the original hammers, remove them and the whippens from the action frame, and order exact replacements. The distances between the hammer shank center, whippen flange center, and capstan are carefully engineered and must be duplicated exactly in order for the action to work properly. If exact replacement parts are not available, rebuild the original parts by regluing all loose joints, replacing felt and buckskin, etc.

Clean the action frame and brackets, replace all worn felt, cloth and springs, polish corroded parts, plug and redrill overdrawn screw holes, and make any other necessary repairs. Replace the damper felts if necessary. Install, space and travel the new whippens.

Grand Hammer Installation

Grand hammer installation is similar to the procedure used for vertical pianos, with a few exceptions: the hammers must form a 90° angle with the shanks, the tails must be shaped and roughened, and because the hammers are drilled all the way through, the shanks must be trimmed if they protrude.

Install the temporary guide hammers and knurl, install, space and travel all the rest of the shanks. Number and draw the striking point on each new hammer. (For details, see p. 114).

Because the grand backcheck catches the hammer itself (as opposed to the catcher in the vertical action), grand hammer tails must be shaped so they are parallel to the backchecks even though the felt hammer heads are angled. Also, because of the angle, the sides of the tails must be shaped so they do not rub on adjacent hammers. A disc sander may be used for shaping the tails, providing that the technician proceeds with caution. Insert an old shank in the head to be shaped. The shank forms a combination handle and guide. Trim the sides of the tail by holding the shank parallel to the sanding disc, keeping the felt part of the hammer away from the sandpaper. Trim the back of the tail by resting the shank on a block of wood on the sander table, lightly touching the tail to the sanding disc, and moving the shank and hammer head in an arc, as in illustration 7-82.

Illus. 7-81 Sanding the sides of the tail so they are parallel to the shank, to eliminate rubbing on adjacent hammers.

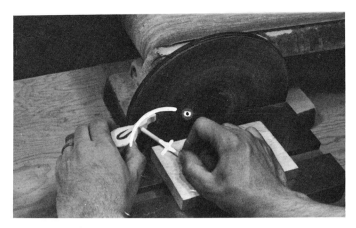

Illus. 7-82 Shaping the back of the tail to make it parallel to the face of the backcheck. Rotate the hammer and shank about the center point indicated to match the original hammer.

Fit each hammer to its shank by reaming the hole with a grand hammer tapered reamer. Reaming the hole slightly makes room for glue in the joint, and enables the hammer to be adjusted slightly to form a perfect 90° angle with the shank. The reamed hammer should wobble 1/16″ (1.5 mm) or less at the striking point.

Install each guide hammer, aligning its striking point with the temporary guides, simultaneously adjusting the body to form a 90° angle with the shank.

After the guide hammers are dry, install the intermediate ones, checking the striking points with a straightedge, and the angle between each head and shank. If the shanks protrude from the heads, unscrew them from the action after the glue is dry and sand the shanks flush with the tails on a disc sander. Roughen the backcheck-mating area of each tail a little with a file card (a wire brush used for cleaning files). If the tails are too smooth, the hammers will not check properly, but if they are too rough, they will wear out the backchecks prematurely. After roughening, reinstall the hammers and regulate the action.

Illus. 7-83 Showing positions of old (temporary) guide hammers numbers 2 and 25.

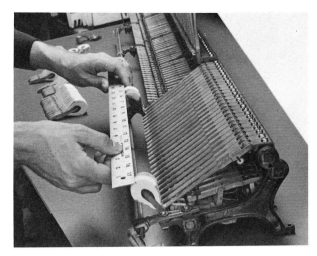

Illus. 7-84 Aligning the new guide hammers, numbers 1 and 26, with the old guide hammers shown in illus. 7-83.

Illus. 7-85 The new guide hammers glued in place.

Illus. 7-86 Trimming the excess shank after glue is dry. No wood should be removed from the hammer tail.

Illus. 7-87 Careful work will result in hammers which are aligned perfectly as in this picture.

Chapter Eight
Electronic Pianos

An electronic piano has a keyboard, mechanical escapement action, and hammers which strike strings, bars or reeds, causing them to vibrate. The vibration is amplified electronically and is introduced into the air by means of a loud speaker (or headphones) rather than a soundboard. The tuning and mechanical servicing of these instruments is akin to conventional piano servicing, while electronic servicing of the amplifying systems is not within the scope of this book. At the time this is written, there are three major brands: the Baldwin Electropiano, the Rhodes, and the WurliTzer. Each instrument is different and is covered separately in the following paragraphs.

THE BALDWIN ELECTROPIANO

Illus. 8-1 Inside front view of Baldwin Electropiano.

Of all brands of electronic pianos, the Baldwin resembles a conventional piano the most, with its strings, tuning pins, pinblock and plate. The plate has two built-in bridges (treble and bass), each consisting of an aluminum transducer rail, a rubber damping strip, and a series of ceramic piezoelectric transducer elements. The transducer rail conducts string vibrations to the piezoelectric elements, which convert physical vibration into electronic signals which are fed into the amplifier. The rubber strip dampens out undesirable harmonics and mechanical noises.

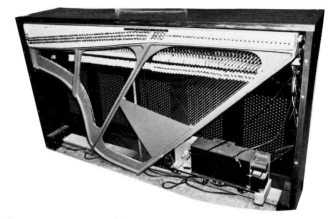

Illus. 8-2 Rear view of Electropiano with outer panel removed.

Tuning

The Electropiano has three strings per treble note and one string per tenor (and bass) note. Standard tuning procedure is followed. The tuning pins go all the way through the thinner-than-usual pinblock, with the strings wound around the inside ends, and the square ends projecting from the back of the piano. Very little "setting of the tuning pins" (see p. 45) is necessary because there is almost no bending or internal torsion; very little "setting of the strings" is necessary because of the low string tension and low string-to-plate friction. Once the tuner becomes accustomed to the "feel" of the tuning pins, he will be able to tune each string with very little back and forth movement of the tuning lever. Normal posture may be used, although it requires a lot of bending over to position the tuning mutes. For maximum comfort, the tuner should maintain excellent posture throughout the tuning. Any more slumping or rounding of the back than necessary will be regretted about half way through

Illus. 8-3 Electropiano pinblock and plate, showing tuning pins projecting from the back of the piano.

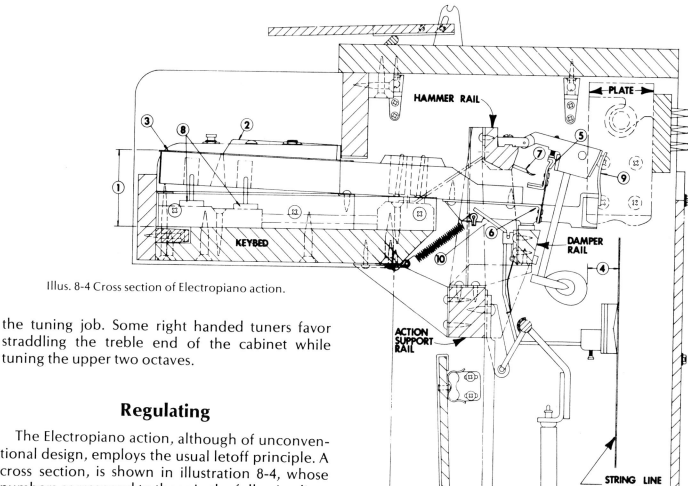

Illus. 8-4 Cross section of Electropiano action.

the tuning job. Some right handed tuners favor straddling the treble end of the cabinet while tuning the upper two octaves.

Regulating

The Electropiano action, although of unconventional design, employs the usual letoff principle. A cross section, is shown in illustration 8-4, whose numbers correspond to those in the following list.

1. Set key height to 2-9/32" (58 mm) by shimming the rail or changing the paper punchings under individual keys.
2. Set sharp key height to 15/32" (12 mm) above the white keys.
3. Set key dip to 13/32" (10.5 mm) by changing paper punchings under the front rail felt punchings, if necessary.
4. Adjust the regulating screw in each hammer butt to bring hammer 1" (2.55 mm) from strings, at rest.
5, 6. Each jack should move approximately 3/32" (2.5 mm) toward the strings when the hammer butt is raised. To adjust, bend the whippen at 6 on illustration 8-4. Do not bend the jack leaf spring. To check for excess jack travel, raise the hammer butt; if the jack moves too far toward the plate, the hammer will not drop.
7. Set letoff to 1/16" (1.5 mm) by bending letoff spoon.
8. Check after-touch by inserting an extra .04" punching under each key (temporarily). When after-touch is correct, key will bottom at the precise moment that letoff occurs. Adjust the

number of punchings if necessary; when correct, remove the test .04" punching.
9. Set hammer checking to 5/16" (8 mm) by bending back checks.
10. Regulate dampers to sustaining rod so all dampers lift together, by adjusting the position where each damper head is screwed to its wire. Regulate each damper to lift when key is half way down, by bending the damper wire.

Tuning Two or More Electropianos Together

Because these instruments often are used in groups for class piano instruction, it is often necessary to tune a number of them together. Using conventional ear tuning, the treble of each instrument will be in tune with the rest. When tuning the bass, select the best sounding piano and tune the bass as usual. Then have an assistant play each bass note on the "reference piano" and tune each other piano to it, one note at a time. If no assistant is available, block the sustaining pedal of the reference piano down with a few rubber mutes, play the desired bass note loudly, move quickly back to the instrument being tuned while the reference piano is still sustaining the bass tone, and tune the new piano to it.

The treble of an Electropiano (including all notes having three strings) may be tuned directly to an electronic tuning aid without recalibrating the aid, because the treble strings have practically no inharmonicity. (The partials are almost perfectly in tune with those of a theoretically perfect string.) For this reason, the treble of each Electropiano in a group may be tuned to an Electronic tuner, and they will all be in tune with each other. Electropiano bass strings are no more perfect than those in a typical console piano, and they should be tuned by ear, as described in the above paragraph.

THE RHODES PIANO

The tone of the Rhodes piano is produced by neoprene-tipped hammers (or in older models, felt hammers) striking tuning forks. The vibration of the tuning forks induces current in pickup coils, which is amplified and fed into a loudspeaker. Wrapped around the lower tine of each tuning fork is an adjustable tuning spring, which is moved in or out to change the vibrational rate.

Illus. 8-5 The Rhodes piano.

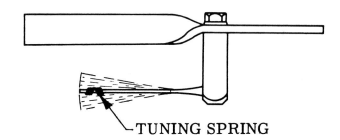

TUNING SPRING

Illus. 8-6 The Rhodes tuning fork.

The Action

The Rhodes action is unlike a conventional action in several important ways: there are no whippens or letoff mechanisms.

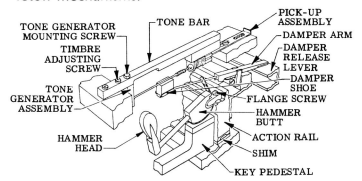

Illus. 8-7 Early Rhodes action.

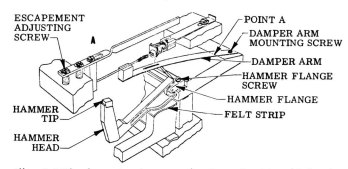

Illus. 8-8 Rhodes action in use at the time of writing this book.

The hammer butt at rest lies on the rear end of the key. When the key is depressed, the hammer "escapes", continues under its own momentum, hits and rebounds from the tine, and lands on the key. The back end of the hammer butt has a bridle tape connecting it to the damper. (In earlier models, the dampers are mounted on levers, while in later examples they are mounted on long leaf springs, but their operation is the same.) As the hammer rises, the opposite end of the butt pulls the bridle tape downward, pulling the damper away from the tine. When the key is released and the hammer falls, the bridle tape is released and the damper returns to rest firmly against the tine.

Tuning

Each tuning spring forms a coil around its tine holding the tuning fork in tune. When tuning is necessary, however, the spring may be moved toward the end of the tine to flatten the pitch, or toward the base of the tine to sharpen it. To tune, remove the harp mounting screws, and rotate the harp to a vertical position. This exposes the tuning springs, and gives easy access for tuning. Turn the amplifier on, and turn the volume up. Tuning may be done by ear or with an electronic aid, as desired, by plucking the tines and sliding the springs up or down as necessary. Because of the relatively pure partial series of the tuning forks, little or no octave stretching is necessary.

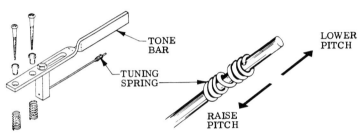

Illus. 8-9 Showing method of tuning the Rhodes.

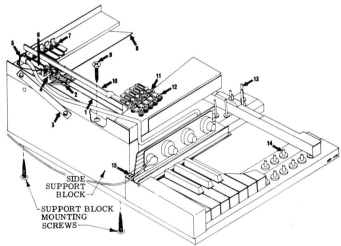

1. Tines
2. Dampers
3. Harp Hinge
4. Pick-ups
5. Preamp-jack
6. Pick-up Arms
7. Pick-up Mounting Screws
8. Damper Release Bar
9. Harp Mounting Screws
10. Typical Tone Bar
11 & 12. Tone Bar Adjustment Screws
13. Action Rail Guide Pins
14. Front Rail Guide Pins
15. Nameboard Mounting Screws

Illus. 8-10

Regulating

Escapement distance, or the distance between tines and hammer tips when the keys are depressed, should be graduated from $5/16''$ (8 mm) for key #1 to $1/16''$ (1.5 mm) for the highest key in the treble. If escapement distance is the only adjustment necessary, it is easier to build up the height of each hammer head individually than to go through the complete regulating procedure described below. Peel off each neoprene hammer tip, glue a $3/8''$ (1 cm) square of $1/16''$ or $1/8''$ thick balsa wood to the hammer as required, and reglue the tip to the balsa wood with Elmer's glue, as illustrated.

STEP 1   STEP 2   STEP 3

Illus. 8-11 Showing method of building up hammer heads.

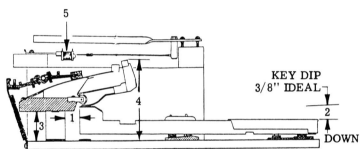

Illus. 8-12 Cross section of the action.

For complete regulation, follow this procedure:
1. Check the position of the action support rail; there should be approximately $1/16''$ (1.5 mm) distance between the rear end of each key and the rear tip of the butt, as illustrated. To adjust, move rail forward or back. For efficient operation of hammers, saturate the felt key pads with graphite, Teflon, or silicone.

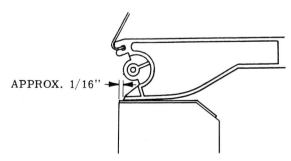

APPROX. 1/16"

Illus. 8-13 Showing relationship of hammer butt to back end of key.

2. Adjust key dip to $^{13}/_{32}$" (10.5 mm) by changing shims under action support rail. Rail height (#3, illus. 8-12) should be 1-$^{15}/_{16}$" (49.5 mm).

3. If #1 and #2 above are correct, hammer should rise to 4-$^{29}/_{32}$" (12.5 cm) from the key frame (measurement #4, illus. 8-12) when key is depressed.

4. Escapement, or distance between tine and hammer when key is depressed, is $^{5}/_{16}$" (8 mm) for key #1, graduated to $^{1}/_{16}$" (1.5 mm) for the highest key. If necessary, shim the harp support blocks to achieve proper excapement distance (Illus. 8-14 #2).

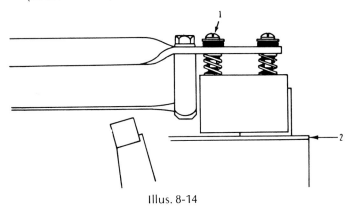

Illus. 8-14

5. After escapement is set, adjust the tip of each tine slightly above the center line of its pickup coil by turning the "timbre adjusting screw" (illus. 8-14 #1). Tine to pickup alignment for proper timbre is depicted in illus. 8-15.

Illus. 8-15

6. Adjust the relative loudness of each note by sliding its pickup closer to or farther from the tine. Average distance for optimum loudness spectrum is between $^{1}/_{32}$" and $^{1}/_{16}$" (.75-1.5 mm).

Illus. 8-16

7. Adjust striking point if necessary, so the distance between the leading edge of the hammer tip and leading edge of the tine is 2-$^{13}/_{32}$" (61.5 mm) for note #1 and $^{1}/_{8}$" (3 mm) for the highest note.

Remove the harp mounting screws, including the hinge screw, and slide the harp forward or back until desired position (or optimum tonal response) is attained. This adjustment is similar in principle to adjusting the striking point of a conventional grand piano action. When the desired position is found, drill two new holes into the maple side support blocks with a #10 drill, and insert the screws. Then drill a new hole for the hinge screw, using care to avoid drilling into a pickup.

8. If the dampers do not seat firmly, bend a gentle curve into each damper leaf spring by lifting near the base. (A gentle curve is better than a sharp bend.) If necessary, align the damper head so it lays flatly on the tine by bending the leaf spring near the head.

THE WURLITZER ELECTRONIC PIANO

Illus. 8-17 The portable WurliTzer electronic piano. This instrument is also made in a conventionally-styled piano cabinet.

In the WurliTzer, the tone is produced by small felt-covered hammers striking tuned metal reeds. The reeds are mounted on a reed bar with their free ends suspended in (but not touching) slots in a "pickup bar" as illustrated. The reed bar and pickup bar form a large capacitor which is wired across the input of the amplifier. When one or more reeds are caused to vibrate by their hammers, the capacitance of the entire bar changes at the frequency of the vibrating reeds; this change of capacitance is translated by the amplifier and loudspeakers into an audible musical tone.

Tuning

Each reed has a small weight attached to the free end, and under normal use stays in tune for long

158

periods of time. If tuning becomes necessary, gently file or scrape the weight to sharpen the pitch, or add solder with a small soldering iron to flatten it. Turn the instrument off while filing or soldering. Any more than the slightest amount of heat will melt the weight; just barely touch it for an instant to flow on a tiny amount of solder. This will invariably make the reed too flat, after which it should be filed to the correct pitch. All metal particles must be removed meticulously to prevent them from shorting out the pickup bar and causing the amplifier to hum loudly or go dead. Do not file the reed near its fixed end, as in reed organ tuning, because this will remove a rust preventive coating and will weaken the reed. If tuning or heavy use injures the tone of a reed, or if a reed breaks, remove it with an appropriate nut driver, and order a replacement from a dealer or the factory, specifying the model number of the piano. All reeds are not interchangeable from one model to another. New reeds are manufactured slightly flat and must be brought up to pitch at the time of installation by scraping. Adjust the reed so it is centered in its slot in the pickup bar when the screw is tightened.

The Action

At the time this is written, four styles of action have been used, and are described below in chronological order.

Regulating the Wood and Brooks Action (Model 112)

1. Set key height to 1-$\frac{13}{32}$" (136 mm) from key frame to top surface of white keys.
2. Regulate white key dip to $\frac{3}{8}$" (1 cm) and black key dip to $\frac{5}{16}$" (8 mm), using conventional procedure.
3. Regulate reed bar height to 4-$\frac{15}{16}$" (12.6 cm) at both ends.
4. Eliminate all lost motion between key and jack. To test, push the rear end of each key down into the back rail cloth. The hammer butt should drop, following the key for $\frac{1}{32}$" (just under 1 mm).
5. Adjust hammer letoff to $\frac{1}{8}$" (3 mm) from the reeds, by turning regulating screw #12. When key dip and letoff are correct, there should be about $\frac{1}{32}$" (just under 1 mm) after-touch. If correct letoff is impossible to achieve, recheck key dip and capstan settings.
6. Regulate each damper (by turning button 32) to begin lifting when the hammer is halfway to the reed.

NOMENCLATURE

1. Front Rail Pin	10. Main Rail
2. Key	11. Butt
3. Music Desk Assembly	12. Regulating Screw
4. Balance Key Pin	13. Butt Spring
5. Key Cloth	14. Butt Flange
6. Capstan Screw	15. Reed Bar
7. Whip	16. Hammer
8. Whip Flange	17. Reed
9. Fly (or jack)	18. Pick-Up Insulator

19. Pick-Up Washer	28. Damper Lever
20. Pick-Up Screw	29. Damper Lever Flange
21. Pick-Up Bushing	30. Damper Lever Spring
22. Reed Washer	31. Damper Washer
23. Damper Rod	32. Damper Let-Off Button
24. Shield	33. Main Rail Stiffener
25. Pick-Up	34. Damper Lever Wire
26. Damper	35. Amplifier
27. Reed Screw	36. Speaker

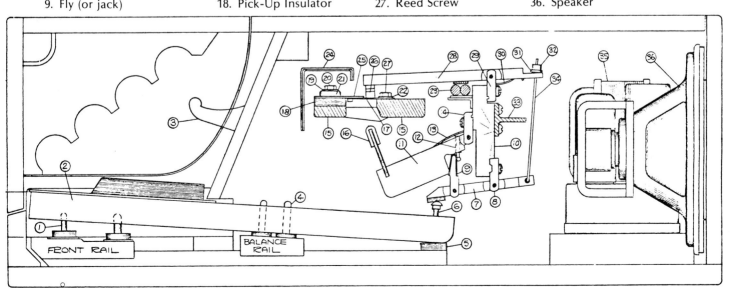

Illus. 8-18 The Wood & Brooks action.

Regulating the
Pratt Read Action
(Models 112A, 120, 700)

1. Set key height to 1-15/32″ (32.5 mm) from key frame to top of white keys.
2. Regulate white key dip to 13/32″ (10.5 mm) by sanding the bottom of the key, or by gluing paper punchings to it. Regulate black key dip to 11/32″ (9 mm) by adjusting regulating screws #41.
3. Adjust reed bar height to 5″ (127 mm) in bass and 4-15/16″ (126 mm) in treble.
4. Regulate capstans to hold the hammers 1-13/16″ (41.5 mm) from the reeds. The hammers are not at the point of lost motion as in conventional pianos.
5. Regulate hammer letoff to 1/16″ (1.5 mm) in the treble, graduated to 1/8″ (3 mm) in the bass, by turning letoff screws #28.
6. The butt spoons (#32) rarely need attention. They are correct when each spoon clears the jack stop cloth (#35) by 1/64″ (.375 mm) after the key is depressed. If there is no space when the key is depressed fully, the spoon is not regulated properly.
7. Regulate each damper (by turning dowel screw #14) so it lifts 3/16″ (5 mm) above the reed when the key is depressed fully.

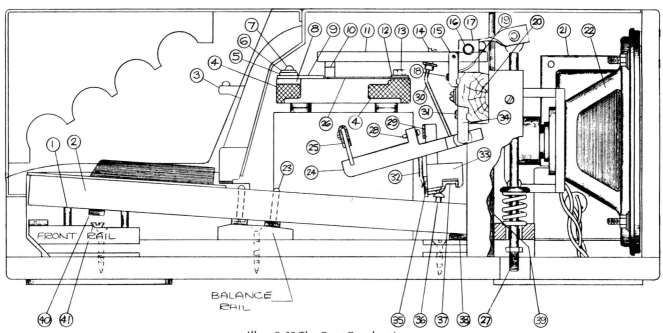

Illus. 8-19 The Pratt Read action.

Regulating the
WurliTzer Action
(Models 140, 145, 720)

1. Set key height to 2″ (51 mm) from keybed to underside of the projecting lip on the front of the white keys, using conventional procedure.
2. Hammer stroke is set at the factory and should be 1-1/8″ (29 mm).
3. Adjust lost motion as in a conventional piano, by turning the key capstan screws.
4. Adjust hammer letoff to 1/8″ (3 mm) from the reed by turning letoff screw.
5. Regulate key dip to 3/8″ (1 cm) as in a conventional piano. When letoff and key dip are correct there should be about 1/32″ (.75 mm) after-touch, and all hammers should check properly.
6. Regulate the dampers to the sustaining pedal. Adjust the nut on the connecting rod underneath the piano so there is 1/32″ (.75 mm) between the damper rail and bottom of the damper levers. Depress the pedal slowly and look for dampers which rise later than others due to packing of the damper rail felt. Shim by gluing paper to the bottom of "slow" damper levers.
7. Regulate dampers to keys by turning damper regulating screws with an appropriate nut driver. Regulation is correct when there is a space of .035″ between the underside of the regulating screw head and the top of the rubber grommet. Check this by slipping a .035″ spacer between screw and grommet.

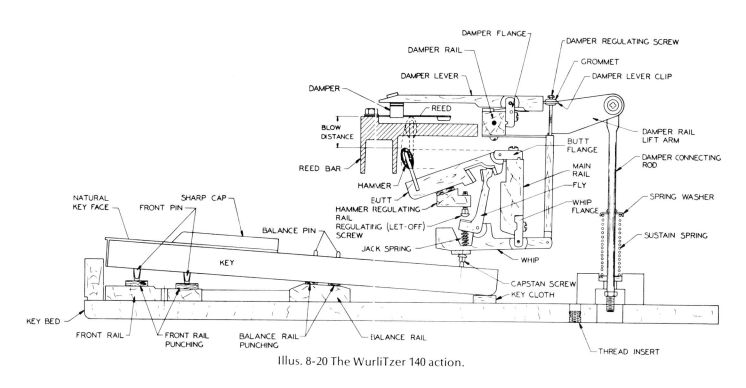

Illus. 8-20 The WurliTzer 140 action.

Regulating the WurliTzer 200 Series Action (Models 200, 203, 203W, 206, 207, 207V, 214, 214V)

The WurliTzer 200 series action is regulated the same as the preceding (model 140 et al) WurliTzer

action, with the following exception: hammer stroke is 1-5/64″ (27.5 mm). It is factory-set and does not normally require adjustment.

For more detailed information on electronic piano servicing, including electronic repairs, refer to the service manuals published by all three of the above manufacturers.

NO.	DESCRIPTION
1	NATURAL KEYFACE
2	FRONT RAIL PIN
3	SHARP CAP
4	BALANCE PIN
5	REED BAR
6	HAMMER
7	BUTT
8	HAMMER REGULATING RAIL
9	DAMPER
10	REED
11	DAMPER LEVER
12	DAMPER RAIL
13	DAMPER FLANGE
14	DAMPER REGULATING SCREW
15	GROMMET
16	DAMPER LEVER CLIP
17	DAMPER RAIL LIFT ARM

NO.	DESCRIPTION
18	BUTT FLANGE
19	DAMPER CONNECTING ROD
20	MAIN RAIL
21	FLY
22	WHIP FLANGE
23	SUSTAIN SPRING
24	WHIP
25	REGULATING (LET-OFF) SCREW
26	WHIP STOP RAIL
27	JACK SPRING
28	KEY CLOTH
29	CAPSTAN SCREW
30	BALANCE RAIL
31	BALANCE RAIL PUNCHING
32	FRONT RAIL PUNCHING
33	FRONT RAIL

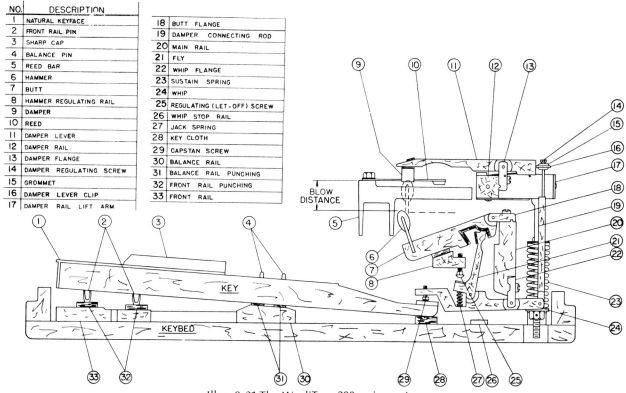

Illus. 8-21 The WurliTzer 200 series action.

161

TOTALLY ELECTRONIC INSTRUMENTS

Some portable electronic organs have "piano" stops which simulate the tones of a piano by means of electronic circuits. Since this type of instrument has no mechanical action, it has the "feel" of an organ rather than a piano, and it is not considered to be an electronic piano. The repair of such instruments is beyond the scope of this book, since it involves an understanding of electronics, but the piano tuner occasionally may be called upon to tune one.

Small electronic organs of this type usually have twelve tone generators, one for all octaves of each pitch. These are exposed by taking the cabinet apart. (Caution: do not touch any of the bare wires inside the organ with a metal tool, unless you have a knowledge of electronics, or you may cause part of the organ to burn out.) Each tone generator is typically tuned by turning a small screw. To tune the instrument, select the 8' piano stop and tune the temperament in the usual way. Adjust each note by turning the appropriate screw, using a television repairman's plastic screwdriver. A metal screwdriver should not be used, because the capacitance of the metal blade might alter the pitch when it touches the screw. Because each screw tunes all octaves of one pitch at the same time, when the temperament octave is tuned, the entire instrument is also in tune.

BIBLIOGRAPHY

Acoustics

McFerrin, W.V., *The Piano—Its Acoustics*, Tuners Supply Company; Boston, 1972.

Business Hints for the Piano Technician

Boles, Don, *The Independent Piano Technician*, The Pinchpenny Press; Atlanta, Georgia, 1968.

Music, General

Apel, Willi, *Harvard Dictionary of Music*, Harvard University Press; Cambridge, Mass., various editions.

Blom, Eric, ed., *Groves Dictionary of Music and Musicians*, Ten Volumes, MacMillan & Co., Ltd; London, England, various editions.

Scholes, Percy A., *The Oxford Companion to Music*, Oxford University Press; London, England, various editions.

Piano Construction and Theory

American Steel and Wire Co., *Piano Tone Building*, Reprint of 1916–1919 volumes by The Vestal Press; Vestal, N.Y.

White, William B., *Theory and Practice of Piano Construction*, Reprint of the 1906 edition by Dover Publications; New York.

Pfeiffer, Walter, *The Piano Key and Whippen*, (English Translation by Jim Engelhardt), Verlag das Musikinstrument, Frankfurt Am Main, Germany, 1955.

Wolfenden, Samuel, *A Treatise on the Art of Piano Construction*, Reprint by Unwin Brothers, Old Woking, Surrey, England, 1916 edition with 1927 supplement.

Piano Dates and Serial Numbers

Michel, N.E., *Pierce Piano Atlas*, Bob Pierce; Long Beach, California, various dates.

Piano History

Dolge, Alfred, *Pianos and Their Makers*, Reprint of 1911 edition by Dover Publications, Inc.; New York, 1972.

Dolge, Alfred, *Pianos and Their Makers, Vol. II*, Covina Publishing Company; Covina, California, 1913.

Loesser, Arthur, *Men, Women, and Pianos*, Simon & Schuster; New York, N.Y., 1954.

Michel, N.E. *Historical Pianos*, Published by the author, Pico Rivera, California, 1969.

Piano Regulating

Mason, Merle H., *PTG Piano Action Handbook, 2nd Edition*, The Piano Technicians Guild, Inc.; Seattle, Washington, 1971.

Piano Servicing—All Aspects

Howell, W. Dean, *Professional Piano Tuning*, American Piano Supply Co.; Clifton, N.J., 1969.

Travis, John W., *Let's Tune Up*, John W. Travis; Takoma Park, Md., 1968.

National Association of Piano Tuners, Inc., *The Tuners Journal*, various issues.

Piano Technicians Guild, *The Piano Technicians Journal*, various issues.

Stevens, Floyd, *Piano Tuning, Repair & Rebuilding*, Nelson-Hall Co.; Chicago, Illinois, 1972.

White, William B., *Piano Tuning and Allied Arts*, Tuners Supply Company, Boston, Reprint of the 5th edition.

Piano Stringing Scales

Travis, John W., *A Guide to Restringing,* Middleburg Press; Middleburg, Virginia, 1961.

Player Piano History

Bowers, Q. David, *Encyclopedia of Automatic Musical Instruments,* The Vestal Press; Vestal, N.Y., 1972.
Roehl, Harvey N., *Player Piano Treasury,* The Vestal Press; Vestal, N.Y., second edition 1973.
Ord-Hume, Arthur W. J. G., *Player Piano,* A. S. Barnes & Co.; Cranbury, New Jersey, 1970.

Player Piano Servicing

Givens, Larry, *Rebuilding the Player Piano,* The Vestal Press; Vestal, N.Y., 1963.
Standard Player Action Company, *Principles of Player Action Operation,* Reprint of the 1924 edition by The Vestal Press; Vestal, N.Y.

Refinishing

Hand, Jackson, *How To Do Your Own Wood Finishing,* Popular Science Publishing Co., Harper & Row; New York, N.Y., 1967.
Kuhn, W.H., *Refinishing Furniture,* Arco Publishing Co., Inc., New York, N.Y., 1973.

Woodworking

Feirer, John L., *Cabinetmaking and Millwork,* Chas. A. Bennett Co., Inc.; Peoria, Illinois, 1970.
Power Tools, Sears, Roebuck and Co., 1969.

CONVERSION TABLE
Millimeters to Inches

Millimeter	Inch Decimal
.1	.0039
.2	.0078
.3	.0118
.4	.0157
.5	.0197
.6	.0236
.7	.0275
.8	.0315
1.0	.0393 (7)
2.0	.0787
3.0	.1181
4.0	.1575
5.0	.1968
6.0	.2362
7.0	.2756
8.0	.3150
9.0	.3543
10.0	.3937
11.0	.4331
12.0	.4724
13.0	.5118
14.0	.5512
15.0	.5905
16.0	.6299
17.0	.6693
18.0	.7087
19.0	.7480
20.0	.7874
21.0	.8268
22.0	.8661
23.0	.9055
24.0	.9449
25.0	.9842
25.4	1.0000
44.5	1.750 (1¾)
47.6	1.875 (1⅞)
63.5	2.500 (2½)
66.7	2.625 (2⅝)

CONVERSION TABLE
Fractions of Inch to Millimeters

8ths	16ths	32nds	64ths	Decimal	Millimeters
			1	.0156	0.397
		1	2	.0312	0.794
			3	.0469	1.191
	1		4	.0625	1.588
			5	.0781	1.984
		3	6	.0937	2.381

CONVERSION TABLE
Fractions of Inch to Millimeters

8ths	16ths	32nds	64ths	Decimal	Millimeters
			7	.1094	2.778
1			8	.1250	3.175
			9	.1406	3.572
		5	10	.1562	3.969
			11	.1719	4.366
	3		12	.1875	4.763
			13	.2031	5.159
		7	14	.2187	5.556
			15	.2344	5.953
2			16	.2500	6.350
			17	.2656	6.747
		9	18	.2812	7.144
			19	.2969	7.541
	5		20	.3125	7.938
			21	.3281	8.334
		11	22	.3437	8.731
			23	.3594	9.128
3			24	.3750	9.525
			25	.3906	9.922
		13	26	.4062	10.319
			27	.4219	10.716
	7		28	.4375	11.113
			29	.4531	11.509
		15	30	.4687	11.906
			31	.4844	12.303
4			32	.5000	12.700
			33	.5156	13.097
		17	34	.5312	13.494
			35	.5469	13.891
	9		36	.5625	14.288
			37	.5781	14.684
		19	38	.5937	15.081
			39	.6094	15.478
5			40	.6250	15.875
			41	.6406	16.272
		21	42	.6562	16.669
			43	.6719	17.066
	11		44	.6875	17.463
			45	.7031	17.859
		23	46	.7187	18.256
			47	.7344	18.653
6			48	.7500	19.050
			49	.7656	19.447
		25	50	.7812	19.844
			51	.7969	20.241
	13		52	.8125	20.638
			53	.8281	21.034
		27	54	.8437	21.431
			55	.8594	21.828
7			56	.8750	22.225
			57	.8906	22.622
		29	58	.9062	23.019
			59	.9219	23.416
	15		60	.9375	23.813
			61	.9531	24.209
		31	62	.9687	24.606
			63	.9844	25.003
8			64	1.0000	25.400

Group 1

Inch	Mm.	Wire Gage	Decimals of an Inch
		80	.0135
		79	.0145
1/64			.0156
	.4		.0157
		78	.0160
		77	.0180
	.5		.0197
		76	.0200
		75	.0210
	.55		.0217
		74	.0225
	.6		.0236
		73	.0240
		72	.0250
	.65		.0256
		71	.0260
	.7		.0276
		70	.0280
		69	.0293
	.75		.0295
		68	.0310
1/32			.0313
	.8		.0315
		67	.0320
		66	.0330
	.85		.0335
		65	.0350
	.9		.0354
		64	.0360
		63	.0370
	.95		.0374
		62	.0380
		61	.0390
	1		.0394
		60	.0400
		59	.0410
	1.05		.0413
		58	.0420
		57	.0430
	1.1		.0433
	1.15		.0453
		56	.0465

Group 2

Inch	Mm.	Wire Gage	Decimals of an Inch
3/64			.0469
	1.2		.0472
	1.25		.0492
	1.3		.0512
		55	.0520
	1.35		.0531
		54	.0550
	1.4		.0551
	1.45		.0571
	1.5		.0591
		53	.0595
	1.55		.0610
1/16			.0625
	1.6		.0630
		52	.0635
	1.65		.0650
	1.7		.0669
		51	.0670
	1.75		.0689
		50	.0700
	1.8		.0709
	1.85		.0728
		49	.0730
	1.9		.0748
		48	.0760
	1.95		.0768
5/64			.0781
		47	.0785
	2		.0787
	2.05		.0807
		46	.0810
		45	.0820
	2.1		.0827
	2.15		.0846
		44	.0860
	2.2		.0866
	2.25		.0886
		43	.0890
	2.3		.0906
	2.35		.0925
		42	.0935

Group 3

Inch	Mm.	Wire Gage	Decimals of an Inch
3/32			.0938
	2.4		.0945
		41	.0960
	2.45		.0966
		40	.0980
	2.5		.0984
		39	.0995
		38	.1015
	2.6		.1024
		37	.1040
	2.7		.1063
		36	.1065
	2.75		.1083
7/64			.1094
		35	.1100
	2.8		.1102
		34	.1110
		33	.1130
	2.9		.1142
		32	.1160
	3		.1181
		31	.1200
	3.1		.1220
1/8			.1250
	3.2		.1260
	3.25		.1280
		30	.1285
	3.3		.1299
	3.4		.1339
		29	.1360
	3.5		.1378
		28	.1405
9/64			.1406
	3.6		.1417
		27	.1440
	3.7		.1457
		26	.1470
	3.75		.1476
		25	.1495
	3.8		.1496
		24	.1520
	3.9		.1535
		23	.1540

Group 4

Inch	Mm.	Wire Gage	Decimals of an Inch
5/32			.1563
		22	.1570
	4		.1575
		21	.1590
		20	.1610
	4.1		.1614
	4.2		.1654
		19	.1660
	4.25		.1673
	4.3		.1693
		18	.1695
11/64			.1719
		17	.1730
	4.4		.1732
		16	.1770
	4.5		.1772
		15	.1800
	4.6		.1811
		14	.1820
		13	.1850
	4.7		.1850
	4.75		.1870
3/16			.1875
	4.8		.1890
		12	.1890
		11	.1910
	4.9		.1929
		10	.1935
		9	.1960
	5		.1969
		8	.1990
	5.1		.2008
		7	.2010
13/64			.2031
		6	.2040
	5.2		.2047
		5	.2055
	5.25		.2067
	5.3		.2087
		4	.2090
	5.4		.2126
		3	.2130
	5.5		.2165
7/32			.2188
	5.6		.2205
		2	.2210
	5.7		.2244
	5.75		.2264
		1	.2280
	5.8		.2283

Metric conversion chart for number, letter, and inch drill sizes. From *Modern Metalworking* by John R. Walker, published by the Goodheart-Wilcox Company. Reprinted by permission.

Inch	Mm.	Letter Sizes	Decimals of an Inch
	5.9		.2323
		A	.2340
15/64			.2344
	6		.2362
		B	.2380
	6.1		.2402
		C	.2420
	6.2		.2441
		D	.2460
	6.25		.2461
	6.3		.2480
1/4		E	.2500
	6.4		.2520
	6.5		.2559
		F	.2570
	6.6		.2598
		G	.2610
	6.7		.2638
17/64			.2656
	6.75		.2657
		H	.2660
	6.8		.2677
	6.9		.2717
		I	.2720
	7		.2756
		J	.2770
	7.1		.2795
		K	.2810
9/32			.2812
	7.2		.2835
	7.25		.2854
	7.3		.2874
		L	.2900
	7.4		.2913
		M	.2950
	7.5		.2953
19/64			.2969
	7.6		.2992
		N	.3020
	7.7		.3031
	7.75		.3051
	7.8		.3071
	7.9		.3110
5/16			.3125
	8		.3150
		O	.3160
	8.1		.3189
	8.2		.3228
		P	.3230
	8.25		.3248
	8.3		.3268

Inch	Mm.	Letter Sizes	Decimals of an Inch
21/64			.3281
	8.4		.3307
		Q	.3320
	8.5		.3346
	8.6		.3386
		R	.3390
	8.7		.3425
11/32			.3438
	8.75		.3345
	8.8		.3465
		S	.3480
	8.9		.3504
	9		.3543
		T	.3580
	9.1		.3583
23/64			.3594
	9.2		.3622
	9.25		.3642
	9.3		.3661
		U	.3680
	9.4		.3701
	9.5		.3740
3/8			.3750
		V	.3770
	9.6		.3780
	9.7		.3819
	9.75		.3839
	9.8		.3858
		W	.3860
	9.9		.3898
25/64			.3906
	10		.3937
		X	39.70
		Y	.4040
13/32			.4063
		Z	.4130
	10.5		.4134
27/64			.4219
	11		.4331
7/16			.4375
	11.5		.4528
29/64			.4531
15/32			.4688
	12		.4724
31/64			.4844
	12.5		.4921
1/2			.5000
	13		.5118
33/64			.5156
17/32			.5313
	13.5		.5315

Inch	Mm.	Decimals of an Inch
35/64		.5469
	14	.5512
9/16		.5625
	14.5	.5709
37/64		.5781
	15	.5906
19/32		.5938
39/64		.6094
	15.5	.6102
5/8		.6250
	16	.6299
41/64		.6406
	16.5	.6496
21/32		.6563
	17	.6693
43/64		.6719
11/16		.6875
	17.5	.6890
45/64		.7031
	18	.7087
23/32		.7188
	18.5	.7283
47/64		.7344
	19	.7480
3/4		.7500
49/64		.7656
	19.5	.7677
25/32		.7812
	20	.7874
51/64		.7969
	20.5	.8071
13/16		.8125
	21	.8268
53/64		.8281
27/32		.8438
	21.5	.8465
55/64		.8594
	22	.8661
7/8		.8750
	22.5	.8858
57/64		.8906
	23	.9055
29/32		.9063
59/64		.9219
	23.5	.9252
15/16		.9375
	24	.9449
61/64		.9531
	24.5	.9646
31/32		.9688
	25	.9843
63/64		.9844

Inch	Mm.	Decimals of an Inch
1		1.0000
	25.5	1.0039
1 1/64		1.0156
	26	1.0236
1 1/32		1.0313
	26.5	1.0433
1 3/64		1.0469
1 1/16		1.0625
	27	1.0630
1 5/64		1.0781
	27.5	1.0827
1 3/32		1.0938
	28	1.1024
1 7/64		1.1094
	28.5	1.1220
1 1/8		1.1250
1 9/64		1.1406
	29	1.1417
1 5/32		1.1562
	29.5	1.1614
1 11/64		1.1719
	30	1.1811
1 3/16		1.1875
	30.5	1.2008
1 13/64		1.2031
1 7/32		1.2188
	31	1.2205
1 15/64		1.2344
	31.5	1.2402
1 1/4		1.2500
	32	1.2598
1 17/64		1.2656
	32.5	1.2795
1 9/32		1.2813
1 19/64		1.2969
	33	1.2992
1 5/16		1.3125
	33.5	1.3189
1 21/64		1.3281
	34	1.3386
1 11/32		1.3438
	34.5	1.3583
1 23/64		1.3594
1 3/8		1.3750
	35	1.3780
1 25/64		1.3906
	35.5	1.3976
1 13/32		1.4063
	36	1.4173
1 27/64		1.4219
	36.5	1.4370

INDEX

Jacket Design by Robinson Art Studios, Vestal NY 13850
Book Design and Composition by Jessamy Graphics, Binghamton NY 13902
Set in Optima with bold & italic
Printed on 70# Patina II paper; manufactured by S. D. Warren Co.
Division of Scott Paper Company
Printed and bound by the Vail Ballou Press, Binghamton NY 13902